Where Was the Working Class?

Where Was the Working Class?

REVOLUTION IN EASTERN GERMANY

Linda Fuller

University of Illinois Press

Urbana and Chicago

© 1999 by the Board of Trustees of
the University of Illinois
Manufactured in the United States of America
1 2 3 4 5 C P 5 4 3 2 1
This book is printed on acid-free paper.

Library of Congress Cataloging-in-Publication Data
Fuller, Linda, 1944–
Where was the working class? : revolution in
Eastern Germany / Linda Fuller.
    p.   cm.
Includes bibliographical references and index.
ISBN 0-252-02442-7 (cloth : alk. paper)
ISBN 0-252-06751-7 (pbk. : alk. paper)
1. Working class—Germany (East)—Political activity—
History—20th century. 2. Labor movement—Germany (East)—History—
20th century. 3. Socialism—Germany (East)—History—20th century.
I. Title.
HD8455.F85   1999
322'.2'09431—ddc21   98-19766
CIP

For Greg McLauchlan and Joyce Carrillo

Contents

Acknowledgments   *ix*

Introduction   *1*

1. Everyday Worlds of Work and Class   *9*

2. Workers in the Gallery: The Single-Class Character of Revolutionary Politics   *33*

3. The Socialist Labor Process   *40*

4. Workplace Politics   *57*

5. The Class Relationship Revisited   *77*

6. Workers on Stage: Activists in the Revolution   *106*

7. A Second Look at the Labor Process and Workplace Politics   *122*

8. Workers in the Wings: Passive Participants in Revolutionary Politics   *142*

9. Class, the Labor Process, and Workplace Politics in Comparative Perspective: Poland and the GDR   *154*

Appendix: Doing Research in the GDR and the Former GDR   *175*

Notes   *179*

Works Cited   *225*

Index   *237*

Acknowledgments

I have many to thank for their support, intellectual stimulation, and friend-ship over the course of this project. Things would never have gotten off the ground if people had not generously shared their GDR contacts with me, as David Abraham, Debra Jansen, Neva Makgetla, Dorothy Rosenberg, and es-pecially Brad Scharf all did. Once in the GDR, Thomas Edeling, the Freier Deutscher Gewerkschaftsbund (FDGB), the Liga für Völkerfreundschaft, Artur Meier, Irene Runge, Gerhard Tietze, and Gerhard Wittich were equally generous with their time and help. I give special thanks to Helga Schmidt, who, though I no longer know where she is, always gave of her gregarious nature, her crafty ability to handle bureaucracies, and her mothering skills. I cannot imagine what this book would have become without Helga. Finally, I thank the many people in the GDR who allowed a perfect stranger to ask them tough and sometimes embarrassing questions and watch them do their paid jobs. Their life experiences are the heart of this story, and I have tried to represent them as respectfully as they were offered.

I was also fortunate to have benefited from fine research assistance in both the United States and the GDR. For this, I thank Ilka Cohen, Beate Lang, Barbara Möller, Antje Pißerak, Helga Schmidt, Sabine Schnug, and most of all Annette Bridges and Uli Müller. Both Michael Burawoy, to whom my intellectual debt is immense, and Jon Miller, a fine and honest friend and a thoughtful critic, made suggestions for revisions, many of which I incorpo-rated into the book. I also thank two anonymous reviewers at the University of Illinois Press and my editor, Dick Martin, for their invaluable support of my work. Jane Mohraz's careful copyediting is also greatly appreciated.

Monetary assistance came through travel awards from the GDR Studies

Association and research grants from the ASA/NSF Small Grants Program, the Summer Research Award from the University of Oregon, the Graduate School of International Relations at the University of Denver, and the Faculty Research and Innovation Fund at the University of Southern California. I am also grateful to Lutz Flöth, the Gewerkschaftshochschule Fritz Heckert, Üte Haarbrücke, and Gregg Kvistad for their hospitality.

Finally, I thank my family and friends. I could not have done without them (though there were surely many times they could have done without me) over the years it took to write this book. They always helped put writing sociology in its proper perspective, and without that, I think I would not have had the will to finish this project. Hugs to Michael Burawoy, Zawdie Ekundayo, Kevin Hansen, Eun Mee Kim, John Lie, Annie Lovitt Olsen, Steve McMahon, Steve McMillan, Sandi Morgen, Jeanne F. Olsen, Russell K. Olsen, Rutsy Olsen, Teresa Sharpe, Vicki Smith, Nancy Solomon, Arlene Stein, Cliff Williams, and Karen Williams. I dedicate this book to two kind and politically committed people, Joyce Carrillo and Greg McLauchlan. Compared with all they have seen me through, the process of writing this book was nothing.

Where Was the Working Class?

Introduction

The demise of the socialist systems of East and Central Europe has been ranked among the most important social phenomena of the twentieth century. Despite the immensity of this event and the chorus of voices now claiming it was inevitable, few had any inkling of what was to transpire in this region of the world during the 1980s and 1990s. "Our jaws cannot drop any lower!" Radio Free Europe exclaimed, and on both sides of the socialist-capitalist divide, scholars of contending theoretical persuasions, journalists, diplomats, social critics, and people on the street were equally surprised.[1]

I include myself among them. In June 1989, less than six weeks before the closings of the West German (FRG) embassies in East Berlin, Prague, Warsaw, and Budapest spelled the beginning of the end of the German Democratic Republic (GDR), I had just returned from my second trip to the GDR. During this and a previous journey, I had collected data for a comparative project on workers' involvement in decision making at worksites and in the larger economy in Cuba and the GDR. My fieldwork was still not complete in June 1989, and my plan was to return to the GDR the following summer to wrap up my research.[2]

The following summer, however, the GDR, for all intents and purposes, no longer existed. My original comparative project permanently scuttled, I decided to use my field data for a new purpose. The research questions I eventually settled on can be posed simply, though their answers have turned out to be complex: to what degree and in what ways were workers, the overwhelming majority of GDR citizens, involved in the politics of the 1989–90 revolution, and how can their involvement best be explained? I was able to use a good deal of the information I had already collected on the GDR to help formulate answers to these questions, because the major concern underlying both projects was the same: a long-standing interest in the politics of social change, an interest stemming from a deep dissatisfaction with the inegalitarian, disempowering, undemocratic, and violent arrangements under which many people exist with one another and with the extrahuman environment.

All investigators must make a series of choices over the course of their research that have a defining impact on the character of their work. In chapter 1, I discuss two of my choices in some detail. The first is my reliance on the insights of feminist scholars, particularly those who have been dubbed standpoint theorists. These feminist epistemologists have shown how science, the most esteemed and influential form of knowledge production in much of the contemporary world, is, like all human endeavors, socially embedded and thus thoroughly gendered.[3] As such, its approach and its products reflect a masculine, as well as an advantaged and particularly Western, piece of the social fabric, even while its trademark mantle is one of universality and objectivity. A principal point of these feminist thinkers is that hegemonic science limits knowledge for all people. There are numerous and significant things about the world we simply cannot find out so long as this one approach to learning so thoroughly, and sometimes so violently, dominates all others. To counter the narrowness of our scientific knowledge, feminist standpoint theorists counsel us to begin inquiries from alternative points, in other words, from the places and the perspectives of the least powerful and privileged groups in society. In the GDR, one such group was the working class. In what follows, I have tried to understand working-class political behavior, as well as the social conditions that influenced it, from workers' perspectives. My debt to feminist standpoint epistemology is not to be found in frequent and direct citation and quotation of its principal formulators. Rather, it is evident in my selection and analyses of issues, which, to the extent I am successful, do not match those of most treatments of the GDR revolution or of the society from which it emerged.

In chapter 1, I also consider the central interpretive concept on which this study hinges: class. Here I present my definitions of the working class and the intelligentsia, the two classes I view as fundamental for understanding GDR society and its revolution. Next I illuminate the dynamics through which both classes were reproduced as enduring elements of GDR social structure. Chapter 1 ends with an exploration of one of three long-standing features of the relationship between GDR workers and intellectuals that influenced working-class politics during the revolution—workers' perception of the intelligentsia as a largely homogenous, rather than a differentiated, social stratum.

Although there is sharp disagreement over the usefulness of class as a tool for understanding socialist societies, my overriding interest in social change is the basis of my continued attachment to it. Theorists, empirical researchers, humanists, and activists alike who take class seriously share an understanding I consider central to the politics of social change: fundamental, though not necessarily large-scale, change cannot be accomplished if workers are not actively involved in its conception and execution. By this, I do not mean that only people who identify themselves as workers first and foremost must be involved or that workers' concerns should take precedence over those of everyone else. All people who cannot thrive under existing social arrangements but who do not necessarily identify themselves as workers, though most of them are also that, have vital roles to play in the process. But I do not see that any such groups can go it alone, without substantial working-class involvement. Nor do I think they should. Social changes implemented without considerable worker participation and support have too often been minimalist, elitist, ephemeral, and nondemocratic. In short, they have not gone to the heart of the matter.[4]

The importance I attach to the working class, instead of some new social movement, in the process of social change makes my analysis decidedly unpostmodern. Beyond this, postmodern scholars, and certainly others as well, will undoubtedly view my treatment of the working class as too undifferentiated, too homogenous. They are, of course, correct that GDR workers were not all alike in terms, for example, of their gender, their race, or their ethnicity, three ascriptive divisions in the working class that have proven of great import in other places. My response to such criticisms relies only partly on the comparative homogeneity of the GDR working class.[5] To those who would look askance at what they judge my "potato sack" view of the working class, I would also reply that I have directed my research efforts toward distinguishing among workers on the basis of their actions rather than their ascriptive characteristics, because I am persuaded that how people act in the world is central to understanding processes of transformative change. I do not view what people do and how we classify them (or how they classify themselves) as unconnected, as my emphasis on class should make clear. Gender, for example, was surely associated in some fascinating ways with workers' political activity during the GDR revolution. But I leave to others the worthwhile task of relating divisions *within* the working class to differences in political behavior in order to explore what differences *between* workers and the intelligentsia can reveal about the revolutionary process in the GDR.

Readers will find this volume diverges from postmodern and some other strains of contemporary social analysis in another way as well. I am much more interested in what people actually do or do not do than in what they think, believe, feel, or write. Readers whose main interests tend toward motivations, opinions, values, ideologies, consciousness, identities, or discourse will thus find this work lopsided. To a point I would agree, because I do not think such things can be cleanly separated from people's actions. At the same time, my concern with the politics of social change keeps redirecting me toward a more materialist, more practice-oriented focus on what people do. Matters of the head, the heart, and the pen are relevant to the study of social change. But whatever amazing things run through people's heads, however they identify themselves, and whatever their literary products and emotional states are, these things are not equivalent to social change. For change to occur, people must act. They must struggle with one another in some concrete way, and thus studies of change that ignore people's actions in favor of their discourse, motives, identities, ideologies, and whatnot fall flat both intellectually and politically.

In chapters 2, 6, and 8, I describe the three principal forms working-class politics assumed during the *Wende* (the change).[6] In chapter 2, I discuss how many GDR workers shunned political involvement of any kind during the tumultuous events. Such workers steered clear of concrete actions, and while some, though not all, admitted opinions about the revolution, they declined to express these in any public or semipublic venue. In chapter 6, I cover the smallest group of GDR workers, those who actively entered the political fray. By their own assessment, their most important actions occurred not in the streets or in association with electoral politics but at their workplaces. Here they set up work councils, radically reformed existing unions, and created entirely original forms of self-representation, many of which embodied elements of a genuine alternative to GDR-style socialism and to FRG-style capitalism. In chapter 8, I focus on perhaps the largest group of GDR workers, those who participated in revolutionary politics but only passively. These workers held definite views on revolutionary matters, which they shared in public. But they were extremely reluctant to act on these opinions, and when they did, their actions were unplanned, individual, and minimal in scope and the time and energy they required. My fieldwork uncovered workers in this third category who engaged in passive political participation both on the side of those challenging the status quo and on the side of those attempting to uphold it.[7]

My discussions of workers who eschewed political participation entirely, of worker activists, and of workers who chose passive involvement in the revolution concentrate on the fast-paced, bewildering, and volatile months from September 1989 to mid-March 1990. I limited my study to this time period because I was most interested in the political manifestations of the revolution and in its indigenous politics, and it was during these months that both politics and indigenous participants dominated the revolutionary process. Both before and after, the economic aspects of the crisis and FRG interventions were far more prominent.

During the first stage of the *Wende* (through approximately December 1989), newly formed citizens' opposition groups—the four best known of which were Demokratie Jetzt, Vereinigte Linke, Demokratischer Aufbruch, and Neues Forum—dominated revolutionary politics. These groups initiated the indigenous political challenge to GDR socialism, and for about four months, their tactics, ideologies, leadership, and hard work defined its course and character. During the late fall of 1989, however, the citizens' opposition groups rapidly began to lose political ground to a variety of new and reborn political parties.[8] The shift from the citizens' opposition stage to the political party stage of the revolution, which was completed before the national election in mid-March 1990, spelled the transformation of revolutionary politics from a more open-ended, less predictable, more creative contest to a more familiar, narrower, more orderly, and less passionate one. It represented, in the words of a West Berlin political scientist, "a transformation within the transformation."[9]

The round tables formed the unstable political bridge between these two stages of the revolution. The round tables brought the citizens' opposition groups together with the government and the old and new political parties. They were first constituted on the local level at the initiative of citizens' opposition groups and for a time ran some of the GDR's major cities. The national round table was convened in December 1989 and temporarily served as a second parliament. Yet as the political parties, in the limelight of international media coverage, began to engage in slick and expensive competition for the sympathies of GDR voters, the politically fragile round tables started to degenerate. On March 18, 1990, with the strong showing of those parties with substantial FRG support in the Volkskammer (the GDR's national unicameral legislature) election, control over the fate of the GDR and its revolution passed decisively from the hands of indigenous political forces.[10]

In chapters 3, 4, and 5, I examine the reasons so many GDR workers avoided political involvement during these months of revolution. In chapter 3, I show how workers' day-to-day experience of several features of the labor process—its disorganization, its dishonesty, and its deficient disciplinary and remuneration systems—is implicated in this development. In chapter 4, I consider the contribution workplace politics made to working-class withdrawal from politics during the *Wende*. The focus of this chapter is union organization in the workplace and how its lack of attention to economic and production matters, its subservience to management and the party, its undemocratic leadership selection processes, and the formalism and central-ism of its political practice all conspired to direct workers away from activ-ist politics. In chapter 5, I explain workers' retreat from political activism more fully, demonstrating how two additional features of the class relation-ship not discussed in chapter 1 contributed to the political paralysis of the GDR working class: the lack of sustained contact between workers and the intelligentsia in the years leading up to the revolution and workers' aware-ness of the vast difference between their lives and those of intellectuals.

In chapter 7, I revisit workers' day-to-day experiences of both the labor process and workplace politics, and in so doing, I reveal that even as some of these experiences left many workers with no taste for politics, other expe-riences helped account for the creative activism of the minority. While on the job, GDR workers were continually called on to exercise their ingenuity and problem-solving capabilities, to perform multiple tasks imparting broad knowledge of the overall production process, and to control and manage their own labor, and all three of these labor process experiences helped prepare them for workplace-based activism during the *Wende*. Likewise, in provid-ing a vehicle through which workers had practice actually doing politics, workplace unions helped prepare a handful of workers to assume activist roles. This occurred when workers at the lowest level of union organization—the *Kollektiv*—selected their own leaders, participated in union activities relatively independent of managers and the party, dealt successfully with economic and production matters, and engaged in both decentralized and personalized political practice.

In the last section of chapter 8, I account for the large number of GDR workers I describe as passive participants in the politics of the *Wende*. To understand the political behavior of this middle group, we need to consider the totality of aforementioned outcomes of the labor process, workplace politics, and class, which simultaneously prompted workers toward and away from activism. As the crisis unfolded, GDR workers were so buffeted by forces at once impelling them toward and channeling them away from activism that many found themselves unable to commit fully to an activist course yet un-willing to avoid revolutionary politics altogether. These workers, as well as the labor process, workplace politics, and class dynamics that lay behind their dilemma, are testimony to the puzzling complexities, concealed contradic-tions, and intricate ironies of socialist societies, which, the better I came to know the GDR and before it Cuba, the more I learned to appreciate.

In the last chapter, I turn eastward to Poland and events in the summer and fall of 1980 that gave rise to Solidarity. During these memorable months, the Polish working class displayed the highest and most sophisticated level of activism of workers in any socialist country in the last half of this century.

As such, their behavior poses an unmistakable contrast to that of GDR workers during the *Wende,* providing a good opportunity to discover whether the labor process, workplace politics, and class antecedents of working-class politics in the GDR were unique or whether they bear some relevance to the political behavior of workers elsewhere in the socialist world.

As I disclosed earlier, my interest in social change is motivated by displeasure with the limitations of existing social arrangements. I am hopeful the last chapter demonstrates that my choice of socialist societies as places to conduct studies of social change originating in such motivations is not misguided. Those who see room for improvement in the largely capitalist social systems under which most of us now live can learn a great deal from critical and comparative appraisals of socialism, despite, indeed partly because of, its demise. We can learn about alternative social arrangements, alternatives that we want to avoid but also alternatives we judge positively. More important, we can discover more about how and under what circumstances both types of alternatives emerge, prosper, and fail. All such inquiries offer lessons invaluable to future attempts at social change, yet few of these lessons will be available to us if we avoid the opportunity to unravel the tangled histories of now defunct socialist countries. Neither the GDR nor Poland, nor the brand of socialism of which they were examples, represented the alternative to the inequality, injustice, militarism, and ecological devastation that continue to accompany the spread of capitalism. Clearly such things were part of the socialist experience as well. Nonetheless, knowledge of the socialist histories of the countries of East and Central Europe can help all of us sharpen our ideas about what we want to change, what we care to aim for, the best paths by which to pursue these goals, as well as those we must avoid.

1   Everyday Worlds of Work and Class

Two major premises guide this analysis of workers' involvement in the 1989–90 revolution. The first is that if we are to develop a full account of working-class politics at that time, we must begin from workers' daily lives under GDR socialism. While their daily lives had many facets, there can be no more important facet of workers' everyday experiences to scrutinize than paid work. The workplace was the concrete locality where GDR workers passed a substantial share of their waking hours. Over their lifetimes, a major portion of their physical, mental, and emotional energy was expended there. GDR workers made and maintained important friendships at work. Many family activities were centered at the workplace, which formed people's organizational link to many desired material, social, and cultural amenities as well. So much of so many workers' lives in the GDR revolved around the workplace that an observer once dubbed it their "second home."[1] As principal spaces in which workers lived GDR socialism, workplaces across the country must be understood as producing much more than coal, health care, automobiles, or reports. They also produced people, as workers, with particular experiences of, relationships with, and attitudes about themselves, other workers, their bosses, and socialism in general, all of which, when the moment broke, affected their willingness to become politically active.

My second premise is that the GDR was a class society, fundamentally bipolar in nature, the principal social fissure of which ran between the intelligentsia and the working class. Many observers of the GDR and of socialist societies in general do not share this premise. Because they understand

Marx's idea of class to apply only to capitalism or because they reject his notion of class entirely, some do not regard the GDR as a class society at all. But even those observers who find class a useful prism through which to analyze socialist countries like the GDR do not always understand the class divide the way I do. Some of these scan the social landscape to report at least three classes (a political elite, an intelligentsia, and workers), and even many of those who agree with my dichotomous portrayal of the class structure do not define the working class or the intelligentsia as I do.

The two premises informing this study of working-class politics during the *Wende* are connected in two important ways. First, the everyday world of paid work is precisely what brings the basic divide between the working class and the intelligentsia into sharp relief. In other words, it is from the standpoint of workers doing their daily jobs that the bipolar rift in the GDR class structure can be most clearly discerned. From the standpoints of other people, who had not shared workers' daily experience of paid work, the major outlines of the GDR social structure would not look this way. While alternative standpoints would be appropriate places from which to launch the study of other topics, because my goal is to understand what *workers* did and did not do during the *Wende,* beginning from where they were, where the class structure appeared dichotomous, is the most sensible. Second, workers' experiences of class and the workplace were overlapping and interpenetrating. Neither experience was external to the other. I do not consider one a micro and the other a macro phenomenon. Rather, the workplace was the principal site in which GDR workers participated in the construction of class most immediately and most continuously. At the same time, class and the workplace were not fully coincident features of workers' lives. Class was integral to workers' directly lived experiences at their paid jobs, but it was a social relationship that shaped their daily lives outside the workplace as well.

In exploring the notions of the day-to-day world of paid work and class in more detail, I begin with a discussion of the importance of the everyday for understanding the social world. I then define the working class and the intelligentsia and detail how my definitions differ from those of others who have been party to the debates over the nature of the social structure of societies like the GDR. In the third section, I examine the conglomeration of educational, family, occupational, and political dynamics that ensured the continuation of the two-tier class structure in the GDR and suggest how their dense overlap sustained workers' view of the intelligentsia as undifferentiated. In the fourth section, I explore the basis of this perception more fully, before arguing that the distrust, animosity, and disrespect it helped breed affected the nature of public political protest long before the fall of 1989. These two final sections help us begin to comprehend how and why, from workers' everyday perspective, class mattered during the forty years of the GDR's existence, and how and why it ultimately counted heavily in workers' decisions about what political actions to take or not to take in the twenty-six weeks of its unraveling.

Everyday Worlds

Feminist standpoint theorists have made a powerful case for beginning social research from other than the abstracted Archimedean point of the impartial, disinterested, and socially unsituated observer, so standard and so venerated in Western, masculine science. Dorothy Smith is one of a number of such theorists, and readers familiar with *The Everyday World as Problematic* (1987) will recognize my debt to her from the title of this section. Smith made an especially powerful case for a sociology that begins from people's local and directly acted-in and known worlds, from the actually lived situations that absorb, tantalize, engage, and infuriate them on a day-to-day basis. Smith's work was full of sensuous descriptions of everyday worlds, but of all of them, I am partial to the following, which I have adapted slightly to correspond more closely to the topic of this study:

> She exists in the body, in the place in which it is. This, then, is . . . the place where her coordinates of here and now, before and after, are organized around herself as center; the place where she confronts people face to face. . . . Here there are textures and smells. . . . Here she has the flu. . . . [Here she is bored. Here she learns. Here she is coerced. Here she is challenged and challenges. Here she cooperates with others and makes fast friends.] Into this space must come as actual material events . . . anything she knows of the world. It has to happen here somehow if she is to experience it at all.[2]

Everyday worlds are thus concrete places, where real time passes, as particularly embodied people, in coordination, engage in various mental, physical, and emotional life activities that create and re-create, if only partially, the webs of social relations surrounding them near and far. The real sites in which GDR workers performed their paid labor are just such everyday worlds.

In contrast, most social research, though its generalized, value-neutral, and socially disconnected starting point allows it to disguise the fact, actually begins from what Smith called the perspective of society's extralocal ruling apparatus, "a set of positions in the structures that 'rule' (manage, administrate, organize, and otherwise control)," which are peopled by those who share similar "problems, experiences, concerns, and interests."[3] Two incidents that occurred at a scholarly conference on the GDR during the *Wende* bring

Smith's point home nicely. At lunch I was seated with six other conference participants, whose hour-long conversation regarding their field experiences consisted almost exclusively of animated exchanges of the names and goings-on of politicians, colonels, musicians, academics, and dissidents in the GDR and elsewhere in East and Central Europe, many of whom were well enough known to have been familiar to any regular reader of the *New York Times*. Although I, too, had done research in the GDR, I had little to contribute to the conversation. It was as if I had conducted my research in a different country entirely, which was, of course, exactly Smith's point. After lunch, the conference ran two simultaneous sessions. The first, which played to a packed house, suggesting a resonance with the interests of the scholars in attendance, focused on the role of intellectuals in the rapidly unfolding events in the GDR. The second session, which was concerned with workers' role in the same events, was three-quarters empty. In the light of her critical view of where most social research begins, neither incident would have surprised or pleased Dorothy Smith.

Throughout her book, Smith stressed two points about the sociology of the everyday, which I tried to keep in mind in my work. First, she reminded us that everyday worlds are neither transparent nor obvious. Smith attributed their opaque and hidden quality under capitalism to the fact that everyday worlds are generated by social relations that originate elsewhere, social relations not completely present in, visible from, or encompassed by the everyday. This was also true, in nonidentical ways, of GDR socialism. In contrast, many researchers assume that everyday worlds are transparent and obvious. By that, they often mean uninteresting, simple, humdrum, or irrelevant, and such pejorative judgments of everyday worlds have been used to justify the scant attention they receive in many research accounts. This I would argue, and I think Smith would agree, is one further consequence of beginning sociology, without reflection, from the perspective of the extralocal ruling apparatus, which has historically excluded, disparaged, and discounted the majority not of its rank.

Second, Smith doggedly insisted, "Defining the everyday world as the locus of a sociological problematic is not the same as making it an object of study." To do the latter would be to isolate the everyday world from the surrounding social worlds in which it is situated. Instead, the everyday world represents the point of entry for the researcher, not the end point of inquiry, as with many ethnographies. Everyday worlds are not complete, autonomous, or self-contained, and any approach that treats them as such is therefore inadequate: "We are restricted to the descriptive, to allowing the voices of women's [or other excluded persons'] experience to be heard, unless we can go beyond what our respondents themselves have to tell us. Important as it has been and is to hear the authentic speaking of women [and other excluded persons], it is not sufficient to ground and guide a sociological inquiry." Smith's interest, then, was beginning from the everyday in order to grasp the whole, using people's local and directly experienced worlds to organize "inquiry into the social relations in back of the everyday worlds in which people's existence is embedded."[4] Understanding how the chronic disorganization under which GDR workers expended their labor was linked to the dynamics of the shortage economy and how class was related to union involvement are two examples from subsequent chapters.

There is one important way, however, in which my emphasis in this study diverges from that of Smith. In her insistence on linking the everyday world to outside structures and processes, Smith most often emphasized how the surrounding world impacts everyday worlds. She often spoke of how the everyday world is ordered, shaped, changed, organized, and even determined by social relations and processes external to it. "This is," Smith asserted, "the problematic of the everyday world."[5] While I, too, have tried to map relevant influences of the external on the everyday worlds of GDR workers, the overall thrust of my analysis runs largely in the opposite direction. That is, my line of investigation concentrates on how the everyday worlds of paid work and class left definitive imprints on working-class politics during the *Wende* and ultimately on the fate of the GDR.

Class Definitions

As noted earlier, I view the GDR class landscape as fundamentally bipolar, incorporating both the working class and, roughly following GDR terminology, the intelligentsia. (Sometimes, for stylistic reasons, I refer to the intelligentsia as the middle class or the intellectuals.) The criteria I have chosen to assign people to these two groups combine their education, the content of the work they performed, and their political position. I include in the GDR working class all paid workers without technical college (*Fachschule*) or university (*Hochschule*) degrees—for example, many direct and auxiliary production workers, transportation and construction workers, office and clerical workers, and many service workers. These people often performed manual labor, but many did not. No one, regardless of education, who held a top- or mid-level decision-making or management position in a governmental, administrative, economic, educational, or political group or unit or in a mass organization, such as a union, was considered a worker. All people without higher education degrees who merely worked for or were members of such groups, units, or mass organizations, however, were. Clerical workers at universities, maintenance workers at national union headquarters, and cooks at the Ministry of Culture thus join most employees of factories and service delivery units as members of the GDR working class. So also do workers who were merely members but not leaders of the SED (Socialist Unity Party of Germany).[6]

The GDR intelligentsia includes all paid workers who had technical college or university degrees and who also performed largely mental labor at the time of this study. I also include among the intelligentsia a second group of mental workers who held positions of some political influence, though not all these people had higher education degrees. These were the top- and mid-level decision-making and management personnel in enterprises, in governmental, administrative, economic, educational, and political groups or units, and in mass organizations.[7] By my definition, most people who were currently working in a profession (e.g., physicians, engineers, artists, scientists, teachers, and attorneys) are considered members of the intelligentsia. So, too, are all people, with or without technical college or university degrees, who, for example, managed worksites, directed unions, led the party, oversaw political and educational institutions, and ran local governments or central ministries. Although I do not regard party membership a criterion for inclusion in the intelligentsia, many of the first group were party members, and virtually all of the second group were members, and often leaders, of the SED.

While the dividing line between the working class and the intelligentsia can be spelled out relatively neatly on paper, in practice assigning real people to one or the other class often involves a degree of arbitrariness. Sometimes this is because the quality of information available is poor, sometimes it is because the real-life combination of traits people possess does not easily fit predevised categorization schemes, or sometimes both reasons come into play.[8] We can, however, get a rough idea of the number of people included in the GDR working class and in the intelligentsia using the definition just elaborated. Education statistics are by far the easiest with which to work. Approximately 21 percent (1,663,000) of GDR citizens employed in the socialist economy had earned technical college or university degrees in 1986; approximately 79 percent (6,861,000) of those so employed had no such degree at the time.[9] The 1,663,000 figure comes quite close to estimates made by observers who define the intelligentsia as college-educated people doing largely mental labor.[10] I therefore use it as my ballpark approximation of the size of the GDR intelligentsia and, by subtraction, the working class.

These numbers, however, are not exactly the same as those that would result if we had data to calculate the size of the working class and the intelligentsia using all three of the classification criteria I have proposed (education, content of work performed, and political position). For one thing, of the people with technical college or university degrees employed in the socialist economy, some would not have occupied positions requiring predominantly mental labor. These people, however, are included in the intelligentsia when education statistics alone are used to delineate it, though, by my definition, they would not be considered members of this class. For another, there were people without higher education degrees performing largely mental labor, sometimes as top- and mid-level decision makers and management personnel, who would not count in calculations of intelligentsia based solely on education but who, by my definition, belong in this group.[11] We get some help figuring the total size of the top- and mid-level decision-making and management group from estimates of the size of the superelite and the party or party-related elite in the GDR. Estimates of the superelite range from approximately 1,500 to approximately 10,000, while estimates of the party or party-related elite, usually designated as the party leadership or the nomenclature, range between 60,000 and 500,000.[12] In both cases, however, only some of these people—those with higher education—would have been included in the 1,663,000 figure cited earlier.

The most notable difference between my class categorization scheme and many others is that my categorization method *excludes* many people others have considered part of the working class, while it *includes* many people in the top social tier other schemes have excluded. The sharpest contrast is with many official GDR portrayals of the class structure, which included almost everyone in the working class. Hence, Walter Ulbricht, head of state until 1973, could once declare that "the scientist, the artist, the technician, and the engineer are now firmly integrated within the working-class community."[13] Besides such technological and cultural elites, administrators, managers, and top government, party, security, and union employees were also lumped alongside white- and blue-collar workers, mental and manual laborers, in the working class. Everyone, in Rudolf Bahro's words, "from the cleaning lady to the highest politbureaucrat" became part of it. Since this official categorization was based on a person's relationship to productive property, the only people not classified as workers turned out to be cooperative and private farmers and fishers, private craftspeople, independent contractors, and private traders and retailers. The official portrayal did not identify any serious structural source of conflict within the social formation. For all intents and purposes, the GDR appeared virtually classless.[14]

Ironically, adherents to what has come to be known as the totalitarian perspective on socialist societies, those who would most shudder to think of themselves sharing anything at all with GDR officialdom, likewise inflated the size of the lower social rung and deflated the size of the upper, in my estimation quite dramatically. Observers sympathetic to the totalitarian view relied almost exclusively on political criteria to distinguish between what they often termed the ruling elite and the masses in socialist societies. From their viewpoint, the nomenclature was usually contrasted with the rest of society, which then incorporated the highly and lowly educated, the mental and the manual laborers alike.[15] In an amendment of Bahro's prior characterization, the politbureaucrat was segregated from the masses, which came to include everyone from the cleaning lady and the hod carrier to the doctor, the department manager, the engineer, and the filmmaker. Two possibly antagonistic classes were now discernible on the socialist landscape, but, just as in the official version of social structure, nearly everybody in the GDR still ended up in only one of them.

There were many other observers, however, who distinguished more than peasants and fisherpeople or a ruling elite from the rest of the people in socialist countries. Their principal addition to the class maps of these countries was an intelligentsia. Yet the criteria they used to locate this group, its political importance, and how they viewed its relationship with the political elite and workers varied greatly. A few examples will help clarify, by comparison, the conception of the intelligentsia I employ.

The content of labor performed, one of the three criteria I use to differentiate classes in the GDR, is the major criterion both Rudolf Bahro and Hillel Ticktin used to delimit the intelligentsia from other classes under socialism. Bahro contrasted intellectual labor, which demands abstraction and differentiation, with other types of labor, while Ticktin focused on whether a person alienated his or her labor power (workers), had partial control over the surplus product (elite), or did some of both (intelligentsia).[16] For Bahro, however, "traditional horizontal" class groupings, such as the intelligentsia and the working class, were not especially useful for understanding the normal functioning of socialist societies, though he distinguished between the intelligentsia and the bureaucracy under this circumstance.[17] Yet in his vision of how an actually existing socialist society might be transformed into a more democratic socialist one, the intelligentsia suddenly assumed a vanguard role in the struggle against the bureaucracy. Bahro was adamant that the abilities needed to lead the progressive transformation of socialism are not distributed equally or randomly throughout society. Rather, these abilities are unambiguously concentrated among "those strata anchored in the higher functional levels of labour."[18]

Ticktin also devoted attention to change in socialist societies, and while he recognized that the boundary between the elite and the intelligentsia is blurry, his discussion of the dynamics of socialism, like Bahro's, depended on its existence.[19] Although both Bahro and Ticktin paid some attention to workers, in neither account did workers appear to matter much in understanding the transformation of socialism. The pivotal struggles occurred between the intelligentsia and the bureaucratic elite, which could be easily distinguished from each other when it came to explaining change.[20] In contrast, I argue that the politics of the GDR revolution can be fully grasped only when we understand that the demarcation between the elite and intelligentsia can be irrelevant. In other words, understanding the most dramatic change in the forty years of GDR existence requires a viewpoint that stresses the similarities, not the differences, between them.

George Konrád and Ivan Szelényi did not hedge from their contention that the class structure of socialist societies was basically dichotomous. Workers, who were "deprived of any right to participate in redistribution," were contrasted with intellectuals, who, on the basis of specialized knowledge acquired primarily through higher education, carried out the redistribution of the surplus that workers produced.[21] Instead of workers receding in prominence, it was the elite, now merged with the intelligentsia, that did so. However, when Konrád and Szelényi began to explore the sociopolitical dynamics of socialism, the vagarious relationship between the ruling group at the apex of the intelligentsia and the mass of intellectuals below it, particularly the technocracy, became critical. Although I agree with much of Konrád and Szelényi's portrayal, I make far less analytical use of the elite-intelligentsia divide than they did for two reasons. First, my explicit goal, which Konrád and Szelényi did not share, is to explain working-class politics by starting, insofar as possible, from the everyday standpoints of workers themselves. Second, my chief interest, also unlike Konrád and Szelényi's, is to account for working-class politics during a period of dramatic crisis. In attempting both tasks, I became convinced that more could be revealed from an analytical lens focused on the gulf that divided the working class from the rest of GDR society than from one riveted on the fissures within the top social stratum, which Konrád, Szelényi, and I all regard as the intelligentsia.

Michael Kennedy's analysis of the massive changes in Polish society prompted by the rise of Solidarity in the early 1980s rested on a much less homogenous depiction of the top social stratum than either Konrád and Szelényi's or my own. Kennedy distinguished four important social groupings—the elite, the vassals of the elite, professionals, and the intelligentsia—within Poland's top social layer. Yet in elaborating his characterization, Kennedy did not drop workers from his account of change. Rather, he pointed to the relations between the working class and professionals, who exhibited significant overlap with the vassals, as key to understanding Poland during this period. Kennedy introduced some interesting criteria for disentangling politically significant social groupings in socialist societies. Political position, personal connections, education, and, to a lesser extent, the content of labor performed all played roles in his demarcation of subgroups within the upper social stratum. Overall, however, his scheme still resulted in an upper stratum that was somewhat less inclusive than I argue it to be. College-educated people in the arts and religion, for example, whose politics and whose pre-*Wende* relations with workers mattered a great deal during the revolution, seemed to slip easily from the top social rung in Kennedy's work. So, too, in all likelihood, did a host of college-educated people who performed largely mental labor as managers of small and mid-size production and service delivery establishments, as well as some mid-level people in state, party, and security organs. GDR producers, however, would have been unlikely to view any of these people as fellow workers.[22]

Class Reproduction

So far, the depiction of the GDR social structure, however complex, amounts to no more than a snapshot. But what of the moving picture of class in the GDR? In other words, what do we know of the social dynamics continuously at work that rendered the division between workers and intellectuals a long-standing and prominent feature of GDR socialism? What processes, institutions, and relations were implicated in the production and reproduction of the class divide during the GDR's history?[23]

If one were somehow to diagram class reproduction in the GDR, the picture would reveal a number of hub processes, institutions, and relations. Among these nodal points would be the educational system, families, the political system, and the occupational structure.[24] None of these, however, would be discrete. Rather, each would be linked to all the others through dense, complicated, two-way paths, the totality of which would represent the overall dynamics of class reproduction in the GDR. I do not attempt to trace all the linkages among all the nodal points in this hypothetical diagram, for there are far too many. Instead, I concentrate on the connections between the four listed above and their contribution to the ongoing re-creation of the GDR class structure. The education system, which Gert-Joachim Glaeßner called the most important instrument of planned social structural change since the early years of the GDR,[25] is my point of departure.

From the beginning, the GDR pursued a conscious strategy designed to uncouple class background and educational attainment. It attempted to achieve this goal through a number of policies, including class-based quotas favoring worker admission to higher education and liberal financial assistance for students. Multiple routes to higher education were also created in an effort to increase its accessibility for working-class students.[26] As a consequence of such policies, the proportion of university students from working-class backgrounds, which had amounted to only 3 percent before the war, reached between 55 and 65 percent by the mid-1970s.[27] While some observers applauded these achievements,[28] others emphasized the ways in which the educational system, through its links to other nodal points in the hypothetical diagram, helped mold and solidify the bipolar class structure of the GDR. In a word, they maintained the educational system perpetuated the division between workers and the intelligentsia, not diluted it.

The first link such critics noticed was the one between families and the educational system, which helped preserve GDR class differences in ways reminiscent of capitalist countries. Children raised in middle-class families were educationally advantaged by their class upbringing throughout their school careers. Observers commented on the superior school preparation enjoyed by youngsters of the intelligentsia. Superior preparation took the form of more ample resources (e.g., wealthier families could afford private tutors to prepare their children for admissions exams); more developed linguistic, mental, and motor skills; heightened motivation for formal learning; and more school-appropriate social skills and behaviors. All this amounted, in János Kornai's words, to a significant "intellectual inheritance" accruing to the middle class.[29] In addition, informal connections apparently played no small role in university admissions, and here young people from middle-class families were clearly advantaged. "Children of different social backgrounds," concluded one GDR scholar, "profited differently from a system of universal education and from the same educational possibilities."[30]

But it was not only that a middle-class background advantaged young people in ways that allowed them to profit disproportionately from a class-neutral educational system. It was also that the educational system and educational policy themselves exhibited class bias and therefore helped create and re-create the existing class division. One place this was evident was in the implementation of GDR-style tracking policies. To begin with, there was an entire subsystem of more generously funded classes, schools, colleges, and institutes (some known as party schools), which offered special curriculums to prepare students for high-status careers in politics and the economy. Second, university-prep tracks designed for working-class students were said to be harder and lengthier than the prep tracks middle-class students were more likely to choose. Third, in the 1980s, a conscious push was undertaken to identify particularly talented students at a very young age, and this gifted core, especially those in natural science and engineering, was provided the best the GDR educational system could offer. Finally, tracking was implicated in the solidification of the dual-class system through its contribution to the class-homogenous marriage pattern in the GDR.[31] By the time they had reached the average age for choosing marriage partners, GDR young people had for years been channeled into either college or noncollege school tracks. Hence, the pool from which many would select their future spouses was essentially limited to one containing young people of like class standing.

That children from intellectual families were educationally privileged before entering the school system and that the system itself functioned to reproduce an intelligentsia of relative educational advantage can be seen in the following figures: in 1985, 53 percent of university students in mechanical engineering, 75 percent of those in social sciences, and 78 percent of those in natural sciences had fathers with technical college or university degrees. Among those studying to be teachers, on whom would devolve much of the responsibility for selecting the students who would move onto advanced education tracks in the future, this figure rose to 82 percent.[32]

The educational system contributed to the reproduction of the bipolar GDR class structure through its relationship with not only families but also the political system. This connection was most obvious in the role the SED played in the educational admissions process. In Thomas Baylis's view, for example, the importance of party membership for entrance into institutions of higher learning was much more pronounced in the GDR than in either Poland or Hungary.[33] One way this worked was that party leaders informally pressured admissions officers to ease their children's entrance into the university or technical college of their choice. The link between politics and education could also operate to deny higher education to some. A number of people I interviewed after the *Wende* said that they were refused admission to a university because they did not belong to the SED or one of the Block parties or that they were denied permission to take the exam (*Abitur*) necessary for university entrance because they had evidenced passive disagreement with some SED policy.[34] Freya Klier argued that not only did applicants' political affiliations and activities color their admission chances but so also did the political reliability and activity of their parents, especially if applicants wanted to study in such fields as pedagogy, language, art, journalism, law, or social science. This situation, she continued, distinctly favored the "intelligentsia and the functionaries."[35] Finally, exemplary party members were provided with multiple opportunities (sabbaticals, time off work, special courses, financial support) to secure their college degrees, opportunities less readily available to those with less political visibility.

The education-politics connection worked in the opposite direction as well. That is, while politics were important for educational success, educational achievement mattered for political success. The SED paid special attention to the ranks of recent higher education graduates in recruiting new members.[36] Such credentials made a big difference to those who sought leadership positions in the SED as well. The close attention the party paid to the educational achievement of its leaders, which it exercised through its cadre selection, training, and mentoring policies, is suggested by the fact that by the 1980s approximately 65 percent of its base-level leaders and nearly 100 percent of its county- and district-level leaders possessed higher education degrees.[37] Education in special party schools was also beneficial for ascending the party hierarchy. Finally, figures indicate that higher education was almost essential for some government positions. By the 1970s, 96 percent of the leaders and scientific staff of the central government apparatus and over 90 percent of both county (*Bezirk*) and district (*Kreis*) council members held technical college or university degrees.[38]

The association between education and occupation was yet a third connection implicated in the reproduction of class in the GDR. One indirect, yet institutionalized, way in which these two were joined was through the nomenclature. The nomenclature assembled lists of key positions throughout the country, whose occupants had to receive party confirmation before assuming their posts. The leadership positions on these lists were not limited to those in the party itself. They also included judges, government administrators, legislators, some members of local government executive committees, as well as high-level posts in factories (e.g., general and department directors of *Kombinate* [conglomerates] and heads of the factories constituting them) and in research institutes, farms, service delivery agencies, mass organizations, the education and health systems, and cultural organizations. The nomenclature system was operationalized through personnel pools, continuously updated at appropriate party levels, from which the positions on the nomenclature were ordinarily filled.

The nomenclature linked jobs to higher education because positions on the nomenclature required occupants to hold a technical college or university degree. Competition for the most prestigious jobs in the GDR was thus formally limited to the 21 percent of the population with such credentials. As a further guarantor of such an outcome, a college degree was also a main qualification individuals deemed suitable for the personnel pools from which nomenclature posts were filled had to possess. In fact, county-level party organizations attempted to keep personnel records on every person in their jurisdiction who had advanced schooling.[39] The education-occupation link achieved through the nomenclature was considerable: Kennedy estimated that between 1 and 4 percent of all jobs in Soviet-style societies fell under the nomenclature system, and in the GDR, by Hermann Weber's calculation, about half a million SED members were listed on the nomenclature.[40]

Although the majority of jobs in the GDR never appeared on any nomenclature, they were also closely tied to educational attainment in a direct and familiar, though informal, way. The more job holders could control their own labor, instead of having it controlled by someone else, the more likely their positions required a higher education degree. Rudolf Bahro called higher education "the entrance ticket to a bureaucratic career, in no matter which branch" in socialist countries,[41] and George Konrád and Ivan Szelényi concurred. Those with university degrees found a multiplicity of good positions open to them, even "including some whose knowledge-requirements do not correspond to the curriculum of the degree-granting university." For Konrád and Szelényi, this was because the knowledge gained through higher education was not viewed narrowly or technically under socialism. Rather, "the teleological element in it is decisive, and that is why it is so easily convertible." "Almost as neutral as capital itself," the knowledge signified by the possession of a higher education degree "serves as a kind of bureaucratic medium of exchange." For Konrád and Szelényi, a higher education diploma at once defined the parameters of the intelligentsia and legitimated the existence and activities of a class whose members held those positions in the occupational structure from which socialist society was controlled.[42]

While the extent to which higher-level jobs demanded higher education credentials was especially pronounced in the GDR, the union between education and occupation was fortified through reverse processes as well. People already occupying positions at the apex of the occupational structure were afforded special opportunities to enhance their educational standing. For example, Eckhard Schröter reported that "a considerable portion" of public administrators were enrolled in correspondence courses or were given leaves to study at universities. Likewise, David Granick showed that education was ongoing for those occupying top slots in GDR enterprises and factories. People in these positions regularly availed themselves of the chance to enroll in postgraduate courses, some of which were offered under the auspices of the regular higher education system and others of which took place in a special school run by the Central Committee of the SED.[43]

Had we begun our exploration of class reproduction from any other nodal point in our diagram besides education, we would have uncovered other ways in which the GDR class division was continuously redrawn as people lived their lives in the midst of privileged or nonprivileged webs of education, family, political, and occupational institutions, processes, and relations. Among these, the conspicuous connection between occupation and politics (variously conceived as party standing, level of political participation, loyalty to superiors, or political conformity) would stand out prominently.[44] Kennedy developed the implications of this connection for class reproduction in a particularly interesting and accurate way. Vassals—for example, managers of large factories, holders of key media positions, important party and government figures, and professional members of the security apparatus—owed their positions to their obedience and loyalty to the political elite.

Inertia, passivity, conformity, and avoidance of responsibility thus became commonplace in this strata. Viewed another way, these traits, emanating simultaneously from every major organization in socialist society, were the behavioral manifestations of powerful systemic arrangements that served to maintain the social status quo.[45]

No matter where we started our investigation of class reproduction in the GDR, we would soon be struck by one of its characteristics that has important consequences for this study. The two-class system was reproduced along the multiple strands of a very dense web of interpenetrating family, education, political, and occupational processes, institutions, and relations. The very density of this web meant that, from workers' perspectives, their bosses, the doctors at the clinic, the managers at the supermarket, the teachers at the school, and the well-known figure skater and poet all approximated one another in important ways. They nearly all had higher education degrees as well as an office in the party, the union, the town council, or a mass or cultural organization. They spoke and dressed in a similar fashion, they sought one another's company, and they were confident their children were college or university bound. Said another way, the exceptionally close linkages between the institutions, relations, and processes implicated in the reproduction of class made it quite reasonable for workers to lump all such individuals, from their boss to the poet, in the same apparently self-contained, self-selecting, self-absorbed, and self-legitimating social category. From where GDR workers stood, they were *all* "them."[46]

Class Relationships

The nature of the pre-*Wende* relationship between workers and the intelligentsia was a social backdrop against which workers made their choices about what they would and would not do during the crisis. The tendency for GDR workers to understand the intelligentsia as a homogenous group, which made sense in the light of the manner in which classes were reproduced in the GDR, constituted a fundamental feature of this relationship.[47]

I anticipate strong objection, however, to my claim that workers, or anyone else, could or should view the GDR intelligentsia as homogenous. After all, volumes have been written detailing the differences within this social stratum, once called the most socially heterogeneous group in the country.[48] Besides the distinction commonly drawn between the political intelligentsia and the remainder of the stratum, which I explore later, extensive attention has been devoted to the difference between the "old" (presocialist) and the "new" intelligentsia. Observers have also distinguished among various sectors of the intelligentsia on the basis of the quality of their training, the economic sector in which they worked, their area of formal study, their modes of domination, and, very often, their political ideologies. The most common distinction I encountered in the GDR—between intellectuals working in production and those working in research centers, schools, and cultural establishments—can also be added to this list.[49]

Were workers, then, simply mistaken in their reading of the intelligentsia as undifferentiated? Did their inability to perceive the ideological, historical, disciplinary, organizational, and other fissures within this stratum, so obvious and so significant to intellectuals themselves,[50] merely reflect their unrefined social sensibilities? I think not. Rather, I suspect we are confronting a difficult epistemological matter here. That is, the heterogeneity often attributed to the intelligentsia is a partial result of the fact that our knowledge about class under socialism has been produced almost exclusively by intellectuals. What we know about the socialist intelligentsia therefore carries the flavor of an insider's account, and insiders are notoriously able and willing to discover great complexity, intricate patterning, and nuanced distinctions within their own ranks.[51] An example is the large body of academic and popular work, mostly authored by whites, that pays inordinate attention to Irish, Italian, Polish, Scandinavian, and other ethnic distinctions among whites in the United States but treats African Americans as if they were all of a single ethnicity.

Thus, where many written accounts described diversity within the GDR intelligentsia, I suggest GDR workers more often perceived homogeneity. The point is not that either the variegated or the flat view of the intelligentsia is the true one. Whichever perspective is most revealing depends on the reasons a researcher wonders about class under socialism in the first place.[52] My goal is to understand and explain *workers'* politics during the *Wende,* and to do this satisfactorily, I join Dorothy Smith and others in insisting that we try to comprehend, as best we can, what things were like from where workers were. And from where they stood, from the bottom of the class ladder looking up, fissures between various strains of the intelligentsia blurred to the point where the group appeared virtually uniform.

In spite of the epistemological prejudices against recognizing the intelligentsia as homogenous, do GDR workers find any theoretical or empirical collaboration of their view that party bosses, chemists, poets, and enterprise managers all pertained to the same undifferentiated social stratum? They clearly do from Szelényi, who wrote that following de-Stalinization, "intellectuals of all sorts, from humanistic intellectuals and ideologues to technocrats, [now joined] the circle of powerholders, merging with the bureaucrats."[53] Others, sometimes inadvertently, painted an analogous picture.[54] But what if we focus more sharply on the relationships among some of the most commonly delineated segments of this stratum, such as the political, the scientific-technical, the managerial, and the oppositional intelligentsia? Might such an approach reveal at least some groups of intellectuals that workers did not lump together with all the rest? It does not seem to. Instead, focusing on the relationships among specific segments of the intelligentsia makes it even more evident why GDR workers viewed them as homogenous.

In the GDR, as everywhere in East and Central Europe, the relationship between the political and all other segments of the intelligentsia came under the closest scrutiny, and this attention revealed that the boundary separating the political intelligentsia from the remainder of intellectuals was quite fluid. Whatever the tensions between sectors of the intelligentsia, M. Donald Hancock argued that "they comprise[d] a leadership *community* with overlapping values, interests, and to some extent membership."[55] The social composition of the party membership and leadership of the GDR can be read this way. At periods between the mid-1970s and the mid-1980s, the intellectual sector of the SED grew more rapidly than its working-class component, the result of a party decision to "saturate" the scientific-technical and cultural intelligentsia. By the early 1980s, 34 percent of the party membership and between 66 and 100 percent of various party leadership bodies had higher education degrees, a trend that continued into the late 1980s, by which time over 50 percent of SED recruits had earned such degrees and nearly all higher education graduates had joined the party.[56]

While it has been suggested that some of these intellectuals were reluctant, even hostile, participants in the party, such ideological subtleties were probably lost on many workers, particularly the vast majority who were not SED members themselves and had little direct knowledge of or access to internal party workings. What was more likely obvious to them was that the members of the intelligentsia with whom they were acquainted outside their paid work—for example, their child's teacher and the engineer across the street—were all party members or leaders. On top of this, as one worker recalled, "Party groups inside workplaces were never as grass-roots as they claimed to be. In mine, the group was mostly people who worked in offices. There were maybe only three or four production workers, so they didn't have that much to say about what went on in the *Betrieb* [factory or work establishment]."[57] These views from the bottom correspond nicely to the post-*Wende* reflections of an intellectual and well-known oppositional figure: "[The ruling clique was] 'allied' with us, as the official phrase was. We were useful parasites, fed by the ruling clique. We were like Buddenbrook's wife, who also had nothing to say, but who nevertheless belonged to the bourgeoisie."[58]

The institutional merger of the political intelligentsia with the rest of the intelligentsia through the party held, to varying degrees, across East and

Central Europe.[59] But if the experience in other countries is any indication, even members of the GDR intelligentsia who were not in the party could have been easily mistaken for their card-carrying social counterparts. They had acquaintances and good friends in the party, they publicly hobnobbed with party figures, and they were beholden to the party in a host of ways. Konrád and Szelényi imparted a flavor of this dependence:

> The highest political leaders will willingly receive him when he calls and will gladly attend to requests of his, as a favor—finding an apartment for a son about to be married or seeing to a passport for a young colleague whom the police had refused one. The other side of the coin is that . . . he has to ask the intervention of his friend on the Central Committee not only if he wants to accept an invitation from abroad, but even if he wants merely to have a telephone installed in his new apartment or to have his name put at the head of the list for buying a car. But if next week or next month the political police should happen to call on him and ask in the politest way possible for information about a young and apparently thoughtless friend, student, or colleague, and if he should hesitate to cooperate in a confidential inquiry, then he will soon learn . . . he is in their hands.[60]

The plausibility of workers' undifferentiated understanding of the intelligentsia is further substantiated when we narrow our focus to the relationship between the political intelligentsia and specific subgroups within the GDR middle class. By 1975, the largest of these subgroups was the scientific-technical intelligentsia, and all evidence suggests that GDR workers would have been particularly unlikely to perceive this group as separate from the political intelligentsia. For decades, the alliance between these two agglomerations of intellectuals had been closer in the GDR than in many other East and Central European countries.[61] Commentary on this relationship repeatedly suggested how easy it would have been for workers to view engineers, economists, accountants, and planners as virtually indistinguishable from the country's political leadership. Manfred Grote regarded members of the scientific-technical intelligentsia as well integrated, unquestioning "partners, not rivals" of the political caste; Michael Sodaro noted that they were "successfully co-opted by the regime" and showed no signs "of wishing to jeopardize [their] stake in [it]"; Mary Fulbrook concurred, casting them as political conformists in the service of the ruling elite.[62]

Pre-*Wende* observations of the GDR likewise indicated that the working class could readily have understood workplace management as the close social kin of the political intelligentsia. Comments recorded during interviews illustrate this:

The boss of the factory was in the Communist party. The bosses of the factory boss were also in the party. That was the problem.

Our management worked with the Politburo and other leaders of the party. And we are pretty sure that they worked with the Stasi too.[63]

Workers' perceptions of a social congruency between management and members of the political intelligentsia were well captured in the common complaint that managers rarely set foot in actual work areas without being totally surrounded by packs of party functionaries and state leaders.[64]

The intellectual subgroup we might least likely expect workers to perceive as socially similar to the political elite would undoubtedly be the oppositional or dissident intelligentsia. After all, the self-identity of this group, many of whom were artists, writers, and the like, hinged on its critical stance toward the country's political leadership.[65] Yet from workers' social location, there was ample reason to think oppositional intellectuals bore a striking resemblance to others of their class—engineers, economists, managers, and so on— who supported, rather than challenged, the reigning political establishment.[66]

For one thing, after the wall was constructed and especially after Erich Honecker (head of the SED from 1971 to 1989) announced a more open cultural policy in the early 1970s, there was a slow, though steady and perceptible, warming of relations between the SED and the dissident intelligentsia.[67] The public face of this gradual warming was the government's erratic, yet highly proclaimed, liberalization of visa, publication, and performance policies and its reluctance to punish vigorously the transgressions of certain dissidents as fully as the law allowed. For another, some members of the oppositional intelligentsia became quite friendly with members of the political intelligentsia, even finding themselves on the best guest lists and the recipients of prestigious public awards.[68] Moreover, organizations with largely middle-class memberships, including those known for their oppositional stance, enjoyed discernible independence from the party and a degree of intra-organizational democracy unmatched in other organizations in the country.

Even the numerous intellectual dissidents associated with the Protestant church, far and away the GDR institution most independent from the government, may have looked like their avowed middle-class adversaries to most workers. Consider, for example, the frequency with which supporters of the church-linked peace movement and other dissident church factions were either party members themselves or children of staunch party families, had trusted party contacts, or exhibited an identifiable party style. Moreover, even as the church grew into a refuge for critical dissidents, some of only peripheral religious bent, it seemed to prosper politically. Despite overt public conflicts with the government, the church was permitted to pursue a wide range of officially sanctioned activities, it was allowed to operate relatively autonomously, and the government even had an affirmative action program for the children of pastors, who thus came to be overrepresented in college-track secondary schools.[69] All these things created pressure on the dissident intellectuals associated with the church to temper their challenges to the regime. For many people, the church's unwillingness to distinguish itself from the political elite was best typified by its 1971 pledge to function as a church within, not a church alongside or against, socialism, a policy that translated into frequent local church actions suggesting subservience to, rather than independence from, the government.[70] The "Church from Below" was apparently concerned that this policy had already moved oppositional intellectuals too close to the regime. At its 1987 founding, the group declared that it had come together "because the church has already lost part of its basis—the workers—and it is about to lose the rest."[71]

Since the *Wende,* the often tortured confessions of oppositional intellectuals have highlighted how easy it would have been for workers to perceive an overlap between the political intelligentsia and its oppositional cousins. There is perhaps no better example than the 1990 statement of Wolf Biermann, an exiled singer and widely revered symbol of intellectual opposition: "We were closely connected to and implicated with our opponents. . . . We were a family, divided in bitter dispute, but a family nonetheless."[72] Considered alongside other indications of their proximity to the political intelligentsia, the expression *corridor dissident,*[73] connoting a pampered insider critic who now and then expressed polite disagreement from a safe party or professional niche, may have seemed to workers an apt description of oppositional intellectuals who nonetheless fancied themselves the regime's biggest political problem. From where workers stood, the political intelligentsia and the oppositional intelligentsia did not appear as arch enemies. Rather, many GDR workers would have shared Konrád and Szelényi's assessment that "the critical intelligentsia . . . is part of the intellectual class, from which neither its structural position nor its value-system will allow it to secede."[74]

Although GDR workers had many concrete reasons for viewing the intelligentsia as homogenous, this was not the only facet of the pre-*Wende* class relationship of importance for understanding workers' politics during the *Wende.* Two others also emerge as central. First, workers were keenly aware of the difference between their own lives and those of intellectuals, and, second, they had few sustained contacts with the intelligentsia in the years before the crisis. Although these two topics are not fully explored until chapter 5, they deserve brief mention here because, in combination with workers' perception of the intellectual stratum as uniform, they had translated into suspicion, animosity, and disrespect between workers and the intelligentsia for years before the *Wende*. This translation was neither automatic nor invariable. Nevertheless, the GDR class relationship had not been a neutral one for decades before the revolution, and, as will be apparent shortly, this left an indelible mark on pre-*Wende* political protest in the GDR that endured through the fall and winter of 1989–90.

The workplace was one location within and around which a miasma of interclass hostility and anger sometimes surfaced. This became palpable during pre-*Wende* interviews when intellectuals let me know they felt workers were coddled by virtual full employment and extensive worker protections and social programs. Workers, I was told, could get away with murder on the job. I am reminded, for instance, of a conversation with the head of the personnel department (a position typically occupied by a party leader) in a farm equipment factory. After a long monologue on what he considered the firm's two major problems—absenteeism and low productivity—I asked what he could do about these problems in the personnel department. I was quickly set straight. Absenteeism and low productivity were not problems in *his* department. Things were different there because "everyone is highly qualified. They are all college graduates. *They* know the importance of what *they* do for society. So problems with the maximum use of labor time aren't *our* problems."[75]

Working-class resentment of the GDR intelligentsia jelled around several worksite matters before the *Wende*. From workers' point of view, intellectuals often did not appear to do much, or much of value, at work; there were far too many of them at most worksites; they were disrespectful of workers and did not take them seriously; they enjoyed too many work-related privileges, and they were paid too much. The joke Michael Burawoy and János Lukács heard from Hungarian workers captures this last sentiment well. It concerns the contributions three people made to socialism: "The first receives five thousand forints a month. He builds socialism. The second receives fifteen thousand forints a month. He directs the building of socialism. The third receives fifty thousand forints a month. For him, socialism is built."[76] Surely such bitterness over class inequalities at the workplace, here blunted by humor, was sharpened by their juxtaposition with reigning ideology and cultural prescriptions, which enshrined the working class as the source of all value and progress and adulated it as the country's leading political class.

The pre-*Wende* bitterness and distrust between workers and the intelligentsia was not confined to work or workplace issues, however. Interclass antagonisms had long spread beyond workers' relationships with their bosses and others higher up the workplace hierarchy. I commonly heard GDR intellectuals recite, sometimes in patronizing tones, a litany of generic critiques of the working class: workers had little concern for such "higher" principles as democracy and freedom; workers were too materialistic (the irony is that intellectuals had more material goods); workers were oriented to the present, not the future, and were thus unable to fathom the importance of political participation; workers could not think for themselves, were untrustworthy, and did not bother to inform themselves; and workers had a hard time processing theoretical problems and comprehending the content and the language of intellectual discourse.[77] In addition, when middle-class people complained about something in the GDR, I probed for their thoughts on how this might be changed, often to be met with elitist renditions of how social change had to originate from the higher social stratum, not from the working class. Dirk Philipsen had the same experience: "We figured [prior to the *Wende*] that if already existing resentment and anger were to break out from below, there would be neither a future for the GDR nor a possibility for a renewal of socialism. So we thought change would have to originate from above, and then could be responded to from below."[78] Finally, at more than one cultural event, I even heard intellectuals make snide remarks about how unfashionably workers were dressed.[79]

Many GDR workers also harbored uncomplimentary views of the intelligentsia not related to work. As far back as the 1950s, a survey of workers revealed that 73 percent either took a "critical position" toward the intelligentsia or expressed "strong aggression" toward them.[80] More recent accounts likewise abound with workers' negative opinions of the intelligentsia: the largely middle-class peace activists were sometimes seen as unprincipled; the nomenclature, party officials, and the Stasi were viewed contemptuously by those who did not share their class position; teachers were resented for their authoritarian and ideologically conformist ways; the cultural establishment was disliked by many; and the privileged class was derided for its fear of speaking out in public.[81] Working-class anger over material privileges in particular was often apparent to outside observers. Carl Bradley Scharf, for instance, related indignation over class differences in auto ownership, and even some less conspicuous material inequalities irritated workers. Helga Michalsky noted that supplementary pensions for intelligentsia had to be handled gingerly and that the difference between general pensions and those awarded some intellectuals had to have provoked resentment.[82]

In the forty-year life of the GDR, working-class antagonism toward the intelligentsia only rarely manifested itself in overt, collective ways. More often, as in much of East and Central Europe, it took more subtle, often individual forms, and people outside the immediate locale of its expression were not likely to hear about it. Workers told, for example, of sending letters and petitions of complaint to union leaders and sometimes even posting these on workplace bulletin boards.[83] So far as we know, however, only once in a while did resentment against intellectuals find more militant expression.[84] The "banana fight" Paul Gleye heard about is one example: "At coffee break one day the story went around of an incident in the nearby city of Erfurt. A group of high-school students had brought bananas to school and were promptly beaten up by other students. Bananas were then only available at the special shops for use by Party functionaries."[85] The "coffee strike" Werner Volkmer reported, a visible collective effort that also required some planning and coordination, is another:

> In one case, East German workers actually went on strike. The authorities had withdrawn one brand of coffee and virtually withdrew another, so that only the most expensive brand was available. The labour force in the Fritz-Heckert-Werke in Karl-Marx-Stadt walked out in protest. Having been told by Ulbricht during the 1960s that East Germany had become a "socialist community of men," East German workers found it difficult to accept new social divisions developing in such a society. All in all, fifty workers were taken into custody because of the strike.[86]

Workers, of course, well understood that hard currency was a main requirement for obtaining many of the material privileges of the intelligentsia. Their publicly demonstrated displeasure with the middle class was therefore sometimes expressed in the idiom of the deutsche mark; travel to the West, a principal means of securing the currency; and the network of Intershops, where hard currency could be spent. At least a decade before the *Wende,* Volkmer pointed out, "In several big companies strikes were threatened should proposed Intershops be opened nearby. And in a big machine construction company to the north of Berlin the traditionally militant work force demanded that their wages be paid partly in hard currency so that they could join in the new Intershop consumerism."[87]

The most memorable occasion on which workers challenged the intelligentsia was the workers' uprising of June 1953. In the context of our current concerns, this event was important not just because approximately half a million workers were involved, making it by far the largest group protest in the GDR before the *Wende,* but also because it reveals a social pattern to protest activities that existed long before the 1989–90 revolution. The June 17 uprising, like the disturbances and strikes that occurred for a time afterward, was almost exclusively working class. Nearly every account of the events of June 1953 highlighted the absence of intelligentsia support for working-class actions.[88] "The middle classes and the intelligentsia played little or no part," according to Arnulf Baring. "The technologists in general," he continued, "either sat quietly in their offices or made their way home when the workers grew restive."[89] The same pattern reappeared in a second wave of unrest, which followed Khrushchev's denunciation of Stalin at the Twentieth Party Congress in the Soviet Union. Yet this time protesters came almost entirely from the intelligentsia. Workers stayed out of the fray.[90]

Conclusion

The pre-*Wende* relationship between workers and intellectuals in the GDR might be envisioned as a complex cloth woven of multiple threads, each spun of the perceptions, experiences, and concrete interactions one class had of and with the other. Of all these threads, three are particularly important to the story of working-class politics during the revolution: workers' understanding of the intelligentsia as homogenous, discussed in this chapter; workers' recognition of the deep social gulf that separated them from middle-class citizens; and the truncated contact between workers and the intelligentsia in the years preceding the revolution, both of which await full development in chapter 5. These three facets had both combined and separate impacts on working-class politics during the 1989–90 crisis. We have just learned of one way in which the three converged to influence workers' politics. Together they generated resentment and distrust between the classes that translated into the pattern of class-exclusive protest witnessed over the course of the GDR's existence. In other words, when it came to the history of public political protest in the GDR, the biographies of workers and intellectuals had moved along divergent courses for forty years.

As chapter 2 shows, the *Wende* proved no exception to this pattern. The 1989–90 revolution in the GDR was largely a middle-class affair. My full explanation for why workers were relatively invisible as the revolutionary drama unfolded and developed considers all three facets of the class relationship, together with workers' day-to-day experiences of the labor process and workplace politics. But before this explanation is rounded out in later chapters, I need to document workers' political retreat in 1989–90, a retreat that might surprise some yet one that, in imitating the long-standing and class-exclusive pattern of political protest in the GDR, was historically unexceptional.

2 Workers in the Gallery: The Single-Class Character of Revolutionary Politics

The end of forty years of socialism in the GDR has often been depicted as a revolution from below, a revolution brought about by "the citizens," the people," "the population," or "the masses" of that country. Yet workers, who constituted about 79 percent of the GDR population, were relatively invisible among the politically active during the *Wende.* Sociologically speaking, one factor that stood out through all three stages of the revolution was its single-class character.[1] It was an affair dominated by middle-class citizens, which fit not only the pre-1989 pattern of the GDR but also the pattern Timothy Ash identified as typical of all the 1989–90 revolutions in East and Central Europe.[2] The *Wende,* in other words, was a revolution of the relatively privileged in GDR society, a struggle that occurred largely between two segments of the intelligentsia—one defending the status quo and the other determined to overturn it.[3]

Working-Class Noninvolvement

It thus comes as no surprise that when I asked workers about their political involvement during the *Wende,* they repeatedly told me they had stayed out of politics altogether, aside from sometimes discussing events among themselves. A sample of typical responses reveals the depth of many workers' noninvolvement:

> Steelworker: Neither my wife [a secretary] nor I were involved. We didn't want to be. I wouldn't know about anything that happened at my workplace.

Brewery worker: We didn't even talk a lot about things. Well, you thought about it, but . . .

Worker in a farm equipment factory: There were no activities here. The union didn't do anything. Neither did the workers.

Construction worker: I wasn't active. I stayed out of it all. I was pretty cautious. My work mates kept their distance from demonstrations and so on. If they even heard the word *demonstration,* they preferred to stay home. They thought: "It will either happen or it won't." They might have walked in a May Day demonstration before, but when things became more revolutionary, they wanted to stay home. People discussed things. But to do something about it—no one wanted to commit to that! Everyone expressed their opinion, but no one felt very strongly about anything.

Switchboard operator: I didn't do anything, I just worked. I didn't take notice of anything happening.

Secretary: I wasn't active. Everybody [in my workplace] said, "I don't want to have anything to do with it!"

Clerk in a personnel department: I was not active in any political way. At first I was simply ignorant about a lot of things, and later, when things became more clear to me, I lacked the courage.

Auxiliary production worker: A lot was discussed in my factory. People were certainly interested—but to be active? Most people weren't so thrilled about that. I thought, "I'd like to have some change, but do I really want to *do* something about it?"[4]

Ironically, in one factory where some workers did become actively involved in politics, the impetus to do so was a coworker's passivity. This coworker had been arrested as she walked on the street near an ongoing demonstration. Everyone at work knew this was "a mistake." The woman was not an activist; she had merely been in the wrong place at the wrong time. The clear injustice of her predicament was what prompted some of her coworkers to attend subsequent demonstrations. But, added one in an indication of how fragile this newfound activism was, "It was probably a good thing she wasn't young. That would have made a different impression on my coworkers. They would just have said, 'Young people always get in trouble anyway, and it's their own fault.' And then they would not have gone to those demonstrations."[5]

Ordinarily workers who insisted they did not participate in politics went on to explain why they had remained on the sidelines as the revolution swirled around them. Chapters 3, 4, and 5 are devoted to answering this question from a more structural perspective, which, while centered around workers' experiences of GDR socialism, does not end with workers' own explanations for their noninvolvement. Nonetheless, what workers shared in this regard is worth recounting here, for it will soon become clear how many of their explanations spoke directly to those contained in these subsequent chapters.

Many workers said that the demands of their paid jobs left them neither the time nor the energy to get involved in *Wende* politics. "For one thing, a lot [of political activities] seemed to go on on Saturday," a construction worker said. "So we couldn't do it. Eighty percent played soccer on Saturday. The rest were just glad it was the weekend!" "This may sound like an excuse," explained a worker in a cultural tour agency regarding her reluctance to work with any opposition groups, "but it had to do with the time involved in such things. Maybe one should make time to work in these groups, but my work is pretty difficult and demanding already."[6] In general, women felt such pressures, together with those stemming from their family responsibilities, most acutely. Sometimes they also had to contend with male partners or family members who assumed they had the authority to grant or deny women permission to take part in political activities.[7] Some other workers judged themselves so politically ineffectual that the slightest suggestion that their actions could have had any impact was simply unfathomable or was met with scoffing cynicism. Still other workers told me they had opted to remain uninvolved because they were unsure whether the outcome of their efforts would make things in the GDR better. A few suggested that the fear of repression was a factor in their decisions to stay out of revolutionary politics. "Our habitual need to be cautious, to remain hidden to some degree" was how one worker related this sentiment.[8]

A more common explanation workers gave for their lack of participation was that they were "politically burned out." Sometimes "politically burned out" meant they had experienced too much official pressure to be active before the *Wende*. More often, however, workers described themselves as politically burned out because they had tried repeatedly to effect some change before the revolution and had never seen any results. One local union officer in Leipzig likened his past activism to beating his head against the walls of a padded cell until he was simply too worn out to try to do anything anymore.[9] Another became quite animated as he linked his past experience as a *Vertrauensperson* (the lowest-level union officer) to his lack of political involvement during the revolution:

> I was a *Vertrauensmann* for six or seven years until 1983. And if you were a *Vertrauensmann*, your coworkers would say, "Why don't you do something?" And you would answer, "Why don't you come with me and listen

to what goes on in the meetings we *Vertrauensleute* have with management?" At these meetings we would say, "We need to make this or that better," like in the area of work safety, for instance. We'd say, "The work suits
are wearing out or the work shoes are wearing out," and management
would come back with a piece of paper and say, "That couldn't be! It says
right here on this paper that work shoes last eighteen months and work suits
last twelve months."

Then I finally said, "It's no use, someone else can do this job [as
Vertrauensperson]." You can bang your head against the wall, but nothing
will change. So I gave up the post. You were just desperate. You never saw
any success. You got so tired. And that's how it is with everything. You can
talk and talk, and it makes no difference. Then you might try going to some
government office and being stubborn. Then you really get tired—too tired
to go to any demonstration or anything like that.[10]

The Middle-Class Opposition

At the same time I found numerous GDR workers who had eschewed activism during the *Wende,* Germans I consulted in both East and West categori-
cally described the citizens' opposition groups as "middle class," "intellectual," or "cultural and academic."[11] "New Forum," a GDR sociologist has
since written, "was no workers' movement, either in its social composition
or its political aims and aspirations."[12] The founding members and leaders
of Neues Forum and Demokratie Jetzt included a painter, a film director who
frequently attended cultural evenings at the U.S. embassy, an attorney, a
molecular biologist, a physicist, a translator-mathematician, a historian, and
a theology professor, while Demokratischer Aufbruch was led by seven par-
sons.[13] In October 1989, the third ranking officer in the U.S. embassy in the
GDR paid a visit to one of these founder-leaders, and his recollections provide a telling glimpse into the social world of key middle-class activists: "I
had asked Heather to introduce me to Neues Forum leaders, and Monday
evening she took Gaby and me to Jens Reich and his wife, who live in a comfortable, high-ceilinged, book-stuffed apartment in the Koloniestraße, off the
Pankow market square five minutes from our house. Their summer dacha,
we learned, is down the road from that of our friends where in August we
had discussed the growing crisis."[14]

Neues Forum, Demokratie Jetzt, Vereinigte Linke, and the other citizens'
opposition groups drew most of their active members from among people
of similar middle-class standing, including, as time went one, from disaffected
members of the SED, many of whom did not give up their membership in
the party. Activists also disproportionately came from workplaces outside the

state sector. A church-employed music therapist, for instance, reported, "About every third or fourth of my coworkers was active with Neues Forum or one of the other little groups that developed."[15] Although the social base of the citizens' opposition groups broadened as the pace of events quickened, recruitment continued to rely heavily on personal social networks, thereby reproducing the class characteristics of earlier opposition activists.[16]

Determining the class composition of the less involved supporters of the citizens' opposition groups, people who only occasionally attended a meeting or participated in a demonstration, is more difficult. It is impossible, for example, to know with certainty the class makeup of the weekly demonstrations held throughout the country in October and November. Some workers surely showed up. But, according to Karl-Dieter Opp, Peter Voss, and Christiane Gern, opposition group members, who we have seen were overwhelmingly middle-class, joined demonstrations more often than those who were not, and a West Berlin political scientist told me that demonstration arrest records reveal a preponderance of highly educated people.[17] We do know that intellectuals sponsored numerous large demonstrations in the fall of 1989 and that the November 4 demonstration in Berlin, attended by an estimated 500,000 to 1 million people and regarded as the high point of the citizens' opposition phase of the revolution, was called by a writers' and artists' association and was organized largely by Neues Forum and other citizens' opposition groups, with the cooperation of local officials. The most prominently featured speakers at this demonstration included well-known writers, actors, and journalists, who shared the stage with high-level government and party notables. Finally, major players in dramatic revolutionary scenarios—for example, the negotiators who averted state-instigated violence against street demonstrators on October 9—were largely cultural, religious, and high-ranking political figures.[18]

All the activists in the citizens' opposition with whom I spoke were aware of the thoroughly middle-class character of their groups. A psychologist active in Demokratie Jetzt recalled that his own and other citizens' opposition groups suffered from the lack of a mass base. "There were almost no connections to large enterprises," he added. A free-lance writer who worked with Neues Forum concurred: "Most of the people [active with Neues Forum] were critical intelligentsia. There were many theologians and artists. There were a few technical intelligentsia, but there were very few workers."[19] "I couldn't believe that so few workers would be part of our and other groups," remarked another middle-class activist. "I was frankly embarrassed about this." The singular class composition of the citizens' opposition groups did not escape the notice of workers and unionists either. "Neues Forum didn't have many workers in it then [fall 1989], and it doesn't have many now [fall

1990]," said an official of the metal workers' union in the southeastern part of the country. Similarly, a worker in a consumer electronics factory in Berlin claimed that at his workplace, "workers didn't do anything with it [Neues Forum]."[20]

The shift of power from the citizens' opposition groups to the round tables and subsequently to the new and reborn political parties never altered the skewed class character of revolutionary activism. The working-class majority was not well represented at the higher-level round tables. Unions were not present at all initially, nor were any other organizations with solid working-class constituencies. The former Block parties, which joined the citizens' opposition groups and the government at the round tables, did attract new members as the revolution progressed. This did not, however, shift their political centers away from the GDR intelligentsia, where they had been firmly lodged before the revolution.[21] Both the CDU (Christian Democratic Union) and the LDPD (Liberal Democratic Party of Germany), according to Carl Bradley Scharf, had historically "derive[d] most of their membership from among the bourgeois middle class, professional people, shopkeepers, and independent craftspeople—in other words among people employed outside the socialist sector of the economy."[22] Scharf's characterization of the LDPD is close to one offered by a long-time member and university researcher, who hinted at a party with little interest in organizing workers: "We were engineers, scientists, and some self-employed doctors, lawyers, and so on. We'd all joined to avoid membership in the SED, while demonstrating our integration into the political system. It was a form of self-satisfaction within the small group of liberals. We met regularly, complained about the government, were happy that others thought that way too, and went home."[23]

The SPD-DDR (Social Democratic Party of Germany in the GDR) and the PDS (Party of Democratic Socialism) were the parties more ideologically inclined to represent workers' interests at the round tables and during the electoral campaign. Burdened by its history and beset by internal debate, however, the PDS apparently made only minimal efforts to organize and politicize workers, who were not even included on a list of the party's potential constituencies.[24] The SPD also ignored workers, and, as a consequence, a technician who claimed no workers she knew would have considered allying with the SPD ("or the CDU for that matter") surely expressed an even more widely held working-class sentiment.[25] Moreover, whether from political arrogance or ineptitude, the SPD made the limited attempts of other political players to organize and incorporate workers far more difficult. To have been successful, such efforts would have required time, and hence a postponement of elections, as well as the limitation of political interference from the Federal Republic. Yet because of the actions of the SPD, a party made up largely of "administrators, teachers, officers, managers, journalists, intellectuals and generally those who had benefited from the upward social mobility afforded to the politically loyal under the old regime,"[26] political groups from the FRG were granted greater access to the round tables, and national elections were moved forward from May to March 1990.[27]

Conclusion

The major internal players in the GDR revolution, both the defenders of the status quo and its challengers, were from the intelligentsia. By contrast, the record offers but scant evidence of active working-class involvement in this momentous event. In other words, many workers chose distant seats in the gallery as the revolutionary drama unfolded. They observed from afar as the clashes between middle-class players set the tone and the course of the *Wende.* Why did so many workers absent themselves from politics during this period, a choice with decisive consequences for the outcome of the 1989–90 revolution? For answers, we turn in the following three chapters to workers' everyday experiences of the labor process, workplace politics, and class. Together these chapters underscore how workers' withdrawal from politics was deeply rooted in forty years of GDR socialism.

3   The Socialist Labor Process

Explanations of workers' noninvolvement in the GDR revolution can be partially found in their everyday experiences of paid work. The first aspect of paid work that provides clues to working-class demobilization is the labor process. Several features of the GDR labor process—its disorganization, its dishonesty, and its deficient discipline and remuneration systems—functioned to help ensure that a great many GDR workers were loath to engage in revolutionary politics. Daily exposure to these features of the labor process produced workers who were frustrated, indifferent, and cynical and saw themselves as powerless and unappreciated, in other words, workers who could muster virtually no enthusiasm for activist politics in the fall and winter of 1989–90.

My argument, however, has moved a step ahead of itself, for we cannot comprehend exactly how working-class demobilization resulted from disorganization, dishonesty, and defective remuneration and discipline systems without first briefly exploring the defining Nemesis of socialist economies—ubiquitous shortage.

Socialist Shortage

The dynamics of socialist economies, which result in permanent undersupplies of labor, energy, materials, imports, parts, investment funds, machinery, tools, and consumer goods, have been described by others.[1] In socialist societies, resources needed to fulfill economic plans are allocated by central organs through a process of bargaining with individual production and service delivery units. In the GDR, as in other socialist countries, the fulfillment of prior plan targets enhanced a unit's bargaining power vis-à-vis the center. As a consequence, in negotiating with the center, all production and service delivery units had an abiding interest in securing both undemanding, loose plans and as many inputs of all types as possible. In other words, a core dynamic of shortage economies is the tendency for all work centers to try to minimize their production and maximize their allotment of resources, setting off a high demand–low supply chain reaction, which ultimately entangles all economic players.

The shortages resulting from this basic dynamic were exacerbated in the GDR and elsewhere by derivative behaviors of firms and central organs, both of which were cognizant of the vortex in which they were trapped. Firms not only bargained for plans they could fulfill easily, thereby enhancing their position in future negotiations with the center, but also were careful never to exceed any plan by too much,[2] lest targets be increased in succeeding years. They not only attempted to extract as many resources as possible from the center but also hoarded resources against the day when they might get stuck with a difficult plan. The hoarding of some inputs reached major proportions in the GDR, where inspections uncovered stockpiles of materials adequate for ten to fifteen years.[3] Finally, since central planners routinely assumed that production and service delivery units worked under looser plans than necessary and always requested more inputs than actually needed,[4] their inclination was to saddle firms with more ambitious plans than they said they could fulfill, all the while allotting them fewer inputs than they had requested.

Shortages of all production inputs were thus an overriding feature of people's everyday experience with the GDR labor process, so much so that jokes about shortages were one of the few things not in short supply:

Q: "What is the difference between capitalist hell and socialist hell?"
A: "Nothing theoretically. Sinners are boiled in oil in both places. But in socialist hell there are never any pots, oil, matches, or wood to do it with!"[5]

Workers continually complained about shortages before the revolution. At a construction site I visited near Leipzig, they half seriously tried to convince me to return a third day, because the days when out-of-the-ordinary visitors appeared were "the only days we get a mechanical shovel to work with." A *Vertrauensperson* who announced her intent to quit her post before a meeting of the entire work center made the shortage of work materials the dominant theme of her unexpected resignation speech. "One has to admit," a plant-level union officer lamented, "that these shortages go on year after year, and nothing is ever done about them."[6] Worker frustration with shortages surfaced prominently in the midst of the crisis as well. A worker in Leipzig, for instance, partially blamed them for the street demonstrations and the flood of émigrés leaving the country. Another publicly volunteered to move from the factory where he had worked for forty years to a different one producing spare parts, "if that would help solve the [shortage] problem."[7]

Socialist Hard Work

Directly and indirectly, shortages lay behind the hard, often very hard, work that characterized most workers' experience of the GDR labor process.[8] As everywhere, some workers in the GDR worked harder than others, and the length and intensity of labor were greater in some establishments and at some periods than in others.[9] Nonetheless, despite many observers' claims to the contrary,[10] hard work remained a significant part of most workers' experience of paid labor in the GDR, and, as we will see shortly, when understood in the context of other elements of their paid work experience, it helps explain the lack of working-class involvement in the politics of the *Wende*.

As any weekend handyperson can attest, the absence of the proper tools, machinery, materials, supplies, and labor power makes completing any job much more difficult, and this was patently obvious to GDR workers. "Year after year we have to try to do our work with only a part of the supplies, like cables, that we need," grumbled an electrician in a chemical factory. "In the GDR we produce computers with stone implements!" exclaimed another respondent. Ancient equipment was the root of another worker's complaint that "it takes six weeks here to do what you can do in West Germany in two weeks."[11] At the municipal sewage plant near Leipzig, the problem was the lack of health and safety equipment and proper work clothes; and in a Berlin cable factory, it was the labor shortage, which required one worker to take over two work stations. A machinist interviewed by Dirk Philipsen expressed the link between hard work and shortage most graphically: "Workers in the shops have always worked hard. On top of that, their work required much more energy than in the West, because they had to make gold out of shit." White-collar workers were likewise cognizant of the hard work necessitated by endemic shortages. Bristling with indignation at a West German's comment that GDR workers were lazy, an administrative assistant retorted, "It's just plain not so! I had to work harder than anyone in the FRG with a job like mine. When they had a report or something to get out and they ran out of anything, they could just saunter down to the store or the supply cabinet and get what they wanted. Me, I'd have to figure out how to finish the job without the typewriter ribbon or the duplicating machine!"[12]

For many workers hard work was symbolized by overtime (above the normal forty-two-hour work week), which became an expected part of many jobs because the shortage of production inputs meant plan figures, which had the status of "sacred cows," could not be fulfilled without it.[13] In many workplaces, overtime hours rose in the years prior to the revolution. For example, Lutz Kirschner reported that overtime in the large factory he studied began to increase in 1983 and then rose rapidly after 1987. As a result, 71 percent of the production workers in this factory clocked overtime hours in 1986, while 89 percent did so in 1987.[14] Overtime did not always require intensive effort. Nonetheless, as the following cabaret skit suggests, it was widely unpopular, and, because workers had the right to refuse it, managers and union officials often had to do a bit of arm twisting to staff extra work stints:

Worker: I am going to stay home and read [not do overtime].
Foreperson: Can't we persuade you?
Worker: Give me a passport to visit Venice, the Canals . . .
Foreperson: That's too expensive, why not Czechoslovakia . . . or Leningrad, the Venice of the North?
Worker: No, I want to see the real thing before it sinks in to the sea. I've worked hard for forty years. Isn't that enough?
Foreperson: No, forty years isn't enough in the GDR.
Worker: Then I'll stay home and read about Paris.[15]

Hard work was also a feature of regular work hours for many GDR workers. For example, fulfillment of production targets without adequate supplies dictated continual shifts of labor and materials from some collectives, departments, or firms to others, forcing intensified effort among workers in the donor units, who still had to make their own targets. Shortages also lay behind the phenomenon of storming, or "fire brigade actions," as I heard them called, those extraordinary bursts of effort demanded near the end of planning periods.[16]

Some women worked especially hard, because they were expected to perform workplace social duties in conjunction with their jobs. Preparing, artfully arranging, and serving snacks and beverages at meetings and cleaning up afterward were examples.[17] Other women spent hours after their workdays formally ended "hostessing" and "mothering" clients or visitors to their work units. For instance, an employee of a cultural tour booking agency said she spent many of her evenings entertaining visiting performers. Another woman employed by the union college spent easily ten hours beyond her required work week offering advice, providing personal counsel, and socializing with students from the GDR and around the world. Perhaps some women found such obligations more enjoyable than their regular job duties.

Nonetheless, these tasks often substantially expanded women's work hours, since they were performed in addition to, not in lieu of, their regular job tasks.

Yet hard work, in and of itself, does not explain why so many members of the working class eschewed political activity during the *Wende*. To understand the connection between hard work and workers' penchant for avoiding politics during the crisis, we must consider hard work in the context of three elemental and pervasive features of the GDR labor process: its disorganization, its dishonesty, and its deficient disciplinary and remuneration processes.

Socialist Disorganization

Despite the hard work required of them, GDR workers often saw their extraordinary efforts subverted by the chronic disorganization of the labor process. Viewed from the top-down, outside-in perspective of free market enthusiasts, the disorganization of the socialist work process is proof positive of the inefficiency of planned economies. From the bottom-up, inside-out perspective of many GDR workers, however, the chronic disorganization at work was significant for other reasons. For one thing, workers were embarrassed to recount how often disorganization left them idle during work hours, and because idleness robbed them of the pleasure of seeing real achievements result from their efforts, disorganization became the source of much frustration and anger.[18] All this was especially clear as a Leipzig construction worker contrasted his ordinary job with his prior experience working on a "special sort of project"—an airport renovation mandated directly by the Council of Ministers: "The design was completed in April. Construction began in May, and it was completed on schedule in August. Every colleague who worked on this project really remembers it fondly, even though we didn't have one Saturday off and we had to postpone our summer holidays to get the work done. The work stopped when the job was finished for the day, not when it was quitting time. Doing the job you're there to do feels good. I hope I'll someday get to be on another project like the airport—one where I can really see some results."[19] Unfortunately, however, the disorganization of paid work in the GDR too often sent workers to their jobs only to "go on break" for much of the day. Too often they ended their workdays not only tired out, partly from waiting around, but also without any sense of accomplishment, of being productive, of making a socially useful contribution through their labor.[20]

The disorganization of the GDR labor process was also obvious to workers in a number of other ways. Sometimes resulting in the perplexing idleness just described, all of these shared common roots in the dynamics of the shortage economy. Not surprisingly, the form of disorganization about which workers complained the most concerned production inputs. Either there were none or too few or, sometimes even simultaneously, there were too many or they were the wrong kind. These input problems disheartened workers, for they squandered labor time and potential, as well as the very production inputs already in such short supply.

Workers' testimonies to the difficulties, dilemmas, and embarrassments resulting from the total or partial unavailability of production inputs were abundant: "More times than I like to think we'd be told to fill, say a ditch, with concrete, when we didn't have any gravel to make it with. So where did we get the gravel? From a heap that you knew wasn't your own. Sometimes you waited until the workers at another site left for breakfast, and you grabbed a few shovels and went over to their gravel pile and stole some. Just like an idiot. You just felt like an old rat slinking into a cupboard where it doesn't belong."[21] Whether of gravel, garbage cans, glue, glycol, garlic, griddles, or gears, analogous shortages at almost every GDR worksite were a daily source of strain and dissatisfaction for workers.

The complete or partial unavailability of production inputs was not the only problem. Other forms of work disorganization associated with inputs could be as annoying. For example, workers continuously had to deal with situations in which production inputs, while technically available, varied markedly in type and quality from those they had expected. Late deliveries were also a source of continual frustration. Construction and maintenance workers at a sewage treatment facility, for example, angrily recalled the "senseless waste of hours" they spent showing up once, twice, and even three times, ready to begin a job, only to discover work could not commence because a promised delivery had not arrived. Not only was the labor of these particular workers wasted, but as one explained, "Since we can't ever depend on when our supplies will show up, but we always need them desperately, we have to have six other workers forever waiting around to be able to unload them from the train on a moment's notice.[22]

Endemic shortages also lay behind the continuous misallocation of resources, which ironically manifested itself in an oversupply of some production inputs at certain times in particular workplaces. Workers were well aware, for instance, of how labor was hoarded at their worksites, a practice which, while ensuring labor power was available at critical production periods, also meant workers sometimes found themselves feeling useless and bored at work. Labor, however, was not the only production input workers were perturbed to find in sporadic oversupply, as an auxiliary worker in heavy industry explained: "Sometimes, for various reasons, we couldn't build a particular kind of machine that was in our plan. But the materials to build it came anyway, so we'd have lots of materials stored around forever that we couldn't use at all." "There were places in the *Betrieb*," this worker continued, "where you couldn't put one foot in front of the other, because this stuff was everywhere. But we couldn't send it back, because, after all, the factories that produced it had their plans too."[23]

Workers blamed much of the disorganization on the errors of worksite management. Undoubtedly, some of the disorganization they attributed to outright management blunder stemmed as much from managerial powerlessness in the face of shortages and from obligatory directives designed to compensate for these as it did from individual incompetence. Nonetheless, GDR workers regularly suggested, and sometimes adamantly insisted, otherwise. For example, workers blamed bosses for the ruin and disuse of desperately needed equipment:

> Three new pieces of a hi-tech cooling system were delivered and set down in the yard. We workers realized they shouldn't just be exposed there in the open air, but it was two years before the administration made a request in the plan for a structure to house them. Meanwhile, we had to take parts off the new equipment to keep other older machines inside the factory working. So by the time the structures to house the new equipment arrived, there were only skeletons left to protect!

> This several million dollar machine was installed by Americans, but it didn't work right because it wasn't installed correctly. But the management didn't deem it necessary to file a complaint or something like that. So the machine just stood there unused.[24]

Workers also often complained that their supervisors could not figure out what should be done when and were unqualified for their jobs:

> We'd get one set of orders from the bosses, only to get new ones half an hour later. Several times I've done work and had to demolish it the next day because they decided it should be different.

> The problem is that the work processes are poorly organized by the leaders who are responsible. The managers just shove the responsibility back and forth among themselves. The party secretary had the final word, and he didn't have a clue.[25]

"Many rank-and-file workers began to wonder whether we had idiots organizing our production," one worker concluded. "If we as workers understood [how badly things were organized], one would assume that someone who went to college should be able to grasp that as well."[26]

A particularly irksome form of disorganization for which workers also held worksite management culpable was the relatively common practice of pulling workers out of one area, firm, or job and reassigning them elsewhere, sometimes to perform tasks they were unfamiliar with and not trained to do:

> We craftworkers are constantly getting sent elsewhere, for example, as temporary help to foreign companies or to accomplish some of the county government's goals. But we're already stretched thin! Doesn't our administration see that the buildings and work areas in both parts of our own enterprise are crumbling?

> Management really creates problems here by yanking workers off one site and plopping them into another, yanking them off one and plopping them into another. We've got no continuity on the job. We get way behind and that causes discontent among the remaining workers.[27]

Shifting labor not only reduced workers' possibilities of ever seeing a job completed but also broke effective work routines and satisfying social relationships for those reassigned, as well as for their former coworkers.

A final form of work disorganization workers found unsettling was the practice of making midyear changes in the plan. That such changes were frequent was alluded to in a statement I heard repeatedly: "The plan is one thing. Real life is another." Plan corrections (*Plankorrekturen*), as these changes were called, often meant workers had to abandon half-completed jobs, orders, and projects: "There are changes in the plan all the time, and we just don't get anywhere. We started this project nearly a year ago, but still have nothing to show for it."[28] Sometimes this happened when a new hard currency customer had suddenly been located, and sometimes it happened because of bottlenecks created by shortages elsewhere. Workers acknowledged that worksite management was not usually to blame for *Plankorrekturen*. No matter the cause or the culprit, when the plan was altered, workers felt they had just wasted a lot of time, effort, and materials. When such corrections happened often enough, they began to look on everything they did as potentially only make-work.

Lying and the Labor Process

Chronic disorganization was but one element of the socialist labor process that left workers feeling frustrated and ineffectual at their jobs. Workers' everyday paid work experience was also plagued by an endemic dishonesty, which both distorted and obscured their hard-won accomplishments. This dishonesty went far beyond the commonly noted discrepancy between macroeconomic projection and performance in the GDR. It was rooted in the disjuncture between the everyday reality of paid labor and its portrayals. The gap between the two did not escape the notice of production and service workers, but GDR workers were more than mere observers of this inconsistency. To engage in paid labor in the GDR was also to participate in, or at minimum to acquiesce to, the construction of lies about it.[29]

Workers both witnessed and cooperated in the fabrication of the webs of duplicity that enveloped their work in various ways. First, nearly every kind of report on every work center was to some degree fudged. Unions were key players in this process, and union leaders admitted this before the *Wende,* though they usually did so circumspectly since it was a sensitive topic. For instance, a factory union leader in a furniture enterprise alluded to the misreporting in which she was routinely involved: "Every enterprise union committee has to write a monthly report on the situation in their workplace to send to union headquarters. So do two other union committees. With all three reports, you'd think they'd get the picture of what was going on at each workplace. But, in reality, that's not so. This really embarrasses me. No, actually, it drives me mad!"[30] A *Vertrauensperson* who had worked in a child care facility was more explicit: "The one major thing that could improve our union work would be honesty in our reports. Too often we write one thing but mean another. If that weren't so, we would probably achieve more."[31] When the lid came off during the *Wende,* more people began to speak openly about union complicity in sanitizing reports. "Each union officer at each level who wrote a report, wrote a rosier one than the one they received, until by the time the report reached Berlin, no problems were mentioned in it at all," declared a former union leader. An enterprise union leader from another part of the country emphasized the same point: "The only opinions that reached our union leadership were those that fit into their understanding of really existing socialism. That is precisely how we got into the currently existing situation in the first place."[32]

No matter who the author, embellished reports of their economic accomplishments, especially the fulfillment of plans, were particularly irritating to workers:

> Do we want to continue wasting valuable work time sitting for hours in meetings during which we try to figure out by which twists and turns we can claim to have fulfilled the monthly plan?

> We feel betrayed by the constant media reports of success in fulfilling the plans. After all, everyone knows, from their own work, what reality looks like.

> It's wrong and dishonest to say we fulfilled the plan, but we didn't have the parts.[33]

This "god-damned looking at everything through rose-colored glasses" became the topic of derisive humor in the GDR: "What are the four economic strengths of actually existing socialism? First, the microelectronics industry in Mongolia, second, the work climate in the People's Republic of Poland, third, the meat supply in Moscow, and fourth, the statistics in the GDR."[34]

While all manner of misinformation became more fictional as it moved up in the union, party, and government bureaucracies, the apex of exaggeration was reached whenever a high-level official actually visited a worksite. Not only were reports of reality blatantly doctored at these times, but workers were required to alter physical reality itself. In anticipation of such visits, GDR workers told of being hurriedly set to work covering roads, walkways, tools, handrails, almost anything, with coats of paint (sometimes red), distributing floral arrangements all over the workplace (sometimes right on top of greasy machinery), and moving classy furniture into workers' break rooms (always to be removed later).[35]

Workers not only periodically conspired in the construction of lies about the labor process during the visits of such dignitaries but regularly did so through formal procedures set up to incorporate them into worksite decision-making processes. The yawning gap between the stated purpose and the actual functioning of such procedures meant many workers experienced them as mere charades. "In the past," claimed a department-level union head, "we were often supposed to express our opinion about all sorts of things. However, we did this without genuinely participating. We welcomed and we regurgitated whatever was expected of us."[36]

Planning assemblies provide a good example. Their ostensible purpose was to include workers in devising their workplace plans. Workers insisted, however, that the production figures sent from above could never be altered, no matter what they said or how they said it, because the figures they came together to discuss were already binding by the time they arrived at the enterprise. A master of satire, one worker described the farce that his annual planning assembly thus became:

> The manager and the BGL [*Betriebsgewerkschaftsleitung*, enterprise-level union committee] members come in and say, "Hello workers! These are our figures. We have this to do. We have more to do than last year. You have to work more." And we workers would respond saying, "Okay, boss, we'll do our best! Next week give us all the materials and equipment and we'll fulfill these figures." "Oh, that's great," the manager would say. "Everything is okay, now everything is okay. Let's vote! Everyone who approves of these figures raise their hands." We would all raise our hands. "*Wunderbar!*" the manager would exclaim. And then it was over.[37]

Under these circumstances, real-life planning assemblies lost nearly all semblance of the democratic proceedings they were touted to be. For the most part, they degenerated into ritualized discussions of certain topics that only underscored the discrepancy between what these assemblies were supposed to be and what they actually were. One such topic was the implementation, as opposed to the stipulation, of plan figures. "Somehow at first the figures always seem too high," a bakery worker explained to me. "But our problem is to figure out ways to do it." With determination, he added, "One must find ways."[38] Another such topic was overfulfillment of the plan, the only planning matter about which workers were certain their opinions would be heard. "Workers only have the possibility to discuss the figures if they want to make more," according to a construction site supervisor, "so it's not a real discussion at all."[39] Planning assemblies thus joined a number of other worksite decision-making forums in which GDR workers were called upon to participate in concocting an appearance of paid work that did not jibe with its reality.[40]

Discipline and Remuneration

While disorganization subverted producers' accomplishments at work and dishonesty obscured and mocked them, GDR workers also saw their hard work devalued and underrecognized by the discipline and remuneration systems. Their frequent inability to translate their hard work into adequate housing or a dependable supply of quality consumer goods was evidence of this, as was the daily unpleasantry of unkept and poorly appointed workplaces.[41] But it is on the failings of the discipline and remuneration systems that I focus in this section, for workers read these as equally and consistently important signals that their hard work went underappreciated.

Observers of the GDR labor process agree that it was extremely difficult to dismiss anyone from their paid job.[42] Managers with whom I spoke, such as the director of a sewage treatment plant of about six hundred workers, continually bemoaned this:

> The *Arbeitsgesetzbuch* [labor code] is too humane on this matter. It's theoretically possible for me to lay off someone, but as a practical matter it is not. The mechanism for getting rid of someone is very complicated and time consuming. The union will always intervene to try to prove management didn't do everything it could have to prevent things from getting to this point. And there's always some loophole in the code that the union and the worker can use. Eventually I just say, "For God's sake, let them stay!" because it's just too big a headache to go through the procedure. Only one person has been dismissed here in nine years. I've heard of a few more in

the entire *Kombinat,* but these were people who hadn't shown up to work for months. They'd effectively already quit themselves.[43]

Workers concurred on the difficulty of dismissing anyone: "That was unthinkable! The person would have had to have done something *really* bad outside of work. But then you would still have had to go through certain processes, and even then you would have had very little chance of getting approval for the firing."[44]

Workers' overall perspective on the issue of dismissals, however, diverged from that of most managers. Their sentiments were also at odds with those of many union officers, such as the BGL chair in an electric motor factory, who proudly told me he would *"never* agree to the firing of *any* worker."[45] Most workers felt that dismissal should remain next to impossible during firm reorganizations and that it should be only sparingly available as a weapon against indiscipline. Many workers nonetheless felt that in *extreme* cases, dismissal should be an option. In any particular instance, workers would undoubtedly disagree over where to draw the line between indiscipline and indiscipline extreme enough to warrant termination. But to recognize no line at all, which is what most workers saw happening at their workplaces, was unacceptable.

For one thing, workers found the consequences of such a lackadaisical state of affairs distressing. They complained that when the union devoted too much time to the defense of total laggards, it was unable to attend to the needs of the remainder of workers, who were doing their jobs. Beyond this, from the perspective of the majority of workers who performed well under far less than ideal conditions, the near impossibility of dismissing anyone for utterly abominable work performance was a sign of disrespect for their own hard-won accomplishments on the job. Their solid records were tarnished by the extreme leniency accorded a few outrageous, yet atypical, workers. The system did not discriminate reasonably between the many, who often made exemplary contributions, and the few who were a burden and a danger to their coworkers. Instead, it lumped both together.

More than anything else, however, workers identified the GDR remuneration system as the culprit in the undervaluation of their labor. In a word, many perceived too little connection between effort and reward and between results, which did not necessarily reflect effort, and reward. It appeared to workers that earnings did not reflect poor or excellent work, good or bad results, demanding or cushy jobs. They were adamant that the seemingly arbitrary connection between pay, effort, and results devalued the dependable and substantial contributions of the majority. In 1990, I was quite unprepared for the deluge of worker criticisms leveled against the lip service paid the highly touted *Leistungsprinzip* (performance principle), which promoted a close connection between effort and reward. Workers simply wanted, in the words of one woman, "to do [their] work as well as possible and then receive the corresponding sum at the end of the month."[46] To their chagrin, many received no such satisfaction.

It is important to be clear exactly what GDR workers found objectionable about the remuneration system, lest their criticisms be confused with others aimed at the connection between earnings and occupational category, which abound in the literature on socialism. Workers' complaints centered on the relationship between rewards and contributions, and sometimes results, not on the relationship between rewards and skill level, qualifications, training, or experience. To put it bluntly, workers were concerned not with how much engineers, technical specialists, and administrators, by mere virtue of their job titles, earned relative to workers but with how the remuneration system glossed over distinctions between *any* job well done and *any* job poorly done.[47] In other words, workers focused on how productively people used their labor time, and such a determination bore no necessary relation to their occupational title or to the amount of training, schooling, or experience they had.

From where workers stood, the invisibility of the linkage between reward, effort, and result translated into a trio of complaints. For one thing, many workers were simply not sure how or if reward, effort, and result were connected, because the whole remuneration system was so complex. "The highly complicated wage system introduced in the GDR in the 1960's," Hartmut Zimmermann wrote, "with its numerous supplements, premiums, etc., soon proved beyond the comprehension of those concerned."[48]

For another, performance-based allotments, that portion of a worker's total earnings specifically designed to bridge reward, effort, and outcome, did not do so satisfactorily.[49] All GDR workers received a base wage according to their job classification, and this was codified in great detail in standardized catalogues.[50] Many also received performance-based allotments above this base wage, which supposedly connected on-the-job performance to reward. These payments took two forms, what Carl Bradley Scharf calls "extra-performance wages" and bonuses of various types. Together these two kinds of performance-based payments made up between 50 and 80 percent of many workers' total annual earnings in the mid-1970s.[51] In 1976, a wage reform was implemented, which was intended to link base wages more closely to performance and to reduce substantially the extra-performance wage portion of workers' earnings. According to many workers, these reforms had succeeded in accomplishing the latter goal, though most reported that between 20 and 30 percent of their earnings still came from performance-based allotments of some type, particularly bonuses.

From workers' perspectives, however, both types of performance-based payments muddied the link between reward, effort, and outcome. To begin with, the absolute size of workers' bonuses and extra-performance wages in a given enterprise could depend as much on the bargaining clout of firm management and the economic importance of what the firm produced as on the results achieved or the efforts expended by its work force. Second, the base wage made up a larger proportion of the total remuneration of workers in certain economic sectors, such as service, than in other sectors, most notably production. As a result, as time passed, workers in certain economic sectors tended to be paid less, partly because bonuses often found their way into calculations of base wage rates whenever these were revised. Under these circumstances, performance-based allotments rewarded workers merely for working in a particular sector of the economy rather than for their effort or their results. Third, there were certain areas of the country to which it was more difficult to attract workers of all kinds. As a consequence, some establishments in these areas automatically paid "illegal" prizes to all workers who moved there, regardless of their performance. Finally, the link between effort, result, and reward was rendered even more tenuous by GDR tax policy, which exempted bonuses and overtime from income tax or taxed them at a lower rate, and by court rulings, which protected some bonuses from being cut for indiscipline, curtailed the right of enterprises to reclaim bonuses paid by mistake, and excused bonuses from liability calculations when a worker was convicted of misconduct damaging to the employer.[52]

For many workers with whom I spoke, the thirteenth-month bonus epitomized the arbitrary connection between effort, result, and reward. As its name implies, this bonus equaled approximately one month's wages, and its payment was theoretically tied to plan fulfillment. The thirteenth-month bonus had many problems, however. For one thing, it had come to be virtually automatic, regardless of whether a work center's plan was fulfilled. Sometimes, to justify the bonus, plan targets were reduced ex post facto, or production reports were simply doctored. A construction worker told me this happened every month at his worksite, because the level of production necessary to earn the bonus was impossible to achieve. Then one month someone actually compiled the production report honestly, and the link between bonus and accomplishment, already next to nonexistent in workers' minds, totally evaporated: "The man who did the report only wrote down what we actually did. Well, the report came straight back to him. He was told to think up something that was done to account for the hours put in, like maybe that 500 meters of ditch had to be dug by hand or other strange stuff, because the report just couldn't be turned in the way it was!"[53] In other worksites, no one bothered with such machinations, and the bonuses were distributed, even when poor work was the reason for nonfulfillment of the plan.[54] Workers revealed that bosses were apparently under some pressure to divide the bonuses equally: "You might have thirty *Kollektive* in a work center, twenty-five that worked well and five bad ones. In the *Kollektive* that did good work, each member would get about 800 marks for the thirteenth-month bonus. But the workers in the *Kollektive* that did bad work would still each get as much as 700 or 750 marks. If the general director is good, energetic, they might really reduce the bonuses for bad *Kollektive*. But sometimes they are weak and will not."[55]

The manner in which thirteenth-month bonuses were calculated also served to detach them further from effort and result. Sometimes this happened because different work units, even those in physically distinct areas engaged in different projects, were grouped together for the purpose of determining the size of each worker's bonus. This left workers confused and disgruntled over the amount they received: "You don't know on which sites workers work effectively and on which they don't. You can work and work, but in the end you may not get what you deserve, because somewhere else the workers just don't do their work. But they'd get the same as you anyway."[56]

Workers' sense that reward, effort, and result were only tenuously associated was further reinforced by the comparisons they could easily make among overall remuneration (base wages plus performance-based allotments) across job categories. For instance, pay was sometimes higher merely because some kinds of workers were, or had once been, in short supply. Carl Bradley Scharf noted the widely cited example of refuse collectors in Berlin. Their wages had been raised in the 1960s because few people wanted to do the physically difficult and dirty job, but the collectors continued to receive "inflated" wages even after their work had been mechanized.[57] The complaints of workers in auxiliary departments of a transport factory revealed that workers sometimes drew analogous conclusions from comparisons within their own worksites:

Our departments are called "production back-up departments." Back-up departments equal back-up wages. Just because we are not directly involved in the creation of products does not mean that we should always hobble along behind the production departments in our pay. Without our departments, nothing can happen in this enterprise. The enterprise can't exist without a stable supply of electrical energy, without tools and raw materials being delivered, without construction and reconstruction, without the repair and maintenance of machinery and technical equipment. These examples make clear the great responsibilities weighing on individual workers in these departments, which have only increased with the installation of new technology.[58]

Class tensions were revealed in many such comparisons. The occupational category workers most frequently singled out as an illustration of the failure of the performance principle was administration. Within this category, workers most often focused on high- and mid-level administrators instead of low-level supervisory personnel, such as forepersons. They viewed many of these people as overpaid relative to their work contributions. "Some around here who look like they do the most work—they might have a car or something—don't do the most work at all," one furniture factory worker wanted me to understand.[59] "What is the one thing you would change at your worksite if you could?" I asked an electrician, whose response disclosed a similar view: "I'd like to see the BGL chair have to approve general directors' salaries every month. It's all spelled out what they're supposed to get done every month, economically and socially. We could control their performance if we had to approve their salaries. It would be more transparent. We'd have a real idea what they were getting done. We don't now."[60] In a number of conversations before the *Wende,* other workers concurred in their low opinions of the work contributions made by administrators, who as a group they often referred to unceremoniously, if unfortunately, as *Wasserköpfe* (swollen ranks).[61] Rudolf Bahro would have appreciated this designation. "Productive expenditure of average labour-time . . . declines in the higher functions," he wrote. "[In] the field of administration . . . far more labour-time is wasted than in immediate production."[62]

Conclusion

Workers' daily experience of paid work in the GDR contributed to the lack of working-class involvement in the politics of the *Wende.* Hard work, often induced by shortages, was a major, albeit often overlooked, element of that experience. But it was not hard work in the abstract that linked the labor process to working-class withdrawal from politics in the fall and winter of 1989–90. Rather, the recognition that hard work was performed in the context of disorganization, dishonesty, and deficient discipline and remuneration systems is key to understanding how the labor process encouraged the political demobilization of the GDR working class. Day in and day out workers saw their extraordinary efforts and their sense of accomplishment and contribution subverted by chronic disorganization at work, and this bred a paralyzing frustration and sense of personal ineffectiveness among them. The pervasive dishonesty of the labor process, in which workers were unavoidably complicit, both mocked and obscured their solid accomplishments, contributing to a debilitating loss of self-respect. The discipline and remuneration systems, which failed to penalize abominable job performance and rewarded good work and bad work almost equally, devalued the remarkable work contributions of the vast majority and engendered a cynical demoralization and indifference among them. None of these labor process outcomes—frustration, inefficacy, self-contempt, indifference, and demoralization—promoted activism among workers. On the contrary, working for pay in the GDR was cumulatively disempowering and fostered a withdrawal from and a distaste for politics among large segments of the working class. Avoidance of active political involvement had thus become common among GDR workers long before the *Wende,* and for a significant number this did not change throughout the political crisis of 1989–90.

4   Workplace Politics

Workplace politics are another aspect of workers' everyday experience of paid work that contributed to their lack of involvement in the GDR revolution. The union was the organization that figured most prominently and directly in workers' experience of workplace politics. The more I learned about how unions were implicated in workplace political life, however, the more I realized that for the mass of GDR workers, regardless of whether they were active unionists, there were really two unions and thus two distinct brands of workplace politics: workplace union politics at the grass-roots level, with which they had the most continuous and direct familiarity, and workplace union politics at levels above this, with which their experience was more indirect and intermittent. Structurally, this corresponded to the difference between the *Kollektiv* (the lowest level of union organization) and the BGL (the highest workplace union committee).[1] The distinction is important to bear in mind, because, as a general rule, workers' experience of workplace politics *above* the level of the grass-roots union, which is the major focus of this chapter, contributed most to their disengagement during the revolution, while their experience of workplace politics at the grass-roots union level, the subject of chapter 7, helps explain the activism of the few.

How did GDR unions contribute to the depoliticization of the working class during the revolution? I answer this question by exploring four interrelated features of union operations at the workplace: lack of attention to economic and production matters, subservience to workplace management and the party, absence of rank-and-file influence in the selection of union leaders, and the formalism and centralism of union political practice. Together these aspects of workplace union operations limited workers' understanding of production and service delivery processes, narrowed their visions of political alternatives, trammeled their opportunity to engage in political practice, eroded the relationship between the rank and file and union leaders, and discouraged many workers from assuming leadership roles at the very historical moment when they might have accomplished the most. The result was that a substantial segment of the GDR working class turned its back on political participation during the *Wende.*

Doing Too Much, Doing Too Little: The Content of Union Work

Workplace unions in the GDR were charged with performing a wide array of economic, production, ideological, social, educational, and cultural tasks. Beginning in the early 1970s, union functions expanded rapidly, until by the late 1980s some people commented that the breadth of union work was even greater than that of the party. "There's no single kind of issue that doesn't concern the workplace union," a BGL member from a bakery told me. "Any worker, even those who don't belong to the union, will approach us with any problem." "You ask what the tasks of the union are?" repeated an ex-*Vertrauensperson* and BGL member:

> Well, we work on the plan, and production problems, and we organize socialist competitions around educational, training, cultural, and economic tasks, and we distribute holiday places and tours, and administer the social insurance funds dispersed in cases of work accidents, illness, retirement, and unemployment. And we defend workers' rights informally or in *Konfliktkommission* [grievance commission] proceedings when there's been some dispute. We arrange parties at Christmas and on International Women's Day and other holidays, hold festivals, organize recreational outings and sports events, and keep in contact with the retired workers from the enterprise. And we're concerned with special problems the young workers and women workers have at work.[2]

Despite the length of his list, this man missed a number of things other workers, in response to the same question, identified as tasks of the workplace union: keeping tabs on sick workmates; staying in contact with workers during their paid year of maternity leave; providing and monitoring health and safety instruction; taking part in health and safety inspections; making proposals for the prevention of illness; allocating stays in health spas; doing political and ideological work; evaluating and encouraging plan fulfillment; promoting more efficient use of work time; securing work materials; helping locate and repair worker housing; calculating and distributing bonuses; organizing volunteer and overtime work; dealing with child care issues and children's camps; overseeing work center cafeterias and other on-site conveniences, such as mini-marts and laundries; buying gifts for workers' birthdays and other special events; organizing educational programs; dealing with work schedules and disciplinary issues; consulting on the introduction of new technologies and work processes; and working with local governments on issues affecting workers' living and working conditions, such as transportation and neighborhood planning.

Despite the breadth of their mandate, GDR unions did not devote equal attention to each of these tasks. In fact, most union activity at the workplace focused on its social, cultural, ideological, and educational functions rather than its production and economic ones. The former tasks were usually the first ones that came to mind when I asked what workplace unions and union leaders did before the *Wende;*[3] when I posed the same question after the *Wende,* these kinds of workplace union functions were sometimes the *only* ones named.

> Our *Vertrauensperson?* Well, Katya was pretty good at organizing little get togethers and so on.

> In a way the unions did something. That's what I think. When I visited my mother I was able to get cheap hotels.

> Many members' ideas of the union equaled the number of vacation places it had. They thought of it as a social service agency.

> The only way the union benefited workers was in regard to vacation times and places. Otherwise, they had nothing to offer.

> The union and management met every Monday morning and what did they talk about? How to change the vacation packages or improve the living conditions of the workers.

> The union before the fall of 1989 was more or less like a travel agency.[4]

How deeply expectations of union work were skewed toward social, ideological, educational, and cultural tasks was revealed when I asked people, both before and after the *Wende,* how they thought unions might be improved. Many were simply unable to conceive of a role for workplace unions outside these areas. One man's list of improvements, for instance, was limited to "getting more and better holiday resorts, better medical services and health spas, especially for workers who live in smaller towns, ending the disorder in the kitchen and dining rooms," and, as an afterthought, "cleaning up dirt in the work areas." Still strongly focused on the union as a "social service" and a "travel" agency in the fall of 1990, another worker responded, "The biggest problem the unions had was that there weren't enough holiday places. Not every worker could get one every year." Finally, when I queried workers about union involvement in worksite planning, their responses often focused on the cultural, social, and educational, not on the economic or production, portions of the plan. In comments echoed by many others, a woman from a bakery remarked, "The manager explains the production targets, then most of our discussion centers on how to improve living conditions."[5]

The imbalance in both workplace union activity and workers' expectations of it attracted certain types of people into the union leadership and molded leaders into a particular kind of functionary once they assumed a union office. Workplace union leaders were often people primarily interested in serving the social and cultural needs of the rank and file. "What do you like most about your work as a union officer?" I often asked workplace union leaders. "Personally, I like organizing festivals and cultural outings. Especially I like organizing events cheaper than other officials could do it. It's great to take union trips to another town, because people have a good time," a typical BGL member told me.[6]

I stress the imbalance of union tasks at GDR workplaces not to detract from the unions' very real accomplishments outside economic and production areas, the details of which both workers and union officers recounted proudly,[7] or to imply that carrying out such tasks did not involve effort and combativeness on the part of the unions. As one worker reported:

> Our collective agreement with management stipulated that a certain number of workers could take a trip abroad each year and that they'd get a travel allowance of 250 marks when they went. One time a manager tried to claim the allowance, and we had to challenge him. It's also in the collective agreement that you get paid for days you take off work if you're doing community activities and that every year some workers could go to the trade union school for three months while still receiving their pay from the factory. But sometimes it's not so easy to do all these things. Management starts quarreling with us, and we have to fight it out to make sure that what's in the collective agreement gets enforced.[8]

Rather, I want to stress that even while economic, production, cultural, social, ideological, and educational tasks were not unrelated and even while workplace unions were sometimes involved with economic and production issues, this was not a major thrust of their work. Instead, as the following workers' comments indicate, nearly everyone recognized that workplace unions rarely focused on economic and production matters, such as planning and managing production and service delivery:

When economic issues came up, the union simply didn't have the strength to express an opinion opposed to that of the boss. It's quite a different thing if you blatantly disagree with the boss about such matters than if you simply want to put some sort of social measure into effect.

In this factory, a whole new method of production was recently implemented. When it was being planned, the union was asked for its comments. "We need new workers' washrooms," was all they said.

No way is the union involved in making economic decisions. All that's party or state, not union, business.

The biggest problem was that we had a union meeting every month and we talked and talked about all kinds of stuff except relevant things like production, the quality of the product, and so on.

We often wished the unionists would support the employees in wage demands. In the beginning when the production area was built, the problem was that management hadn't paid us any supplement for the difficulties we had to suffer through. So we turned to the union, but nothing happened. We would have been happy if competent people had been there who were familiar with the legal situation and could have done something. But the union did not support the workers.[9]

The skewed agenda of workplace unions contributed to the dearth of working-class activism during the *Wende*. The unions' restricted, and in many workplaces nearly exclusive, focus on social, cultural, ideological, and educational topics limited workers' chances to gain information and develop knowledge about economic and production matters, especially those concerned with the enterprise as a whole and its relationship with other worksites throughout the country. Investment, planning, personnel deployment, work scheduling and process, research and development, product mix, clientele, organizational structure, work norms, decision-making procedures, pay, budgeting, financing, and management strategies were among matters that, to a large degree, fell outside the purview of workplace unions before the *Wende*. As will be seen in chapters 6 and 7, these kinds of knowledge and information emerged as critical in workers' attempts to refashion workplaces, unions, and other representative bodies in the midst of the crisis. Yet, many workers, lacking the exposure to economic and production issues that union involvement in these areas could have provided, did not have the knowledge, information, or confidence to participate actively in such efforts. But there is more. As will be seen in the conclusion to this chapter, the restricted focus of union work, along with other aspects of workplace politics about to be explored, made additional contributions to the demobilization of workers during the GDR revolution.

Partners, Helpers, Mascots, and Third Fiddles: Union Relations with Workplace Management and the Party

At the top of many workers' lists of preferred discussion topics was the unions' relationship with the two other major political players at their workplaces—state management and the party. Workers felt the union had too little autonomy from either organization, a situation that ultimately curtailed their ability to engage actively and effectively in revolutionary politics.[10]

Union dependence on state management and the party was so popular a theme among workers that it came up in their responses to a variety of questions I posed. "How would you describe the relationship of the union to the party and to management at your worksite?" I asked many times. "They all sit together," a Leipzig construction worker commented figuratively. Yet on many occasions when I was visiting a worksite around mealtime, I observed this to be literally true as well. Day after day, top managers, the head of the worksite party group, and the BGL chair ate together, away from the workers. "There are no differences between the union and the party. Their relationship is very good. They have the same goals," according to an electrician. "In a way the union here was the arm of company management. They functioned as an extension of the government party, in other words, the government leadership of the company," a woman remarked during the *Wende*. A Berlin construction worker likewise recalled, "The BGL head was very close and friendly with the enterprise managers. They did a lot of personal things together."[11] *Assistants, appendages, mascots, helpers, partners,* and *third fiddles* were terms I frequently heard used to describe the unions' relationship with worksite management and the party.[12]

"What are the main tasks of the union at your workplace?" was another question I posed that often elicited comments on union dependence. "I think the main task of the union is to support the leadership of the party, to really carry out and help enforce party policy," explained a child care worker. "Our main goal," a *Vertrauensperson* responded, "is to create a harmony of interests between management and the union, and generally we have no problems in this area. We have a trustful relationship. There are no secrets. We always work towards a common objective, which is to fulfill our economic tasks."[13] "How then," I would press upon receiving such answers, "are the unions' main tasks different from those of the party and management at your workplace?" Again I often received responses underscoring the low degree of workplace union autonomy. "Unions and management have the same general aims, and there are no conflicts about this. It's important not to forget that workers and managers have common interests in the enterprise—to make sure the production process isn't disturbed," explained a BGL chair in an electric motor company. "The functions of state management and the union are not very well differentiated, and they don't ever confront each other," replied another man.[14]

Finally, my queries about the protection of workers' rights, union shortcomings, and changes workers would like to see all evoked further responses suggesting the centrality of union dependence to workers' daily job experiences:

> Formally, GDR workers have lots of rights, but in practice they have far fewer. That's because union leaders are "*ja, ja*" people. That's the word that always comes out of their mouths when managers and party people are around.

> The union's biggest problem was its dependency on the party. Our BGL checked all its decisions with the enterprise director, which meant they served the purposes of the party. So the enterprise director and the BGL, who were mostly party supporters, stood against the employees.

> There are too few union leaders in plants who have the courage to say to the manager, "No, you are wrong, the worker is right!" That is something our unionists should learn to do, so that the workers really see that they are behind them.

> If I could make any change I wanted, I'd separate the union from the management and from the party. Everybody mixes into everybody else's affairs. And I'd pay all voluntary union officers, because they need to stand up to management more. As it is now, it's very difficult to do. They have their job in the work center, so they're dependent on managers, and sometimes when they get too critical of managers, they end up not getting a raise.

> The entire union was a facade. The union was based on a single lie. They said they represented the interests of the employees, but they represented the interests of the leading party. It was a joke.[15]

Workers' judgments of the unions' relationship with the party and state management are corroborated by other evidence. For example, during the summer of 1988, I heard several versions of a story, which was rapidly making the rounds of worksites I visited, about a work brigade in the Leipzig area that had stopped paying union dues because union leaders had "typically" sided with management in a grievance commission case that enterprise management had brought against workers. Likewise, management representatives were ordinarily present at every union meeting, whether of the *Kollektiv,* the *Vertrauensleute,* or the BGL; union officers at each worksite level held regularly scheduled meetings with their management and party counterparts; and there were informal meetings among the three whenever needed. While inclusion in these tête-à-têtes with other workplace leaders might be read as an indication of union power, union incorporation into these elite workplace gatherings was less a reflection of their influence and more an indication of how much their workplace authority depended on cultivating a tight relationship with management and the party. A cabaret vignette I saw performed by a work center troupe humorously illustrated the junior status of the union. A lone player was situated at the center of the stage, trying to nap. He was being pestered by a mosquito buzzing around his ears, selectively stinging him on the left arm, the right cheek, through the pant leg. The player endured the bother for awhile, trying to ignore the pest, occasionally brushing it aside. Eventually, however, his patience wore thin, and he sat up, waited for the mosquito to alight, and then bashed it. The mosquito was the union, I was told. It was a constant nuisance, but in the end the party could squash it with one hand.[16]

Nothing, however, was more apt to be viewed as evidence of union dependence than the membership and leadership overlaps between the unions, management, and the party. In my visits to worksites around the GDR, I came across numerous managers who also held workplace union offices. These people were always from the mid- and low-rungs of the management hierarchy. Department heads, supervisors, and forepersons filled *Vertrauensperson*, AGL (*Abteilungsgewerkschaftsleitung*, or department-level union committee), and BGL slots. I could not find out precisely how common the management-union leadership overlap was, though some workers I talked to claimed it was increasingly the norm.[17]

No one I met felt this situation was ideal. Mid-level managers who were also union officers described themselves as being "pulled in two directions" or as "schizophrenic," and they readily admitted that their union jobs were secondary to their managerial ones. Workers who had experienced this kind of overlap were not happy with it either. For example, a construction worker argued, "When you're a foreperson, you're kind of a tiny little boss, aren't you? So forepersons shouldn't be *Vertrauensleute*. I'm not for that!" Then, revealing how low his expectations had sunk in terms of management-union leadership overlaps, he added, "The BGL should always be at least 50 percent workers." Similarly, when I asked a construction worker from another city what he would do to improve the union, he replied without hesitating, "There should be a separation of personnel between managers and union leaders. It's now so comfortable and convenient for bosses to work with the union because they're often the same people." "But how would this improve things?" I pressed. "Because, as we say in German, the unions are now in management's hip pocket. Union leaders don't have minds of their own. There's not enough fight in them."[18]

A bigger problem for workers was the personnel overlap between the party and the union, which existed at multiple levels. To begin with, the vast majority of the party's approximately 2.7 million members were union members, making party members as much as 28 percent of the total union membership. Yet, if these people were abiding by party policy, they would have been not just union members but also union activists. According to party statutes, the party's leading role vis-à-vis the union was to be sustained by individual party members working within the unions, not by the party ordering the unions about. Party discipline, which bound individual members to support party decisions, thus kept the "union line" in sync with the "party line."

Of course, one of the most logical ways for party members to fulfill their activist obligations was to assume a union leadership position, and apparently this was common, if not condoned, by ordinary workers.[19] Just before the revolution, I was told that one-quarter of the *Vertrauensleute* in the country were also party members (though not necessarily party leaders); roughly the same proportion of union members were probably also party members.[20] Many saw problems with this overlap at the lowest level of union leadership. "Sometimes it's not such a good idea to have party members as *Vertrauensleute*. Sometimes workers have prejudices against party members. 'How can they really represent my interests, they ask?'" "It's like having a party person in the unions. It's not like having the union represented in the party, which would be something else."[21]

The higher up the workplace union leadership hierarchy, the more SED members there were. I came across worksites where one half the BGL was in the party, and a railway worker's comments suggest one way this proportion was kept high: "The union asked me if I wanted to join the party, because I was interested in working in the BGL. But because I declined to join the party after several conversations with them, I was never able to advance into the BGL."[22] When it came to BGL chairs, nonparty members were the distinct exception.[23] The party was keen to have the BGL chair be a party member, I was told. Many workers did not approve of this overlap. A steel worker, who had also been a *Vertrauensperson* for seven years, explained what it was like having the chief of the enterprise union also be a party representative: "Our BGL leader was a member of the party, and he was present at every important union meeting I went to. And if you said anything, he said, '*Kollege*, the party thinks like this about that.' Well, you could say whatever you wanted in those meetings, but what the party, that is, the BGL head, said was right. And so I asked myself many times, 'How is this party related to the union?' There it sat right in the middle of union meetings."[24]

The union-party leadership overlap was even more pronounced in the many places where the BGL chair was not only a party member but also a worksite party leader.[25] Just as nonmembers were asked to join the party upon assuming a BGL position, BGL chairs who were not in the party leadership were "automatically" integrated into this enterprise political elite. "It's an 'unwritten law,'" I was told by a union college professor, "that BGL chairs be at least party members, but they are usually party leaders as well. That's what makes union-party consensus so easy to achieve." "In reality," he added, "BGL chairs were members of the party leadership and therefore bound by the decisions of the party. And because of this, they were limited in their ability to represent the interests of the union members, if they were in opposition to those of the party. That was the biggest problem we had with the unions."[26]

The multifaceted personnel overlap between the union, the party, and management (union and party leaders were part of management, management and unionists were part of the party leadership, bosses and party members and leaders were part of the union leadership) made autonomous union activity extraordinarily difficult and often impossible at GDR worksites. Interorganizational implosion fostered union dependence, but worker assessments and other evidence suggest that even *dependence* is not a strong enough word to describe the worksite relationship between union, management, and party. Unions were also subordinate to these other two bodies. As we will soon see, forty years of union subordination to management and the party, in conjunction with other features of workplace politics, help explain why so many GDR workers chose to remain uninvolved in the politics of the *Wende*.

"Pre-chewing" Union Leaders

The unions' lack of autonomy from state managers and the party was both an outcome and an underpinning of the process through which worksite union leaders were chosen. In theory, rank-and-file union members chose their numerous union officers in secret-ballot elections held approximately every two years.[27] The percentage of union members who cast ballots in the last pre-*Wende* round of union elections was very high, between 80 and 94 percent in the workplaces I knew best.[28] Candidates could not assume their union post if they did not receive a simple majority of the votes cast, which they most often did. "It's never happened here that a candidate hasn't been elected," a Leipzig worker told me, and his report mirrored those from most other worksites with which I was familiar.[29] Successful BGL candidates, for example, were ordinarily said to garner between 90 and 100 percent of the votes,[30] and in 1989, the FDGB (Freier Deutscher Gewerkschaftsbund, or the Confederation of Free German Trade Unions) reported that 81 percent of the

BGL chairs in the country received over 91 percent of the votes cast, while a mere 59 failed to receive a simple majority.[31]

Despite such impressive voting statistics, I detected little enthusiasm for union elections before the *Wende*.[32] Reflecting on her previous job in a paper mill, a woman explained circumspectly, "Union elections were just a formality for some members. You see, the theory and the practice of union elections are often different. I come out of practice, and it's got a lot of differences with the theory." Or, as a construction worker put it the previous summer, "Workers aren't too interested in union elections. Elections have to be held, and that's why they're held. It's the 'rain effect.' Some things, like rain, happen so predictably in the GDR, without us having anything to do with them, that no one really cares."[33]

Workers highlighted several more specific problems with the union elections at their workplaces,[34] the worst of which was how candidates were selected. Candidates for the BGL and AGL, and to a lesser extent even *Vertrauensperson* posts, seemed to have been chosen by almost anyone *but* the rank-and-file union membership—an excellent example of what Paul Gleye heard referred to as "pre-chewing."[35] "Pre-chewing" union leaders meant that the "real" union elections took place long before union members dutifully marked their ballots. "Pre-chewing" usually resulted, a BGL chair told me quietly, in the number of candidates and the number of posts "balancing out,"[36] and it occurred in various ways. I was told the party might suggest, appoint, or blackball candidates. Or management might make union leadership appointments or hand pick certain workers to stand for election. Thus, 62 percent of the 234 unpaid AGL and BGL functionaries interviewed by Lutz Kirschner said management had asked them to take on their union leadership functions.[37]

The union itself, however, was just as involved as the party or management was in candidate recruitment, if not more so. One of the least popular ways this occurred was when union leaders from outside the workplace, such as county and district leaders or union college officials, decided who would fill some union posts in an enterprise. The result was often union leaders who were completely unknown to the workers and completely unfamiliar with the people, the products or services, and the work processes in the places where they assumed union duties. At a hi-tech brewery in Frankfurt Oder, for instance, the BGL chair, who appeared to know virtually nothing about the plant, had previously been the BGL chair in a service enterprise. The county union organization reassigned her to the brewery chairship after she had taken a one-year union training course.[38] Many workers commented quite unfavorably on this practice of "importing" worksite union leaders. It set the union up, many argued, for failure.

More commonly, workplace BGL and AGL officers were the ones who agreed on a candidate list prior to elections. A member of the metal workers' union recalled how, after a five-year stint as *Vertrauensperson,* "The BGL chair came up to me and asked me to be a candidate for the BGL. Actually, he came to see me frequently about this, and when I finally agreed, I was also put up as a candidate for the executive board of the whole union." Once elected, this man then participated in BGL-orchestrated candidate searches himself: "The BGL knows the workers well. You look for someone who's critical and realistic and then you keep an eye on them. Workers aren't so ready to take on unpaid union positions anymore. But it depends on how you talk to them. They'll often do it if you convince them right."[39] As the report from a brewery worker suggests, candidate selection by the unions was at times driven by cynical efforts to diversify the union leadership corps: "Well, I was a member of the CDU. So the BGL members said, 'We'll pick him, then we can say, look, we have a man in there who doesn't always have the same opinions as everyone else.' "[40]

Before the *Wende,* the ranks of the workplace union swelled with pre-chewed leaders. As will be seen in chapter 8, pre-chewing of workplace union leaders was the mark of their vassalage and as such contributed to the passive political involvement of some workers during the revolution. At the same time, the entire process through which union leaders were chosen was so stained by the hypocrisy reminiscent of that surrounding the reporting and planning procedures discussed earlier that it encouraged numerous GDR workers to renounce political participation entirely. Shortly I will explore how the pre-chewing of the workplace union leadership also combined with the other three features of workplace politics discussed in this chapter to bring about this same outcome.

Formalism and Centralism of Union Political Practice

A fourth feature of workers' everyday experience of politics at their workplaces was the stifling formalism and centralism of union political practice. The one seemed to feed off the other in a deadening pattern that ultimately quelled activist inclinations in the GDR work force.

Internal union political practice and the political practices through which the union engaged workplace party and management were both often highly formalized, that is, bound by rigid protocol, hyperbureaucratized, and governed by detailed rules and regulations. Union leaders at the grass-roots level voiced a loud chorus of complaints about this, often targeting the tremendous amount of paperwork their union jobs demanded. "I had to go to clean out the offices of the BGL and AGLs that were dissolved in January 1990," one said. "You can't imagine how much official paper I had to throw away, even though some was already missing by the time I got there. Based on that, I can only begin to imagine the tremendous burdens those union people worked under."[41] The following, which surely accounted for some of the trash this man removed from the union office at his plant, were just some of the written reports enterprise union officers had to prepare as part of their union duties: yearly financial and business reports; at least biannual progress reports on the fulfillment of the annual collective agreement; monthly general reports from AGLs to BGLs and from BGLs to higher union committees; reports from enterprise union committees (e.g., on housing, health, women) to the BGL; reports from the *Kollektive* to the AGLs and from the AGLs to the BGLs on nominees for union office; *Kollektiv* plans for socialist competitions and reports at different union levels on the fulfillment of these plans; reports on the outcome of special production campaigns (e.g., those staged in conjunction with important anniversaries and holidays); and reports of workers' suggestions on and criticisms of the work center's annual production plan. For many workplace union officers, doing union politics meant completing reams of paperwork, a task they found boring and impossible to keep up with and, most ominous in terms of working-class politics during the *Wende,* one that kept them out of touch with the rank and file, as these comments reflect:

> The reporting system has got to be reduced! The BGL members spend too much time writing at their desks, pushing paper, when they should be down at the actual worksite. When most of what you're doing as a union officer gets done behind a desk, you just lose contact with the workers.

> How could the union be made better you ask me? Well, there are too many required reports. They hamper our work. That's a major concern. If those were reduced, we'd have more time for union members. Why can't district and company union officials come down *here* once in awhile? We wouldn't have to write so many reports that way. I think all layers of the union leadership should direct their attention to the workers at the bottom. Workers need to actually *see* them. A good union leader is someone workers really know, because workers have actually seen them around.[42]

Many union officers also targeted their complaints about formalism at the number of meetings they were required to attend, and they were unhappy about how these, too, kept them separated from ordinary union members:

> I want to be in the enterprise meeting workers and discussing things with them personally. But I don't have much chance to do that because of all the meetings I have to go to, especially meetings with managers and with higher

levels of the union that are held outside the *Betrieb* [enterprise]. Meetings for us are a real burden. Like yesterday, I had to go to a meeting about a district sports event. So I had to go to a meeting beforehand to prepare for that meeting and then by bus to Bernau and back for the meeting, which all took three hours. Workers measure the BGL by how often they go to them and resolve their problems, not by how many meetings they can sit through.[43]

Formalism was apparent not only in workplace union leaders' criticisms of the frequency of meetings but also in their comments on the quality of the meetings. Too often grass-roots union officers found them frustrating and negative experiences:

All *Vertrauensleute* have to meet with the BGL once a month. Well, sometimes it's informative, but usually we could finish in half an hour what we do in two. I'm aghast at the overformalization of these meetings. We hold the meeting just because it's scheduled to be held. I mean, they're not effective because we only discuss trivia, or things we can't do a thing about anyway, or we just rubber stamp someone else's decisions. The majority of what happens at these meetings is meaningless and a waste of time.

In our meetings between *Vertrauensleute* and management, managers, and even our union superiors, talked a lot about numbers. They read long lists of numbers to us. But to us, this was useless. We didn't know what the numbers meant, and we didn't understand what all their abbreviations meant. And the super-abstract words like *solidarity* and *proletarian internationalism* that got thrown around didn't have any meaning for us either.[44]

The formalism of union political practice was also a regular complaint of the rank and file. Echoing many union leaders' assessments, ordinary workers were highly critical of what transpired in the workplace meetings they had to attend. State, union, and sometimes party leaders, they said, decided which topics would get discussed, often dutifully and inflexibly reproducing agendas sent down from above. The meetings had a decidedly closed character. Some workers claimed they could not even ask questions, unless these were okayed ahead of time. There was little dialogue. Instead, workers were subjected to dry, pedantic monologues, in the form of long-winded, prepared speeches, which functionaries read page-by-page and word-for-word before their glazed-eyed worker audiences. This passionless and disempowering brand of political practice was parodied in a cabaret skit that made the worksite rounds in 1989. The player read verbatim from the *Arbeitsgesetzbuch* as fast as he possibly could in a monotone voice. Every so often he pretended momentarily to lose his place at the end of a line or a page ending with a hyphenated word. He uttered the first half of the word, the meaning of which was, by itself, often comical, then looked about distressed and puzzled while shuffling through the pages of the book until he found his place. He then victoriously pronounced the second half of the hyphenated word, which standing alone was also humorous, ironic, or carried a clever double meaning. The audience was hysterical with laughter as he repeated this several times.[45]

Although workers' complaints about formalism did not often include excessive paperwork or frequent meetings, union leaders' sense that the time they spent writing reports and attending meetings was interfering with the cultivation of solid contacts with the rank and file was right on the mark. Numerous workers from a variety of workplaces grumbled that worksite union leaders were inaccessible, distant, and unresponsive to their problems:

> It's just extra work to get the union to do something. It takes a lot of initiative on the part of individuals. Some workers, though, make requests or suggestions to the union, year in and year out. And every time the response is the same—"It's not possible."

> The union listened if we brought complaints. But then nothing much ever happened.

> We didn't ever look to our BGL for support. We didn't really have much contact at all with them.

> In my view, the union was an organization that didn't do any real work. If you came to them with a problem, they just put you off. They said they couldn't do anything about it right now. They never came to you to help.

> I think the union shouldn't just push papers around but should go directly to the workers sometimes. They should ask if we have problems. The worker shouldn't have to go to them after a long work day.[46]

Centralism, an operating feature of the majority of large contemporary organizations, was greatly magnified in the GDR. The centralism of GDR organizations did not escape the notice of most who studied them before the revolution, and commentators drew attention to the many imprints it left on political practice in the country. Such people have demonstrated how upper levels of the unions habitually exercised tight control over subordinate levels, even when it came to relatively trivial matters. They have shown how the sectoral unions, all of whose decisions had, by statute, to agree with those of the FDGB, were also financially dependent on the umbrella organization. An ex-BGL member summed up this situation: "In reality, the FDGB was everything. The sectoral unions were nothing."[47] They have explained how lower-level union leaders could do little without the go-ahead from their union, party, and management superiors. This modus operandi was so deeply ingrained that even after the GDR began to unravel, some district-level FDGB officers still could not bring themselves to respond directly to critical letters from workers. Instead, they passed them up the ladder, to be answered by their immediate union and party superiors, who were in turn immobilized by their habitual deference to their own superordinates and relayed them unanswered up to the next rung.[48] Finally, commentators have shown how centralism was reflected in the reduced group of individuals, ever smaller as one ascended the union hierarchy, whose members simultaneously held leading positions in multiple organizations.

Here, however, I focus on a particularly salient way in which centralism affected how ordinary workers experienced politics at their workplaces. Union centralism meant that the principal day-to-day working orientation of workplace union officers was upward—toward their superiors in the union and in other organizations and even toward their organizational equals and subordinates in higher-status organizations. Since the unions, the party, and the state bureaucracies that jointly managed production were all intricately stratified organizations, this meant that workplace union leaders had plenty of superordinates to keep their eyes on. Considering only their superordinates in the union, BGLs had up to six separate union leadership levels outside the firm to which they were subservient.[49] *Vertrauensleute* had all these plus the AGL and the BGL inside the enterprise. Workplace union leaders took up their most consequential business with this gaggle of superiors. Their political energy was focused on and consumed by their relationships with these people.

As a consequence, ordinary union members, who were organizationally superior to no one, were effectively excluded from many of the most significant political deliberations in which the workplace union was involved. The formalism of union political practice thus limited the quality of the meetings workers attended, while centralism precluded their involvement in many workplace deliberations entirely. The "smoke-filled room" metaphor, routinely used to characterize political practice in the United States, fit workplace politics in the GDR equally well. Only rarely did rank-and-file union members take part in political discussions at their workplaces, and the more important the issue, the less likely they were to be involved in resolving it. Instead, such deliberations were hidden from their view, prompting Lutz Kirschner's comment that discussions between union leaders and management in the enterprise he studied were "opaque" to workers.[50]

In the course of describing their work, many workplace union leaders I interviewed corroborated the perception that centralist union political practice shielded workers from politics. Some, for example, called it "bad democracy" for the union to present a collective agreement to workers if some of them might ultimately vote against it. All the wrinkles needed to be ironed out before the workers considered it, they argued. The union in a service enterprise that handled everything from laundry to the maintenance of movie theaters embraced the smoke-filled-room principle even more extensively. There, I was told, not just the collective agreement but also "every work issue and problem is discussed twice a month among the party secretary, management, the BGL, and the FDJ [the Communist youth organization] representative *before* we start discussions of these things in larger worker forums."[51] Doing politics behind closed doors, an important manifestation of the centralism of union political practice, thus rendered vast reaches of day-to-day workplace politics off limits to GDR workers.

Conclusion

Earlier, I argued that the narrow substantive agenda of union work discouraged activism during the *Wende* because it restricted workers' opportunities to develop grounded knowledge on a range of practical and technical topics central to the production and delivery of goods and services. As a consequence, workers found themselves at a decided disadvantage, compared with many intellectuals, when it came to actively participating in the struggles over how to restructure their workplaces and the wider political and economic system, which engulfed the GDR in 1989–90.

Beyond this, we have seen that workers' everyday experience of workplace politics exhibited three additional elements, which combined with the first to solidify further the foundation for the widespread political demobilization of the working class. We can understand one way this happened if we consider workers' ability, when the opening occurred, to formulate their own visions of what work, unions, politics, and production might be like. All four features of workplace politics discussed in this chapter conspired to hamper workers' capacity to conceive and to inspire their own agendas for change. For forty years, formalized and centralized union political practice, the political dependency of the unions, the union retreat from economic and management matters, and the brand of union leadership that flourished when the rank and file was denied input into the selection of its officers had smothered workers' creative energy and imagination under a pall of resignation, indifference, timidity, and cynicism. Hence, many reported feeling "directionlessness" during the crisis—a vague desire for change in the absence of any ideas about the kind of change they wanted. As one woman expressed it, "We could not even imagine that there could be any other way [things could be done]. Thinking was basically taken away from us. You just couldn't imagine anything else, or at least I couldn't."[52]

The four characteristics of workplace politics discussed in this chapter also encouraged working-class withdrawal from the politics of the *Wende* in a second way. Together they thwarted workers' opportunity to gain firsthand experience *doing* politics. Many workers, in other words, were political novices when the *Wende* began. The closed-door nature of union political practice, the unions' eagerness to play political tag-along with managers and the party, the narrowly prescribed bounds of union activity, and the contrived nature of leadership selection contests combined to deprive many workers of the chance to actually practice doing politics. Yet there is no substitute for on-the-ground political engagement as preparation for continued activism. For one thing, doing politics means acquiring and refining political skills—learning to organize, strategize, chart agendas, anticipate outcomes, speak persuasively in public, deal successfully with disruptive personalities, and run a productive meeting. For another, there are important gains to be had from doing politics. Doing politics successfully imparts a sense of efficacy and agency. It is empowering. Likewise, firsthand experience with political failure can produce valuable and maturing lessons for future engagements. Yet the nature of workplace politics routinely denied GDR workers opportunities to amass such political skills and knowledge or to accrue the psychological benefits that can accompany participation. In this way also, the cumulative, direct, and daily experience of workplace politics militated against any widespread display of working-class activism during the GDR revolution.

Everyday workplace politics did not just discourage activism among workers in a direct fashion. Workplace politics in the GDR also crippled working-class political activism indirectly, both by souring the relationship between workplace union leaders and union members and by rendering the experience of workplace union leadership overwhelmingly negative for many workers who tried it before the revolution.

I have maintained that the formalism and centralism of union political practice and the pre-chewing of candidates for union office, in particular, served to insulate workplace union leaders from the mass of union members. Together these two elements of workplace politics virtually ensured that many workplace union officers were severely out of touch with the rank and file. The predictable flip side of this coin was that many workers distrusted their union leaders, viewed them as illegitimate representatives of their interests, and openly wondered whether they even tried to act on workers' behalf. Some workplace union leaders were aware of this and understood that workers' feelings could be attributed to deficient union practice. A BGL member, for instance, perceived how even the occasions when union officers tried to represent workers might appear otherwise to the rank and file:

> We've got to have an agreement with management about the plan beforehand. Consensus doesn't just happen, though. Only hard debate gets us there. But this happens before the workers consider the plan. Managers and the BGL don't want to come into the workers' planning meeting disagreeing with each other. So we settle things beforehand. But then, when we all come to the planning assembly, it looks to workers as if this consensus on the plan was just automatic. And so they naturally ask themselves, "What the hell is going on here with this union anyway?"[53]

Regardless of union leaders' awareness of their strained relationship with the rank and file or the causes of it, the distance and suspicion that had built up between the two groups of workers, layer upon layer for forty years, had a detrimental effect on working-class activism during the *Wende*. Although not all workplace union leaders chose to organize and encourage workers' involvement during the revolution, those who did were hampered by workers' distrust of their leadership. Many workers thus turned a deaf ear to leaders' pleas for activism, leaving many of the workplace union leaders most inclined toward political involvement without an effective constituency.

At the same time the legacy of union political practice convinced many rank-and-file workers to turn away from workplace union leaders urging activism, it also encouraged many former and current union leaders to shy away from assuming activist roles in the first place.[54] Many people who had been workplace union leaders before the *Wende* harbored bitter memories of their experiences. Some felt disheartened by workers' lack of confidence in and appreciation of their work. A BGL member, for example, recalled how the enterprise union leadership had once gotten into a debate with managers over the low quality of meals served in the cafeteria, a debate so heated that management was forced to call in the state prosecutor, who settled the conflict. Once the issue was resolved, however, the managers claimed credit for calling the prosecutor, and the workers ended up praising them, not the union leaders, for the improved quality of the food.[55] Although workplace union leaders could understand that union subordination to management and the closed-door nature of union political practice lay behind such worker reactions, they still felt resentful and discouraged in their union posts. Their experiences in union leadership positions, in other words, provided little inducement to activism during the *Wende*. Instead, disgruntled and even angry, many workplace union leaders retreated to the galleries during the crisis.

Many workplace union leaders shunned activism during the crisis as much from their own frustration with workplace politics as from workers' negative evaluations of their performance. These were the workplace union leaders of chapter 2, who often spoke of themselves as "politically burned out":

> I used to be chair of the union work protection commission. So I dealt with complaints about poor lighting at the workplace, missing or inappropriate seating, and things like that. So I tried to approach the boss and the BGL with these things. And I had to get angry each time, because we were supposed to explain these things to them and express the suggestions and opinions of the workers, but when I did that they got enraged and said I had too many suggestions. The BGL always said they couldn't do anything. No one ever had the courage to just write up an order and say we need this and that, so I made no progress, ever.

> As *Vertrauensperson* I really tried to apply the labor code, like the part that says the union has a right to take part in deciding the collective agreement. But I didn't succeed because the managers and union leaders were old-guard party supporters, and so I was just ignored most of the time.

> I wrote petitions to Erich Mielke [national director of the security police], I wrote petitions to Honecker, I wrote piles of petitions throughout all those years. I always received the answer that "according to section so-and-so, we are not required to provide you with an answer to your request."[56]

We can now understand more of what lay behind the statements made by such "politically burned out" workplace union leaders. Shortages, union subordination and dependence, the innervating centralism and formalism of union political practice, and the union's narrow agenda, contributed to their inability to accomplish much, despite repeated attempts.

Since leadership burn-out was often accompanied by poor relations between workplace union leaders and the rank and file, not only did many experienced working-class leaders refuse to lead, but also the few who were so disposed found it very difficult to attract support from workers. Had circumstances been otherwise, had many workplace union leaders not already sworn never again to take on any leadership responsibilities, they would have been the logical group to have encouraged, organized, and cultivated activism among union members. Had the relationship between so many workers and workplace union leaders not been so unsatisfactory for so long, those workplace leaders who did rise to the challenge during the crisis would have found themselves joined by more of their rank-and-file comrades. As it was, however, the everyday politics of the socialist workplace left the workers' proverbial ship with neither rudder nor crew when the storm finally broke.

5   The Class Relationship Revisited

We have seen how the labor process and workplace politics contributed to the relative invisibility of workers during the GDR revolution, but there is more to the story of the political demobilization of the GDR working class than has so far been uncovered. The extent of the political paralysis that gripped so many GDR workers during the 1989–90 revolution cannot be fully understood unless we revisit the issue of class.

I argued in chapter 1 that from where GDR workers stood, the intelligentsia had long appeared socially uniform, and I posited one way in which this feature of the relationship between GDR classes helps explain workers' reluctance to become politically active during the *Wende*. Together with two other features of the pre-*Wende* class relationship, discussed in the present chapter, it resulted in a class-exclusive pattern of political protest decades before the *Wende*, which was not surmounted in the fall and winter of 1989–90.

In the first section of the chapter, I consider the lack of interaction between workers and the intelligentsia in the years leading up to the *Wende*. In other words, a notable feature of the pre-*Wende* class relationship was how abbreviated it was. For a good illustration of this feature of the GDR class relationship, one that had important implications for the single-class character of revolutionary politics, I focus on civil society. In the GDR, the intelligentsia was the dominant class in a host of important networks and organizations making up civil society—representative government bodies, political parties, professional associations, and opposition groups, to name a few. After documenting the middle-class composition of these arenas of civil society, I explore two ways this contributed to the relative lack of working-class presence among revolutionary activists.

In the second section of this chapter, I suggest not only how GDR workers perceived the intelligentsia as homogenous but also how they came to recognize intellectuals, whether biologists, party functionaries, dissidents, school teachers, painters, or managers, as quite different from themselves. We will see that the social gulf separating them from intellectuals was apparent in numerous ways as they went about their daily business. Both in and outside their workplaces, GDR workers continuously saw, heard, smelled, and lived this class difference long before the *Wende*.

The third section of the chapter relates workers' cognizance of the class divide to the decision of many to avoid oppositional politics during the *Wende*, despite the numerous changes they would like to have seen in the GDR. I contend that the link between the pre-*Wende* class divide and the relative absence of workers in the ranks of the revolutionary opposition was the behavior of the middle-class challengers themselves. Too often they ignored, disparaged, or rebuffed workers, and in some instances, they purposely excluded them from their activist efforts. In other words, from workers' standpoint, the chasm between the working class and the middle class was reinforced during the *Wende*, leaving many workers with no desire whatsoever to actively enter the political struggle on the side of the opposition.

The conclusion to the chapter summarizes my explanations for the paucity of GDR workers among the revolution's activists, which have been presented in chapters 1, 3, 4, and 5. This explanation is woven of many threads. Class, the labor process, and workplace politics are all implicated in multiple ways. Although I have tended to treat each explanatory thread somewhat discretely, in the conclusion we see that a thorough understanding of workers' political withdrawal from revolutionary politics only comes when we remember how all these are all interwoven.

Interclass Contact, Civil Society, and the Single-Class Character of the Revolution

Prior to the *Wende*, one characteristic of the GDR class relationship was the absence of one. By this I mean that workers and intellectuals passed relatively little of their lives in one another's company. In terms of its impact on the single-class character of the revolution, civil society provided the best illustration of this lack of interclass contact. The term *civil society* refers to a miscellany of formal and informal networks and organizations that are at least somewhat autonomous from, though not necessarily opposed to, the state.[1] In the GDR, members of the intelligentsia dominated nearly all such civil society networks and organizations. In other words, the GDR intelligentsia associated mostly with one another, not with workers, in these forums.[2] These class endogenous civil society involvements represented an important way in which intellectuals and workers could be said to occupy different worlds, and they helped ensure that the ranks of revolutionary activists were heavily intellectual during the fall and winter of 1989–90.

Civil society organizations and networks exhibiting only minimal autonomy from state authorities have received relatively little attention from those interested in civil society and its relation to political activism in socialist societies. In my view, however, understanding why the GDR revolution was largely a middle-class affair requires a close look at these state-dependent, or at least state-sponsored, networks and organizations. Among the civil society groupings most identified with the GDR state were certainly its formal political bodies and organizations, and the middle-class presence was substantial in all of these. Take, for instance, representative political institutions. After the mid-1980s elections, the absolute majority of elected officials at all except the lowest government level had university or technical college degrees. Seventy-three percent of those in the Volkskammer and between 52 and 64 percent of those in the county, district, small town, and city councils possessed such diplomas.[3] The work of local governments in the GDR was supplemented by numerous standing citizen commissions concerned with, for example, housing, schools, and transportation. People with university and technical college degrees dominated the membership of these bodies as well. They held absolute majorities at the county (64 percent) and district (51 percent) levels and were overrepresented, considering their percentage of the population, at the two lowest levels of government as well.[4]

Similarly, all GDR political parties appear to have been middle-class havens. Despite the SED's periodic efforts to strengthen its working-class character, SED members with higher education degrees steadily increased between 1970 (about 19 percent) and 1988 (about 41 percent), and this trend was even more pronounced in the party leadership. The same was true of the Block parties, long institutionalized SED-financed features of the GDR political landscape. The CDU, the largest of the four with a 1987 membership of 137,000, drew the majority of its members, 20,000 of whom were important state functionaries or elected government representatives, from the various segments of the middle class.[5] Moreover, according to Robert Goeckel, the CDU provided "some political protection to small businessmen and creative 'space' for those in the fine arts."[6] The LDPD, with 104,000 members in 1987, drew largely from the same social strata. As one LDPD member told me, "Before the 1970s the party was mainly composed of private owners. The people who've joined since then are mostly skilled craftspeople who want to get a license to work privately, and other nonstate workers, for example, some who work for the church. There are also engineers, scientists, technical workers, and other professionals, some of whom are self-employed, like doctors and lawyers for example, and some of whom are not." At an LDPD meeting I later attended with him, he revealed, "We meet regularly in small groups, and many of us have known one another for years."[7] Even the DBD (Democratic Farmers' Party), whose name might imply otherwise, was said to have many members with degrees in agronomy or animal husbandry.[8]

Intellectuals also dominated another sector of state-organized participation in civil society through their appointment to committees constituted to study national and international issues and to offer opinions and recommendations on these matters to state and party authorities. A history professor I met at the union college, for example, had served for about seven years on one such commission, which analyzed and prepared reports on changes occurring in the Soviet Union. Another was a member of what she called a "scientific problem-solving" council concerned with Southern tier nations. This woman also told me of a variety of analogous councils focused on different issues and explained how each brought together party, academic, state, and enterprise representatives under the tutelage of an appropriate carrier institution, for example a university.[9] Her comments highlighted a noteworthy feature of many predominantly middle-class groupings operating throughout civil society: their memberships crosscut organizations and professions, putting subgroups of the intelligentsia, which might otherwise not have interacted with one another, in regular contact.

Civil society organizations and networks that enjoyed a higher degree of autonomy from the state have often been the only ones examined in discussions of civil society and its effect on politics in socialist countries. Intellectuals in the GDR were involved in a number of such state-sponsored but technically nongovernment and nonparty organizations. Included among these were the Kulturbund (Culture League), which had a preassigned number of seats in the Volkskammer, and the Kammer der Technik (KdT—Chamber of Technology).[10] The KdT, with 85 percent of its over 282,000 members holding higher education degrees in 1987, "probably constitute[d] a semi-elitist subgroup within their respective local unions."[11] Organized in 1946, with its prototypical member an engineer, the KdT had sections in various work centers and higher education and research institutions, and it carried out its function of improving production through special committees and study groups, lectures, technical publications, trips, and the like. The Kulturbund was begun in the early years of the GDR explicitly to bring bourgeois intellectuals together and to integrate them into the new system. It attracted the humanist elements of the intelligentsia, and probably 50 to 60 percent of its over 270,000 members came from the middle class. Described by Duncan Smith as the "National Front" of cultural organizations, the Kultur-bund had chapters in higher education institutions and a Berlin headquarters described as a meeting place for intellectuals.[12] In addition, it was affiliated with *Klubs der Intelligenz* (intelligentsia clubs), which numbered approximately 170 in 1987.[13] According to Thomas Baylis's account from the early 1970s, these clubs, some with relatively luxurious headquarters, were mostly social organizations, which "aroused considerable resentment" and were the object of "much rumor and speculation."[14]

Besides joining such semi-autonomous organizations as the Kammer der Technik and the Kulturbund, numerous GDR intellectuals became members of a variety of professional organizations, ranging from associations and unions for national jurists, architects, journalists, artists, and writers to campus-specific faculty clubs at individual technical colleges and universities.[15] Like the Kammer der Technik and the Kulturbund, these organizations served social and professional purposes, and the relationships formed among their middle-class members reflected both. Observers of other East and Central European countries have commented on the dearth of such semi-independent organizations for workers and the proliferation and heightened importance of those primarily attracting and serving the intelligentsia. In this regard, the GDR was no exception. These "kernels of civil society" were sites where intellectuals interacted with their own kind, separated from workers.[16]

The groupings within GDR civil society most independent from the state, however, were not the professional associations, the Kammer der Technik, the Kulturbund, and the like but peace, human rights, homosexual, ecology, women's, and radical religious opposition groups; less formally constituted discussion circles; and some social service groups. Estimates of the number of opposition groups in the years before the *Wende* vary between 150 and 2,500.[17] Because these grass-roots opposition groups were underground, semi-underground, or at least straddling the fence of official approval, we do not know their precise class composition. Available evidence, however, strongly suggests that they, too, were the indisputable province of the intelligentsia. The political scientist Gero Neugebauer, for instance, characterized them as "mostly middle-class," and he is joined in his assessment by numerous others.[18] Anecdotal assessments from every member of the intelligentsia I interviewed fully corroborate these judgments. For example, a music therapist involved in a women's ecology group during most of the 1980s described the members as "intellectuals, artists, teachers, but no workers," and many others of like class standing reported varying degrees of association with such groups before the *Wende*.[19] Some of these groups, which existed around the country, engaged in daring political challenges to the government. Many were

linked in some fashion, either programmatically or through their memberships, and the undisputed hub of this network was the Protestant church.
Although tensions periodically surfaced between the church and the opposition groups, the church has often been described as the sponsor, the coor-
dinator, or the protector of the opposition groups and the groups themselves
as tied to the church, church-inspired, church-led, and even merging with
the church.

Less formally organized and more private were the often nameless discussion circles, usually made up of small groups of friends with opposition sympathies. Many hundreds may have existed in the GDR, and many members
of the intelligentsia who later became revolutionary activists recall them as
among their most meaningful pre-*Wende* involvements. Some get-togethers
focused on national and international political topics—Solidarity and the
arms race, for example. Others concerned participants' families and personal
lives—the ideological pressure children faced at school and alcoholism, for
instance. Sometimes circle members even engaged in joint political action,
such as sending petitions to the government or party, organizing the defense
of people who had been arrested, and printing and distributing flyers.[20] Some
of these circles had functioned for decades before the final months of confrontation that ended the GDR.

A final niche at the more autonomous end of the civil society spectrum
was occupied by a variety of social welfare agencies that provided services
supplementing those offered by the state. Some of these groups were tied to
churches; others were not. I learned in interviews that many of these groups
served as work sanctuaries for middle-class oppositionists who would otherwise have had difficulty finding employment. Carl Bradley Scharf was likewise under the impression that the majority of people involved with these
nonstate agencies had technical college or university degrees, that these
groups had strengthened their links with universities and academic institutes
in the 1980s, and that they represented "the beginnings of coherent interest
group participation" in the GDR political process.[21]

Certainly not all members of the GDR intelligentsia participated in any
of the previously mentioned networks and organizations during the decades
before the revolution. Yet even exceptional middle-class people with none of
these involvements might still have been part of civil society networks established in the course of performing their paid jobs. Many middle-class jobs
required their holders to be in daily communication with other intellectuals, both inside and outside the workplace. Managers met with counterparts
from other establishments and with their superiors in the government and
the party; academics attended disciplinary seminars; doctors and jurists spent
days at conferences; artists and writers held and attended exhibits, openings,

readings, and so forth. Moreover, phone calls and written communications with other members of the intelligentsia filled a good portion of their work time. Each of these meetings, openings, phone calls, and so forth represented a structurally guaranteed opportunity for GDR intellectuals, even those who shied away from participating in any of the civil society groupings discussed, to establish and renew acquaintances with others of their class rank throughout the country.[22] The upshot, according to Marc Rakovski, was an "inner public sphere" inhabited by intellectuals and facilitating "institutionalized communication" among them.[23] Working-class jobs were different. Workers often found themselves either physically isolated at machine posts, in cubicles, or at jobs where rules or noise precluded interaction with anyone, even those in close proximity. The comments of a construction worker, whose job allowed him more mobility and more opportunity to converse with others than those of many of his working-class peers, underscored this contrast: "I don't even know many people in my own company, not even how many of them their are. You know those on your particular site, but the rest are unknown to you. You maybe see them every six months. You never go to the company office. You are just totally isolated."[24]

So far we have explored one example of the lack of sustained contact between workers and intellectuals before the *Wende:* middle-class dominance of a wide assortment of civil society networks and organizations. Many GDR intellectuals, by virtue of their involvements in these networks and organizations managed to interact regularly with their class peers for many years before the *Wende.* The ascendancy of intellectuals in large swatches of GDR civil society had important implications for the class character of the *Wende.* The full significance of one of these will not become clear until the conclusion, where I compare working-class politics in the GDR in 1989–90 with those of Polish workers in 1980. Here I only point out that in contrast with the intelligentsia, GDR workers had few social spaces in which they could interact with others of their same class. GDR workers were involved in some prerevolutionary forums in which they spent time in one another's company—for instance neighborhood associations, sports groups, and base-level union groups, which are discussed in chapter 7—but they had neither the quantity nor the quality of pre-*Wende* opportunities for intraclass contact that the GDR intelligentsia enjoyed.

There were additional ways in which the class-skewed nature of GDR civil society helped ensure that the social character of revolutionary activism was unbalanced. The distribution of political skills was one of these. On the whole, as a direct result of their pre-*Wende* participation across the spectrum of civil society groupings, many members of the GDR intelligentsia, both those who eventually supported and those who eventually opposed the status quo, had been able to acquire political and administrative skills and experience that would serve them well in 1989–90.[25] As local government representatives, political party stalwarts, members of policy-making and advisory committees, workplace managers, and participants in professional, social service, and opposition political groups, many GDR intellectuals had frequent practice speaking before groups, leading, compromising, chairing meetings, debating, envisioning alternatives, raising money, building alliances, planning programs, recruiting supporters, isolating opponents, evaluating options, and so forth.[26] In addition, as a particular consequence of their pre-*Wende* civil society activities, especially those involving policy making and implementation, intellectuals had acquired knowledge of many economic and political issues that became the central topics around which revolutionary politics were waged. Put simply, in terms of their political experience and skills, the GDR intelligentsia was advantaged when the struggle began. Members of all segments of the middle class, not just those critical of the regime, had practice doing politics and some familiarity with the major topics of revolutionary debate, and their comparative advantage in both areas partially explains their high political visibility during the critical months of the revolution.

The civil society involvements of the intelligentsia help account for the middle-class character of revolutionary activism in a second way as well. These networks and organizations provided the grounding for a range of personal and intimate relationships that proved essential to the initiation and development of the many middle-class citizens' opposition groups and parties that challenged the status quo.[27] In other words, their pre-*Wende* civil society involvements, in particular the oppositional political groups and discussion circles, constituted a pool of homologous middle-class persons to which oppositional intellectuals turned first and most often as they initiated and mounted their revolutionary political challenge. The middle-class complexion of major arenas of pre-*Wende* civil society was thus reproduced, through activists' personal friendship networks, in nearly every one of the citizens' opposition groups and political parties of significance during the fall and winter of 1989–90.[28]

Several points lend credence to this line of argument. First, it is not difficult to understand why middle-class oppositionists would have preferred doing politics with people they knew quite well during the fall and winter of 1989–90. As members of pre-*Wende* opposition groups, many of these people had experienced police harassment and infiltration of varying degrees of severity firsthand or had known opposition group members who had. Being able to trust their co-conspirators was thus a paramount concern of middle-class activists, especially in the earlier months of the revolution. "We even went so far as to write pledges to raise each others' children," one woman explained, "because we all knew we could be arrested."[29]

Second, from pre-*Wende* descriptions, we know that politics was not the sole purpose of many opposition groups or the smaller and less formally structured discussion circles. Both intentionally (some transformed portions of their meeting spaces into lounges and cafes) and unintentionally, they also served as the social hub of many intellectuals' lives, as the sites where many intellectuals made and nurtured their most important friendships. For many, they functioned as "small support groups in which the individual could find recognition, strength, security, warmth, comfort, and encouragement."[30] Those people with whom they had established friendships in these settings, sometimes decades before the *Wende*, were precisely the ones many oppositional activists recalled working alongside during the revolution: "It was in my human rights group, during all the meetings we had in the cold church basement, that I really got to know very well all the people who got active in the citizens' organizations later on."[31]

Third, details of the formation of many citizens' opposition groups and new and reformed parties are testimony to the importance of tight middle-class friendship networks for the birth of the revolutionary opposition. A prominent founder of Demokratischer Aufbruch recalled asking "six or seven friends of mine secretly to meet somewhere during the vacations" to talk about the feasibility of forming a political group.[32] The establishment of Neues Forum followed a similar pattern. Its thirty initiators, who secretly collaborated on the founding document at a country retreat in early September 1989, were handpicked by two women, and although none of those invited knew every single one of the others tapped, one founder knew each of them.[33] Certainly the intellectuals who started the revolutionary opposition groups had not all been acquainted through pre-*Wende* civil society networks and organizations, but this was very often the case, as an interview with one such activist revealed: "At the beginning, we were ten people, and we met in a little apartment. We began with people who knew each other from the Ecology Library. I knew Ulrich pretty well. I think he was the main contact person. Ulrich knew other people, and they knew some other people and so on. I brought people along too. One of them I knew very well because we'd wanted to establish a real communist party at one point."[34] Not only had the initiators of many individual groups previously been friends or friends of friends, but also the initiators of different groups were frequently well acquainted. One Neues Forum founder, for instance, had known four of the seven people who wrote the PDS party program for nearly a decade, and one was a close friend. In an interview, another declared, "I have friends and people I really respect [who] are with Demokratie Jetzt and the SPD and Demokratischer Aufbruch."[35]

Finally, the initiators of the middle-class challenge to the status quo would have gotten nowhere if they had not been able to widen their activist net. They had to convince others to become organizational stalwarts; come to meetings; sign petitions; plan, publicize, and participate in group activities; raise money; attend demonstrations; distribute literature; and recruit additional activists. To do this, they adopted the same strategy that had originally enticed them into the activist fold. They activated their networks of personal friends, networks that mirrored the middle-class composition of the pre-*Wende* civil society groups from which they were often drawn.[36] "Starting from about ten or twelve people," one Neues Forum activist recalled, "we spread the word by each making lists of people we knew and contacting them."[37] Many people active in citizens' opposition groups thus remember being "invited" or "convinced" to participate by a personal friend. "I was asked into Neues Forum by a friend who was one of the founders. Which group a person joined depended on this kind of personal connection," one man remarked. "People in one group," he continued, "knew people in all the other groups. I knew a writer in Vereinigte Linke and other people in Demokratie Jetzt, for instance. So at some level we all trusted each other, so there weren't really strict boundaries between the groups."[38] In an alternate pattern of group expansion, entire discussion circles, our "preschool[s] of nonviolent upheaval," according to a prominent activist, transformed themselves into chapters of citizens' opposition groups.[39]

The GDR Class Divide

Even though some observers have maintained that the GDR could best be described as a classless, homogenous, egalitarian society,[40] it did not look this way to workers. At the same time GDR workers viewed all intellectuals as fairly similar, they also regarded the intelligentsia as quite unlike themselves. Their own lives looked demonstrably different from those of the intelligentsia, and, to some extent, they defined themselves in juxtaposition with this demographically exclusive group.[41] There are other reasons, aside from their disparate levels of involvement in civil society, why GDR workers perceived themselves as distinct from the intelligentsia, which I elaborate on below. Here suffice it to say that this distinction was visibly symbolized for all, in every city and town at the beginning and end of every workday, as some East Germans headed toward their destinations donned in well-used, roughly styled, blue work uniforms, alongside others whose paid jobs allowed them to dress as they wished.

Paid work is the first place on which to focus attention in exploring the reality of the class divide for GDR workers. In his two volumes on the labor process in socialist countries, Michael Burawoy argued that the transparency of class difference distinguished these societies from capitalist ones and that this transparency was personified at work by the division between those who rendered surplus product and those who appropriated and redistributed what these workers created.[42] Was this class divide so obvious at GDR workplaces, and, if so, can we be more precise about how it was manifest and what it meant to workers?[43]

The first thing to consider would be the official remuneration structure. The extent to which pay differentials constituted a significant aspect of the divide between classes was complicated, however. On the one hand, typical of socialist countries, income distribution in the GDR was more egalitarian than in capitalist economies. The ratio of CEO-to-worker earnings in U.S. firms can often run as high as 200:1, while even in large socialist firms it rarely topped 5:1. In the GDR, economists told me the average general director of a *Kombinat* made somewhat less than three times what the average production worker earned.[44]

On the other hand, middle-class employees as a group clearly earned more than their working-class counterparts.[45] Yet there were (and apparently always had been) some working-class posts whose remuneration was equal to or greater than others requiring a higher education degree. Artur Meier, for example, reported that the technicians who developed machine tool programs in one plant were generally paid less than skilled operators, and other sociologists of work have related examples in which top managers earned the same as unskilled workers.[46]

After a 1988 interview with two GDR economists, however, I began to suspect that the relatively small pay differential between workers and intellectuals belied its significance for both groups. In the course of this interview, I learned that a new management system had been tested the previous year in sixteen *Kombinate* and that the goal was to have all *Kombinate* operating under it in 1991. A major feature of this new system was an increase in the wage gap between workers and the technical intelligentsia and between workers and top management. Upon learning of this planned change, I began to ask both workers and intellectuals what they thought of the idea. Emotions ran high in both groups, even though the increases were modest. (I was told that the ratio between general directors of *Kombinate* and workers would widen from less than 3:1 to between 4:1 and 5:1.) Most members of the intelligentsia supported the plan in the strongest terms, in the process often revealing bitterness and embarrassment over the personal and professional damage the current "irrational," "outdated," and relatively egalitarian pay scales had caused them. Many workers, who were usually unaware of the change being implemented, shook their heads and frowned, without saying much. But not all of them: "Managers getting more pay? More money? [as if she had misheard me] What for? You mean managers? [again incredulous] They don't earn enough already? Well, probably you could say that about workers. No, I wouldn't agree to that change. I wouldn't agree that the difference between the two should be increased. I don't think we can let the tension between the two be any greater. This would aggravate it."[47] Such reactions were consistent with those often noted elsewhere in East and Central Europe whenever schemes to reverse income equalization trends were proposed or implemented, often as part of economic "reform" packages.[48]

Even though pay was one workplace axis that differentiated GDR workers from the intelligentsia, it was only the most obvious, not the most important.[49] Classes were also dissimilar with regard to working conditions, control of the labor process, and involvement in workplace decision-making bodies, and GDR workers experienced these contrasts more immediately and less intermittently than they did pay differences. Disparities in working conditions, control of the labor process, and involvement in workplace decision-making bodies kept the workplace difference between classes palpable, even when the relative narrowness of pay differentials tended to obfuscate it. Many of the nonremunerative class differences at GDR workplaces may sound familiar. They are reminiscent of differences service, white-collar, and blue-collar workers the world over understand as badges that distinguish their work from that of people with higher education degrees and that they often consider among the most trying features of their jobs. Others may have a less familiar ring, for they are more unique to socialism as it had developed over forty years of GDR history.

GDR workers complained quite openly about working conditions and clearly realized conditions were not the same for many of the intelligentsia. Workers were annoyed, for instance, because they had to wait much longer than their middle-class coworkers for good vacation spots. In addition, they saw many middle-class employees able to capitalize on the influence, knowledge, and power they possessed by virtue of their jobs, thereby securing, with relatively little risk, all sorts of material favors, from private autos on down: "'The man with the big plastic bag,' that described our boss. He received lots of presents from diplomats. They gave him all kinds of stuff, especially cigarettes, sweets, and alcohol. He probably had enough Schnapps for years to come!"[50] Other middle-class job perks also piqued workers. They never tired of telling me, for example, about the higher quality food served in managers' dining rooms and about the coffee and snacks to which their middle-class coworkers had ready access.[51] Too many GDR workers made do without reliable hot water in their lavatories or without any comfortable spot to take their breaks, while managers passed their work time in comparative luxury. Even white-collar office workers were cognizant of differences between their own and their bosses' physical work surroundings. "It takes me over a year just to get my office curtains cleaned!" one man griped. "But it seems like the administration around here gets a brand new set every three months."[52] Working-class jobs, with the exclusion of many in the white-collar sector, were also more dangerous and more unhealthy than those of most middle-class employees. In 1989, for instance, one in three GDR production workers reportedly labored under unhealthy conditions. Contorted working postures and exposure to searing heat, bitter cold, deafening noise, and toxic chemicals were the hallmarks of many working-class jobs in the foundries, mills, mines, and plants of the GDR.[53] Despite the exalted position of production workers in socialist ideology, the dirt, dust, and grime of many of these jobs were not usually glorified by those who did them. "My construction job is plain filthy work," one worker asserted, adding, "Sometimes I'm embarrassed to be seen by people passing by. Well, you might smile, but I feel stupid looking like that."[54]

Of all the working conditions setting them apart from the intelligentsia, time issues were among the most salient for many workers. It was not, however, the difference in total hours worked that was at issue.[55] Rather, it was that workers had far less flexible schedules, and they had to work at more inconvenient and disruptive times. Working-class, not middle-class, jobs were the ones that began and ended at the crack of dawn or in the middle of the night, the ones where time clocks tracked arrivals and departures to the minute, and the ones where taking time off to run personal errands was rarely an option. A prime example of the time issue was shift work, overwhelmingly a feature of working-class jobs. In Martina Jugel, Barbara Spangenberg, and Rudhard Stollberg's 1978 study of 832 employees in production, 41 percent of the unskilled and semiskilled workers, 54 percent of the skilled workers, but only seven-tenths of 1 percent of the engineers were shift workers.[56] In 1987, over 37 percent of all GDR production workers were on shift, and although that percentage had declined slightly since 1980, the percentage of production workers on the most onerous three-shift schedule (6 A.M., 2 P.M., 10 P.M.) had been on the rise from 1962 through most of the 1980s.[57] While shift workers were offered certain inducements, such as shorter work weeks and longer vacations, many reports cited workers' widespread "lack of enthusiasm," "coolness," and "antipathy" toward multiple shift work, because of the numerous physiological, familial, and social disruptions it caused in their lives.[58]

The classic managerial dilemma is how to retain maximum control over producers' work without smothering their initiative, judgment, and creativity, all of which are absolutely necessary if production and service delivery are to be carried out successfully. Managers must aim, in other words, to transfer as much independent thinking as possible away from the point of production, at the same time they require workers who think independently.

GDR managers were in no way immune to this dilemma. As will be seen in chapter 7, however, the optimal balance between controlling workers and allowing workers to control themselves was necessarily different under socialism, where, largely as a result of shortage, managers found themselves more dependent than their capitalist counterparts on workers' managing their own labor. While the managerial leash was surely longer in the GDR, this did not mean workers ran free. The difference between going to work to give orders and going to work to take them constituted a third prominent element of the class divide at GDR workplaces.

Managers the world over have devised an impressive array of methods for controlling and organizing the labor of others.[59] The methods they have relied on have varied according to the nature of production and service delivery, and new ones have been perfected as old ones lose their effectiveness in the face of changes in economic organization, the occupational structure, or the character and resistance of the labor force. Of all the forms of managerial control to which the GDR working class was subjected, however, I heard the most complaints about what has been termed personal or simple control. Continuous, direct, microinterventions by bosses typify personal or simple control. This form of control, which is notoriously unpopular with workers and well known for engendering resistance among them, is often exercised in an arbitrary and idiosyncratic fashion. This is because personal or simple control is lodged with actual people (rather than in technology, in a set of rules, etc.), a fact that also renders its social source readily identifiable to workers. In the GDR, heavy reliance on this form of control was also a result of shortage. GDR managers were ultimately powerless to control shortage in any permanent and systematic way. Frustrated with their own powerlessness, they resorted to desperate and unpredictable interventions in the labor process in their attempts to correct production irrationalities. Yet all concerned recognized the futility of such interventions, which usually only exacerbated shortages elsewhere, thereby compounding workers' resentment over management's use of this heavy-handed and capricious control strategy.

Although some members of the intelligentsia were also controlled in a similar manner at work, it was GDR workers who were disproportionately subjected to the indignities of this control strategy. John Borneman's ethnographic study of seven cases before worksite grievance committees provided examples of the maddening, embarrassing, and belittling exercise of personal control to which GDR workers could be subjected. An unskilled sales trainee was ordered to make up a 66-mark discrepancy in the register tally from his own paycheck, though he was one of many who had operated the cash register on the day in question; a hotel manager docked the pay of a cleaning person who had emptied a waste basket in which a guest had stuffed his mud- and snow-caked shoes, inquiring sarcastically whether the worker would have thrown away a gold chain too, if she had seen one of those in the wastebasket; another hotel manager denied a receptionist his bonus (between 30 and 40 percent of his base salary) because a trainee he was supervising, after writing up over a thousand theater vouchers correctly, had undercharged one guest by 60 marks.[60]

But it was not just that workers had to put up with personal or simple control at their jobs. It was also that their labor was in general more tightly controlled than the intelligentsia's, whichever control strategies or combinations of strategies managers employed. As I have suggested, the result of any management success at controlling and organizing the work of their subordinates is decreased workers' control over their own labor. As management control tightens, jobs demand less of the people who fill them. Work becomes more stupefying, more repetitive, and more boring, and those designated to perform it exercise less creativity, less autonomy, less initiative, less skill, and less responsibility during the workday.[61] Hopes had originally run high that the "scientific-technological revolution," the highly touted party thrust of the late 1970s and the 1980s to increase economic productivity and efficiency with new technologies, would greatly reduce the number of such jobs in the GDR and thereby attenuate workplace differences between classes. Empirical data, however, never bore out this optimistic prediction. Rather, with the introduction of lasers, robots, CAD/CAM, and other technologies at the heart of the scientific-technological revolution, numerous studies highlighted the continued, if not heightened, polarization in the occupational structure between creative and autonomous jobs and controlled and monotonous ones.[62] It was this matter of being controlled instead of being in control during the many hours spent at paid work that, as much as anything, distinguished the workdays of the GDR working class from those of the intelligentsia.

A final way the daily experience of paid work varied by class pertains to involvement in workplace decision-making bodies. Since the 1970s, for example, reports had pointed to different levels of participation by class in the Innovators' Movement, a national group organized at the workplace. Jonathan Steele recounted a 20 percent participation rate for unskilled workers in 1974 yet a 51 percent participation rate for university graduates, and others have reported the same pattern.[63] Similarly, Thomas Baylis reported skewed class participation in the innovator collectives, which appear to have predated the Innovators' Movement; the workplace production committees, which existed from 1963 to 1974, were also dominated by the intelligentsia.[64] Moreover, a close look at the *Konfliktkommissionen* (grievance commissions) suggests some significant class differences in how workers and managers related to them. For one thing, at least in the late 1970s, management initiated nearly three-quarters of all the cases these committees heard. For another, it was rare for top-level personnel to have cases brought against them. Finally, my interviews with commission members confirmed what a union college student who had just completed her thesis on the topic had told me: higher education helped a person secure a seat on the grievance commission. Even though top managers could not sit on these grievance bodies, many mid-level managers and professionals, who undoubtedly wielded disproportionate influence in deliberations, certainly did.[65]

Class had the biggest impact on differential involvement in workplace decision-making bodies when it came to unions. Unions were irrelevant to the workplace experiences of many intellectuals most of the time. While certainly union members, many intellectuals ignored the organizations. They had little interest in or knowledge about them. One intellectual admitted, "It's hard for me to say what the union does at my workplace. I really couldn't tell you." Some intellectuals even voiced overt contempt for the bodies.[66] I discovered this early in my fieldwork when I was introduced as a U.S. sociologist interested in GDR unions before a social gathering of about twenty academics, artists, and party members. A split second of silence was followed by giggles and snickers. People figured this just had to be a joke. I no doubt looked perplexed, whereupon my host decided to make more of the occasion. In a voice intended for all to hear, he turned to me and exclaimed, tongue in cheek, "Oh, they're not really laughing!" As calculated, the snickers and giggles thereupon turned into gales of uproarious laughter.

This scene prompted me to query intellectuals about unions whenever I got the chance. I soon learned that many of their workplaces were essentially union-free, since many of them worked in groups or organizations where everyone, or nearly everyone, was a party member.[67] Consequently, there was almost a total overlap between union members and party members at their worksites, workplace meetings of the party and the union were usually combined, and the organizational identity of the unions dissolved into the folds of the more powerful political organization. "The union where I work is really redundant," a research sociologist explained. "We didn't even notice the unions," a teacher told me. Or as a university worker put it, "I was in the SED and the union. But they both have the same aims where I work. You can't give up the SED, so I just ignored the union."[68]

For many members of the working class, however, unions were the political organizations most central to their day-to-day work experience. This is not to say that all workers held unions in high esteem, that workers controlled the unions, that all workers were active in the unions, or that the motivations of those who were active were other than cynical, instrumental, or self-protective.[69] In fact, we will soon see that GDR workers had multifaceted and schizophrenic relations to unions before the revolution. But it is to say that unions, union work, and union concerns normally loomed much larger in the daily lives of the working class. For better and worse, unions were bodies with which workers, far more often than their middle-class colleagues, continuously had to reckon.

Even though GDR workers were confronted with plenty of reminders of the class divide at their workplaces, paid work was not the only part of their lives where this social gulf was obvious. Their perception of class difference also went home with them at the end of each workday. For many workers, the experience of the class divide outside work was probably a more intermittent and less conspicuous feature of their lived experience of socialism. Nonetheless, workers' experiences of the class cleavage outside and inside the workplace reinforced each other. The consistency of their experiences across diverse social terrains presages the class distinction as a more entrenched and politically consequential feature of GDR socialism than has been apparent up to now.

Whenever the topic of class difference outside the workplace has been broached, the discussion has commonly gravitated to the issue of material goods. The relative material privilege of the intelligentsia depends on the perspective from which this issue is considered. From the standpoint of the GDR intelligentsia, it sometimes seemed minor. Dorothee Wierling, for example, wrote, "It seems important to me that there were so few opportunities in the GDR for individuals to differentiate themselves from other social groups according to specific consumption patterns and lifestyles."[70] From a global perspective as well, the material gap between workers and intellectuals in socialist societies appeared small compared with that in industrialized capitalist and certainly "developing" countries. "I am inclined to believe," Ivan Szelényi once wrote, "that even if we can speak about a new ruling class in Eastern European state socialism then it is the most miserable privileged class in the history of mankind."[71]

GDR workers, however, shared neither assessment. From their social locations, the possession and consumption of certain material goods, especially those from outside the GDR, was one obvious and long-standing badge of intellectual privilege: "More and more people found out that there were those who had no problems acquiring anything. . . . This injustice was really quite unbelievable. . . . And it got worse and worse; after a while, they did not even make any attempt to cover it up."[72]

In the GDR, material privilege ran the gamut from grapes and bananas (which I carted across the border by the kilo in response to never-ending requests) to beer in cans to any number of personal effects (stylish eyeglass frames come to mind), which provided surefire clues to an individual's social standing. Consumer durables—TVs, washing machines, and especially autos—were also highly visible material markers of class difference. Workers owned demonstrably fewer private autos than the intelligentsia did, and they reportedly had to wait a decade to purchase one at more than two years' average salary.[73] One side of the East German ten mark bill, so the joke went, showed a young woman the day she registered to buy a car. The flip side of the bill (a picture of Clara Zetkin, an early German Communist in her seventies) depicted the woman on the day she got the car.[74] Moreover, workers' wheels were more likely to be the legendary, cheap-end, two-cylinder, domestic Trabis, not the Western makes. The class divide in autos was so pronounced that Wandlitz, the housing compound for high-ranking party officials northeast of Berlin, came to be named after the car most highly coveted by the elite. In popular parlance Wandlitz was known as Volvograd, a clever semantic hybrid suggesting characteristics of compound inhabitants beyond their preference in automobiles.[75]

The GDR middle class was able to gobble more grapes and cruise the countryside in more Volvos for at least two immediate reasons. First, they owned more hard currency, which they often amassed through their jobs and foreign travels, the latter an additional and envied privilege differentially bestowed on sectors of the GDR intelligentsia.[76] Their hard currency holdings, together with their relative wealth in East German marks, afforded them greater access to luxuries for sale legally and on the black market. Legal purchases of luxury items could be made in the well-known chain of high-priced "Delikat" and "Exquisit" shops, where East German marks purchased otherwise unavailable imported and licensed goods, and in "Intershops," which accepted only hard currency for their array of quality items. Over the two decades prior to the *Wende,* the availability of some highly desired goods became increasingly restricted. At the beginning of the 1970s, GDR citizens could legally purchase in ordinary stores what later became available only at Exquisit and Delikat shops; by the early 1980s, many of these same products had been moved onto Intershop shelves, thereby available only to those with hard currency.[77] Besides the Delikat-Exquisit-Intershop network and the black market, there were other ways those at the very apex of the intelligentsia secured scare material goods. For example, they might arrange special off-market exchanges of East German marks for imported goods, and, throughout the GDR's history, there were rumors of semisecret shops open only to the tiny group at the top of the socioeconomic ladder.

Second, the conspicuous material privilege of the GDR intelligentsia was a consequence of its relatively greater ability to use personal influence and connections to acquire scarce goods. Pulling strings to improve one's material lot was in no way confined to the GDR middle class. The satisfaction of many needs and desires in shortage economies depends heavily on personal associations that, in Peter Marcuse's words, "soften the impact of central controls."[78] Nonetheless, the strings the middle class might pull were longer and more plentiful, and the rewards to which they were attached were more substantial than those commonly within the grasp of workers. Knowing the right people could get workers some house paint or a toy for their children. But for members of the intelligentsia, who could more easily reciprocate monetarily, whose connections were more extensive, or who might themselves control desired goods or services, knowing the right person could mean not just getting the paint but getting it in an uncommon color, not just getting their children's toy but getting one made in the West. It could also mean securing a VCR, a better position on the waiting list for a new automobile, or even more spacious living quarters in a desirable quarter of town.[79]

For many people, housing was the most poignant material reminder of class advantage in the GDR: "What was the dividing line between ordinary people and the privileged? Apartment size. . . . There were other criteria—access to cars, permission to travel—but apartments were the main thing. You could measure the distinction between the privileged and the non-privileged by the number of square meters in their apartments."[80] At the apex of privilege-measured-in-square-meters were the top government and party officials, whose first homes were, and apparently always had been, palatial compared with workers' quarters, and who were also likely to have second-home retreats in the country.[81]

The privileged housing position of the GDR intelligentsia was one example of how the middle class in socialist countries benefited inordinately from some categories of public spending. Housing distribution was a main focus of Ivan Szelényi's seminal article, which concluded that higher-status groups had better access to state owned (i.e., publicly subsidized) housing. "Consequently," he wrote, "through the redistributive sector of the housing economy, the State reallocates surplus in favour of higher income groups."[82] Szelényi suspected this also was true throughout East and Central Europe. Although his research did not include the GDR, if the pattern held there, the potential transfer from the less to the more well-to-do would have been significant and growing since housing was the third largest category of expenditure in the 1987 state budget (over 15 billion marks), more than double what it had been in 1980.[83]

Szelényi's study raises the question of whether other categories of public spending might not also have contributed to the material difference between classes in the GDR, of which many workers were conscious. Although empirical information on this topic is not plentiful, understanding the extent of class-based material privilege in the GDR warrants mention of any public expenditure that seemingly added to the advantage of the 20 percent who were already the best off. In this regard, the following expenditures merit attention:

Culture: Multiple sources pointed to differential rates of attendance by class at cultural events, which in the GDR received generous state financing. Marilyn Rueschemeyer, for example, suggested that in the 1980s between 50 and 70 percent of the visitors to many art exhibitions were technical college or university graduates or students. Moreover, in 1987 nearly 64 million marks were turned over to such groups as professional writers' and artists' organizations, while unions were financed by members' own dues.[84]

Vacations: Approximately 63 percent of this 438 million mark budget expenditure went to support the FDGB's vacation program. Yet workers often complained they could get good vacation spots, or sometimes even any vacation spot at all, only when union and management bigwigs did not want them. Sectors of the intelligentsia also enjoyed their own private vacation retreats, such as the luxurious island resort of the Stasi.[85]

Health: Most of a 1.92 billion line item expenditure in the health area was for medical services in the technical colleges and universities and for medical clinics in the Academy of Sciences. This suggests a possible middle-class advantage in both the quality and quantity of health care, as does Duncan Smith's report that higher functionaries were required to use chauffeurs to help reduce the stress in their lives.[86]

Education: A special outlay of more than 145 million marks went for schools that were likely to draw their student bodies disproportionately from the intelligentsia. These included boarding schools for children whose parents were abroad and special language, science, and music schools.[87]

Pensions: Honorary pensions for state functionaries, together with supplemental pensions for the intelligentsia (up to 90 percent of preretirement income), were introduced in the late 1950s. Later, special pension schemes were implemented for leading ministerial employees (1969/70) and for teachers (1976), the net result of which was to continue the economic differentiation of the working population into retirement. The intelligentsia was "pampered" by such special pensions, according to one of its number.[88]

The final public spending matter deserving scrutiny is price subsidies for basic subsistence items, especially food. At over 49 billion marks, this was by far the largest single expenditure item in the 1987 state budget.[89] There has been some debate about who benefited most from price supports for basic necessities in socialist countries. In 1989, Carl Bradley Scharf, focusing on the percentage of income that lower- versus higher-income GDR households spent on subsidized goods, argued that the lower-income households were the clear beneficiaries, while a decade earlier Hartmut Zimmermann maintained that upper- and lower-income groups both benefited "to the same extent." Neither author, however, presented evidence to substantiate his claim, and the only research I have seen (from Hungary), after taking absolute differences in consumption level into account, concluded that those at the upper end of the socioeconomic ladder received a greater, not a lesser, percentage subsidy than those at the lower end.[90] Scharf argued in 1984 that when heavily subsidized items were considered alongside many manufactured and luxury goods, which were taxed at an average of 56 percent of their purchase price, the result was a "marked distinction," a "magnified" pattern of difference in consumption patterns by class. The majority of GDR households could make few, if any, purchases in the highly taxed manufactures and luxury market, leaving it to become the shopping haven of the well-to-do, who also received an additional boost in their disposable income from the heavy subsidization of basic necessities.[91]

The Class Divide and Workers' Political Withdrawal

The preceding section argued that GDR workers understood their lives to be significantly different from those of the intelligentsia and that there were many good reasons why they should do so. Although individual sensitivities varied, GDR workers had recognized the class rift decades before the country's demise. But what of the connection between workers' awareness of class difference and the reluctance of so many to become politically involved during the 1989–90 revolution? In other words, how and why did the abyss between the classes figure in workers' decisions to retreat to the galleries in the midst of the political crisis?

Both chapters 6 and 8 reveal that the class divide mattered for understanding the political responses of both activist workers and some workers who were passive participants in the politics of the *Wende*. Both groups often oriented their politics around issues of class difference, opposing in word and deed class-based material and power inequities of all types—middle-class job perks; arbitrary, ineffective, and authoritarian workplace supervision; poor worker housing; weak and dependent unions; party meetings during work time; special management dining rooms; and so forth. Moreover, we will also see in chapter 6 that the preexisting class division often interfered with the political efforts of worker activists in a number of ways. This section, however, concerns a different political impact of the GDR class division. While the class divide left imprints throughout the stories of worker activists and some passive worker participants in revolutionary politics, its deepest and most politically consequential impression came through its contribution to the thoroughgoing demobilization of so many GDR workers during the *Wende.* Anger over class inequality induced some workers out of the galleries. But as a festering reminder of their social inferiority and powerlessness, recognition of class inequality paralyzed many others, who kept their distance from revolutionary politics.

In what follows I pose the question of working-class demobilization from a new angle. Here I ask why, despite the troubled, often tortured, relationship between workers and intellectuals before the *Wende,* their relationship did not improve enough to permit joint political action in the midst of the revolution. This is a complicated question, so I focus on only half of it, asking why workers did not actively join the middle-class challengers in their opposition to existing GDR socialism. The answer to this question is closely bound up with the topic of workers' long-standing awareness of the difference between themselves and intellectuals. During the *Wende,* instead of attenuating this difference, the middle-class revolutionary oppositionists actually magnified it. Both advertently and inadvertently, they reinforced workers' recognition that they were different people who led different lives, had different interests, and harbored different aspirations for the future of the GDR. Workers' cognizance of the class divide, firmly rooted in the structures and systems of GDR socialism, was intensified to the point where even many of those who shared the opposition's critique declined to become involved in their political challenge.

Let us first consider how the middle-class challengers thought and talked about workers during the *Wende.* In chapter 1, we saw that the GDR intelligentsia harbored some decidedly negative views of workers before the *Wende,* and the oppositionists did not magically shed these uncomplimentary attitudes during the crisis. Instead, many challengers retained their low opinions of workers over the course of the struggle, and in some cases these low opinions further deteriorated.[92] The most forceful way to illustrate this is to let a few members of the middle-class opposition speak for themselves:

> You keeping asking about the workers! I think that is archaic thinking, because the working class is not a class that will ever change anything. They will adapt to changes. The majority of workers will focus on what is con-

cretely most effective for them. My hopes to win the masses with appeals to their understanding or consciousness are small.

The people who had just recently been striving, with a noble vision, for a promising future, turned into a horde of brutes . . . who stormed . . . [West German department stores] with cannibalistic lust.

The workers didn't really care if the system was democratic as long as it worked for them. They were interested in material things. It isn't immediately obvious to them that democracy is essential, because democracy, in terms of a free press, free speech, and the kind of culture necessary to develop independent thought and emancipation, is mostly an issue intellectuals care about.

[All this] has to do with the value system of the workers. So, for example, they are more interested in consumption, a car, or a trip than in economic democracy. They don't see that as an issue. They are not interested in taking part in the decision-making process or in formulating production strategies. And that is the problem.

Party platforms and political concepts are something for intellectuals, a small elite of less than 20 percent, but not for the people.[93]

It is striking how closely the substance of these views paralleled those many intellectuals harbored before the *Wende*. The working class of both periods was often seen and spoken of as a materialistic, simple-minded, politically passive, apathetic, narrow-minded, and authoritarian-leaning "horde of brutes." Further consideration of these views reveals they were intertwined with oppositionists' perceptions of themselves. Beholding their own class kind as idealistic, intellectually sophisticated, democracy-loving, and socially responsible activists, the challengers embraced the common social practice of defining themselves in opposition to, as different from, the other. The unsurprising result was an enhancement of workers' long-standing perception that they were different from the intelligentsia. Even workers who were least aware of the class divide before the *Wende* had less problem accepting its existence as the crisis unfolded. Growing numbers of workers came to distrust, even dislike, the oppositional intellectuals and to find their arrogance, whether spoken or unspoken, humiliating. As a consequence, many GDR workers could never view the oppositionists as political comrades and thus kept considerable distance from the challengers' political projects.

If it had been only the oppositionists' views of the working class that magnified the difference between the two groups, far fewer workers would probably have eschewed activism on behalf of the regime challengers. But it was not just the challengers' words and thoughts that made the class divide more obvious to workers during the *Wende*. Much of what those opposing GDR socialism actually did during the fall and winter of 1989–90 had the same effect.

At the most basic level, most opposition groups made few sustained efforts to organize and recruit workers.[94] Workplaces would have been a logical place to begin such efforts, but, by and large, opposition intellectuals avoided them. "I don't think that people from New Forum ever made any attempt to contact us, or to form a factory group inside the plant," recalled a worker from the second largest heavy machinery concern in the country.[95] Some middle-class activists appeared oblivious to the importance of broadening their base of political support. Others were simply so unfamiliar with working-class life, so clueless about how to begin reaching out to workers, that the very thought of doing so was daunting. "Well, going into enterprises was difficult. They had to come to us first. But by the time that happened, it was often too late," a Neues Forum activist remembered.[96] Too late indeed. It was not until the third week of March 1990, after the revolution was essentially over, that a Neues Forum group was formed and called its first meeting in a Leipzig transport factory.[97] Even in the relatively rare instances when opposition intellectuals reported going into workplaces, their success was limited. These visits often had the flavor of rather casual information-gathering missions, and oppositionists often came away dismayed at workers' lack of enthusiasm for their activities. The challengers' erratic appearances at GDR worksites bore some political fruit only when, as one oppositionist put it, "we somehow didn't come across as intellectual, in the sense that the differences between us and the workers weren't emphasized."[98]

Even if they were not inclined to recruit workers into their groups directly, middle-class challengers might have tried to attract them to their cause indirectly by, for example, staying alert to what workers themselves were saying and doing and perhaps offering support to these efforts. Since contact between workers and intellectuals was generally limited before the *Wende,* and since only a minority of workers became politically active during the crisis, opportunities to connect with workers in this fashion would not have been plentiful. Nevertheless, there is little evidence that the challengers made much of those opportunities that did present themselves. Christian Joppke, for example, was told that several delegations of workers approached Neues Forum leaders in early December to ask that they support a general strike, a strike that at least one opposition leader felt would garner substantial support. But instead of doing as requested, a Neues Forum member recalled, "We tried to calm the workers down. We missed the opportunity, we ducked in the decisive moment."[99] In a similar vein, though middle-class challengers were quick to assert that nothing could be accomplished through the existing unions,[100] a number of working-class activists were attempting to do just that through the radical reform of these bodies.[101] Middle-class opposition-ists commonly disparaged such worker efforts as naive, misguided, and noth-ing more than the party's effort to continue leading workers by the nose. At the end of an informal discussion with a long-time oppositionist, during which I related what I had learned about worker efforts to radically reform existing unions, this woman responded, "But surely nothing good could come of such work with the FDGB! Aren't they nothing but party people? They couldn't offer workers anything!" Perhaps my silence belied my disagreement, for she added, somewhat sheepishly, "Or, are you implying that's just exactly what us intellectuals with no union experience might think?"[102]

Oppositionists might also have tried to muster more working-class support through the mountains of literature (flyers, newsletters, articles, platforms, etc.) they produced and through the many speeches they delivered in both formal and informal gatherings. These efforts, however, were mostly ineffec-tive in rallying working-class support to their cause, even if that were their intention. Workers complained that these communications were long on ide-ology, theory, philosophical calls for abstract rights and freedoms ("typical intellectual demands"), and dense academic language and short on concrete programs and practical ideas for implementing them, expressed in a straight-forward fashion. A brewery worker near the Polish border summed up a por-tion of this sentiment when he told me, "The intellectuals [in groups like Neues Forum] failed. They just didn't have anything to offer except ideology, but the workers were just sick and tired of living on ideology."[103] "Cultural revolution," the oft-repeated political slogan of some oppositionists, a core idea of which seemed to be open dialogue, was one example of a concept that was not especially attractive to workers. Nor did the terminology used in com-municating this and other ideas tempt many workers to join forces with the opposition intellectuals. Workers sensed something disingenuous about sup-posedly "all-class," "above class," and even "classless" appeals to "citizens," which emanated from predominantly middle-class groups.[104]

But while many oppositionists avoided GDR workplaces, it was here where the examples of middle-class oppositional activism most guaranteed to turn workers away from this type of political involvement also surfaced. Some-times this occurred when groups of workplace intelligentsia pushed demands for their own inclusion in enterprise decision-making bodies, while failing to mention workers; other production-based intellectuals arranged retrain-ing programs, but only for themselves; still others promoted their own plans for the firm's survival, which often stressed worker layoffs and wage cuts.

But the height of middle-class oppositional behavior sure to make work-ers skittish about allying with regime critics came, in a sharp break with the

GDR tradition of industrial unionism, when some intellectuals tried to form their own separate unions. The Kammer der Technik openly advocated this idea, while other professions took similar steps to organize separate unions all over the country.[105] The first news of such attempts hit the FDGB "like a bomb," and throughout the *Wende* the old union strongly opposed this development and tried, as best it could, to halt it.[106] Yet rejection by the FDGB was exactly what intellectuals seeking separate representation had expected, for one of their biggest complaints concerned their poor treatment at the hands of the old unions. Instead of representing the interests of engineers, scientific and technical workers, managers, and the like, the Initiative for Independent Unions (IUG) reported in its newsletter, "the FDGB acted as if we were all a unified mass with the same interests. In the hypocritically entitled 'Workers' and Farmers' State' the concerns of *Angestellten* [white-collar workers] were given lowest priority and viewed with distrust."[107]

Some of the intellectuals' calls for their own unions waxed on unabashedly about how important they were to the economy, how their creativity and independence had been so badly stifled, how they had been denied the social recognition they deserved, how the gap between their earnings and those of workers was unjustifiably narrow, and how their taxes were too high and their pensions inadequate. Some engineers in Leipzig summed up what many such intellectuals understood as the solution to such grievances: "One must depart from our previous orientation toward the masses and work for an organization whose membership is characterized by expertise."[108] How could GDR workers, encountering such an appeal in their factory newspaper where many were published, find in such a statement any encouragement to join the activist intellectuals around the country who were challenging the status quo? The more likely result would have been—and was—the precise opposite: GDR workers were confronted with yet another reason to shun all versions of middle-class oppositional activism, the message of which, especially blatant in this quote, was too often exclusion of the working class.[109]

Conclusion

Why did so many GDR workers shy from political activism during the 1989–90 revolution? In the last three chapters, we have learned that the answer to this question involves class, the labor process, and workplace politics. All three, in powerful combination, contributed to the scant worker presence among revolutionary activists, and the best way to understand how this was so is to stand in shoes of GDR workers.

To start with, every workday for decades before the revolution, GDR workers had participated in a labor process in which they saw their hard work continuously subverted by chronic disorganization, dishonesty, and a deficient discipline and remuneration system. As a consequence, most workers had become, to some degree, cynical, frustrated, indifferent, and apathetic, all outcomes that had a negative impact on the development of political activism in the working class.

On top of this, workers had to deal on a daily basis with workplace unions that played third fiddle to the party and management, were reluctant to deal with economic and production matters, minimized rank-and-file input in the selection of their leaders, and operated in an highly formalized and centralized fashion. This, too, militated against working-class activism during the revolution by impeding workers' acquisition of technical knowledge, stunting their political imaginations, limiting their political experience, and leaving them distrustful of collective action through unions.

Were all this not enough, GDR workers faced still another impediment to activism when the revolution began: their long-standing relationship with the intelligentsia. To say it simply, despite the official cloak of class harmony, workers did not fully trust or respect intellectuals and harbored a fair amount of hostility toward them. In other words, the class relationship was not neutral before the *Wende*. How then did this poor relationship between the two classes undermine the possibility of working-class activism during the revolution?

Recall that GDR intellectuals of the oppositional stripe can be credited with initiating the political crisis and helping to sustain it through the citizens' opposition groups and the new and reformed political parties. There were two important reasons they were better positioned to do this than workers. First, before the *Wende*, intellectuals had acquired useful political skills and experience in the various networks and organizations of civil society they dominated; second, these very networks and organizations provided them an important, class endogenous pool of personal friends on whom they chose to rely as they wove their activist networks of revolutionary oppositionists.[110]

But from the workers' perspective, who exactly were these politically experienced and well-networked oppositionists challenging? Other intellectuals. We saw in chapter 1 that long before the *Wende*, workers were prone to view all GDR intellectuals as pretty much alike. Even though intellectuals may have been keenly aware of variations within their class, especially between the political elite and other segments of it, for workers, the many obvious indications of support, agreement, cooperation, and even friendship among intellectuals of all kinds eclipsed these differences. Nor did workers' perception of intellectual homogeneity dissolve very readily during the *Wende*. For one thing, activists in many different citizens' opposition groups and in new and reformed parties were clearly well acquainted, and sometimes they were even the same people.[111] For another, in the midst of the *Wende*, the intellectual opposition was often observed working alongside, cooperating and sympathizing with, expressing confidence in, and making exception for intellectuals of the political elite, or at least those well connected with it. As a consequence of all this, many GDR workers likely interpreted the revolution that swirled around them as someone else's struggle, as an internecine squabble in which both sides exhibited the face and flavor, the language, and the tactics of society's upper stratum. The way many workers figured it, the revolution neither concerned them nor held out much hope of bringing about changes they deemed desirable. Many workers thus made an understandable, if politically momentous, decision. They would offer their activist allegiance to neither of the protagonists; they would wait it out on the sidelines.

The pre-*Wende* relationship between classes dampened workers' attraction to activism in an additional way. Not only had intellectuals all tended to look alike before the *Wende,* but also workers perceived the intelligentsia as quite different from themselves. They had long been, in other words, conscious of a chasm between the two classes, and structurally speaking, they were correct. The society that gave rise to the *Wende* was a society fractured by class. Both at their paid jobs and in the rest of their lives workers and intellectuals could reasonably be said to inhabit separate worlds, and from where workers stood, the world of the intelligentsia was characterized by all manner of advantages and privileges in which they did not share. This perception of class difference as inequality, which had been wearing on workers for forty years, was not erased in the few short months of crisis. Rather, we have seen how it was exacerbated during the *Wende.* Oppositional intellectuals bear much of the responsibility for this, for in the course of conducting their activist challenge, they frequently excluded and disparaged the working class. GDR workers, even those who, like the middle-class oppositionists themselves, were quite unsatisfied with the status quo, therefore turned their backs on activism.[112]

The final facet of the class relationship to which workers' reluctance to join the ranks of revolutionary activists can be traced is, oddly enough, the virtual absence a relationship between the two classes before the *Wende.*[113] We saw in chapter 1 that workers and intellectuals lacked any history of joint political protest before 1989, and we learned in this chapter that the two classes had had little sustained interaction in any other social arenas. In other words, I could find little evidence that many workers and intellectuals had spent other than irregular and superficial time in one another's company before the fall of 1989.[114] To put it simply, workers and intellectuals did not "know" one another very well when the *Wende* broke. If they had, there may have been a chance that working-class perceptions of all intellectuals as homogenous and the debilitating and immobilizing consequences of their recognition of the class divide might have been partially overcome, thus opening the way for more workers to assume active political roles in the revolution. As it was, their lack of prior interaction with intellectuals, a "fatal separation" in Patty Lee Parmalee's words,[115] converged with other effects of the labor process, workplace politics, and class relations to confine many GDR workers to the galleries.

6 Workers on Stage: Activists in the Revolution

Had all workers succumbed to the pressures to avoid political involvement, there would be little more to say in response to the question, Where was the GDR working class during the 1989–90 revolution? But all workers did not. A minority of GDR workers were extremely active during the period. Although the political positions these worker activists embraced varied, their words were always accompanied by concrete political deeds. Their political practice was often purposefully planned, carefully organized, innovative, well coordinated, and, most important, undertaken collectively. Moreover, their actions often entailed considerable risk, not only because they attempted them as a decided minority but also because they posed a direct challenge to many intellectuals who upheld the status quo and to many who defied it.

Most accounts of the revolution have taken scant notice of working-class activism during the *Wende*. This is partly because they have not looked for it in the right places. While middle-class activists were forming and reforming citizens' opposition groups and political parties, calling for or squelching street protests, issuing ultimatums and platforms, holding news conferences, running election campaigns, and deliberating at round tables, some GDR workers were engaging in revolutionary acts of a different sort at their workplaces. Although some workers could certainly be counted as participants in the undertakings of middle-class activists, the activist workers with whom I spoke considered their workplace political activities more significant. By centering their political activism at their workplaces, these activists followed precedents set by workers elsewhere at the height of political crises. In Algeria, Portugal, Iran, and early twentieth-century Germany, to cite a few examples, activist workers took advantage of the political vacuum, which appeared after the collapse of the old authority yet before any new social force had replaced it, to expand control over their workplaces.[1]

In the GDR, activists' attempts to transform their workplaces assumed a variety of forms, at times even in the same enterprise. This chapter focuses on three: the organization of *Betriebsräte* (enterprise-level work councils), the radical reformation of existing unions, and the creation of original forms of self-representation for workers. All these efforts required substantial commitments from the workers who undertook them. Meetings had to be organized, supporters had to be recruited, demands had to be formulated and presented, activities had to be publicized, delicate negotiations had to be entered into, goals and tactics had to be settled on, elections had to be organized, and workers had to fill the positions on the newly created workplace representation and management bodies they had designed and promoted.

A Glance toward the Past: The *Betriebsräte*

Betriebsräte have a long history in Germany, first becoming important during the radical phase of the 1918–20 revolution.[2] After being dissolved by the Nazis, *Betriebsräte* in the FRG were fully institutionalized throughout industry and commerce in the decades following World War II, functioning alongside the unions. The history of *Betriebsräte* in the GDR, however, was quite different. In the aftermath of World War II, work councils were formed spontaneously in many firms, at times even becoming involved in plant management. *Betriebsräte* thus existed in most GDR enterprises prior to the postwar unions. Indeed, the FDGB had a difficult time establishing its legitimacy in the GDR, partly because of the competition it faced from the autonomous, Social Democrat-identified *Betriebsräte.* The struggle between the FDGB and the *Betriebsräte* did not subside until 1948, when the *Betriebsräte* were finally disbanded.[3]

With their strong historical link to opposition politics in the GDR and their high visibility in the FRG, it is not surprising that a segment of activist workers should revive *Betriebsräte* at the height of the 1989–90 revolution. Although some claimed the first revolutionary *Betriebsrat* was formed in a Leipzig transport enterprise at the end of December 1989 and that the *Betriebsrat* movement showed little evidence of activity beyond the Leipzig area before April of the following year,[4] a number of workers I interviewed from outside that region reported attempts to form *Betriebsräte* well before April 1990. The revolutionary *Betriebsräte* were generally elected, though nomination and election procedures varied by workplace.[5] The ones I heard of often encountered significant opposition from management.[6] According to one woman, whose coworkers purposively elected her to the *Betriebsrat* so she could not be fired for her workplace activism, "Management tried to slander most *Betriebsrat* candidates, to show their faults or prove they were incompetent. They had a pretty strong campaign against the candidates the workers suggested in the *Betriebsrat* election, since they had their own favorites from the old union leadership. Management didn't like the idea of dealing with worker representatives who didn't support management interests. But management candidates didn't do well in the *Betriebsrat* election."[7]

The *Betriebsräte* formed during the revolution operated in various ways, some carefully patterning their work after *Betriebsräte* in the FRG, where management is legally mandated to consult and cooperate with *Betriebsräte* on social, personnel, and business matters. Most of the six *Betriebsräte* Brigit Grabsch and Karel Kschischan studied, for instance, adopted this advisory role.[8] All revolutionary GDR *Betriebsräte*, however, did not behave as carbon copies of their FRG counterparts. Sometimes, because of members' inexperience, the confusion of the times, or worker inertia, they were less assertive than *Betriebsräte* in the West. For example, according to one *Betriebsrat* member, "Our *Betriebsrat* should have fought against the dismissal of coworkers. We expressed our concerns and, in several instances, demanded that the formal dismissal state that we opposed it. But we should have informed coworkers better about their rights and encouraged them to challenge layoffs. But we didn't, even though we now realize workers' chances of winning would have been pretty high."[9] An electrician who quit the *Betriebsrat* to pursue his activist agenda independently because he thought the work council was passive and ineffective, told a similar tale: "The *Betriebsrat* demanded to be part of negotiations over the sale of the company. A couple of times they included us, then they just went ahead without us. The first people began to get fired, and the *Betriebsrat* couldn't do anything. Workers stopped coming to us with their problems. The most we did was post appeals and discuss what was going on. We had no influence over anything. We had no rights. We never addressed the important questions of the time."[10]

Other *Betriebsräte*, however, took advantage of the uncertainty of the times to step beyond the usual operating boundaries of the FRG *Betriebsräte*. One fledgling *Betriebsrat* in a Berlin steel factory, for example, voted to fire the enterprise director and its decision stuck. Another *Betriebsrat*, by publicizing the negotiations, blocked a surreptitious agreement between the firm's management and a West German investor, thus averting the layoff of half the employees of the enterprise. Other GDR *Betriebsräte* threatened to strike or seriously considered such action as a way to achieve their aims.[11]

The relationship between the *Betriebsräte* and preexisting workplace unions varied over time and among worksites. In some workplaces, the impetus for the foundation of *Betriebsräte* came from workers' outright rejection of the old unions: "Everyone yelled, 'We want *Betriebsräte!*' even though they weren't even sure what they were. But it was something new, and the workers just didn't want the old thing anymore. They would have taken anything. The FDGB just had to be substituted."[12] Union leaders occasionally opposed—sometimes more, sometimes less aggressively—any moves to form *Betriebsräte* or to transform new, worker-initiated representation structures into *Betriebsräte.*[13] But at other times, workplace union leaders (AGL chairs, BGL members, and sometimes BGL chairs) were key to the establishment of *Betriebsräte.* For instance, two of the three original workers in what one study claimed was the first revolutionary *Betriebsrat* were AGL chairs, and this pattern was repeated elsewhere.[14] When a *Betriebsrat* was successfully established in a workplace where the old union continued to exist, the relationship between the two ranged from hostility to grudging tolerance to harmonious cooperation. For example, a *Betriebsrat* member in a farm implements firm claimed as late as October 1990, "If we have important decisions to make, then the *Vertrauensleute* are always part of the process."[15]

My interviews suggest that *Betriebsrat* activism owed more to the initiative and involvement of the intelligentsia than did the other two forms of revolutionary worker activism to be discussed shortly. Others affirmed this observation, noting that *Betriebsräte* spearheaded by workers were the clear exception.[16] Members of the production-based intelligentsia (e.g., engineers, firm architects and economists) commonly constituted the majority of *Betriebsrat* activists at a workplace. A shipyard on the Baltic was a case in point. The *Betriebsrat* initiative was begun by five or six engineers, some of whom were familiar with FRG *Betriebsräte* from contacts there, and most of whom were eventually elected to the shipyard *Betriebsrat.* Differences between *Betriebsrat* supporters and workers surfaced quickly. While workers called for a reduction of engineers in the company, *Betriebsrat* supporters argued that some workers would have to go. While workers demanded higher wages and better benefits, the engineers insisted that preserving the enterprise be given top priority.[17] Intellectuals not based in production were sometimes involved with *Betriebsrat* initiatives as well, either indirectly, through their personal acquaintances with production-based intelligentsia, or directly, as members of citizens' opposition groups and political parties. Vereinigte Linke, the PDS, regional citizens' committees, Neues Forum, and assorted academics all initiated, promoted, or advised *Betriebsräte* at one time or another.[18]

This is not to say that ordinary production and service workers were uniformly unenthusiastic about *Betriebsräte.* In some places, workers supported and were actively involved in their development. For example, 70 percent of the workers in a Leipzig establishment attended a meeting to decide whether to organize one of the earliest *Betriebsräte*. They voted almost unanimously to do so, and subsequently 70 percent of those eligible voted in the *Betriebsrat* election.[19] Nonetheless, middle-class activists' close association with many *Betriebsräte* undoubtedly figured in some workers' exclusion from, disinterest in, and sometimes hostility toward *Betriebsräte* at their workplaces. As one worker explained:

> My construction brigade only learned about the *Betriebsrat* election after it took place. The bureaucrats in the administration were actually the ones who voted. The rest of us were just told who won. The old BGL chair became the new *Betriebsrat* chair, and he was in cahoots with the enterprise director. This guy was dismissed shortly, and a new *Betriebsrat* was elected, but I didn't take part in and don't know anything about that election, except that only about two or three of the twenty or twenty-five people in my department voted. I don't know the chair or anyone from that *Betriebsrat* and neither do most workers. The new *Betriebsrat* chair announced several times that he'd come by to introduce himself during our lunch break. So we all sat in a room waiting for him, but he never showed.[20]

In other enterprises, workers' lack of commitment to the *Betriebsrat* was illustrated by the difficulty of finding anyone willing to run for a seat on the body. Overall, Theo Pirker, Hans-Hermann Hertle, Jürgen Kädtler, and Rainer Weinert, who studied the movement in some detail, described support for the *Betriebsräte* as "broad but mostly passive." The *Betriebsräte*, they continued, "represent [for workers] a vague hope for increased security but not an instrument of self-conscious, collective interest representation." The position of the *Betriebsräte*, they concluded, rested more on management's willingness to cooperate than on the ability of the *Betriebsräte* to mobilize workers from below.[21]

Radical Reform of the GDR Unions

A second focus of worker activism in the revolutionary period, one which owed less to middle-class involvement, was the radical reform of the existing GDR unions. In some firms, workers participated in elections for new union officers at the grass-roots level, while the old union was left basically unchanged. Yet other workers, commonly workplace-level union leaders, moved beyond minimal reform to challenge not just the leadership of the old unions but their structure, process, and functions as well. Activist workers who steered this course tried to capitalize on certain strengths of existing unions, while attempting to recast them as more militant and effective representatives of working people.

Union structure and process were intertwined, and worker activists targeted both for radical reform. Their demands and accomplishments included open union books, local control over union finances, direct union involvement in worksite management, new electoral procedures, and union independence from all political parties. In some worksites, the last two reforms meant barring appointees from union leadership bodies and extending the use of direct elections. Some also revamped their previous leadership structures, paring the number of officers and refocusing their tasks. Finally, some reformed union leaders began to welcome members of worker-initiated representation bodies, such as the *Gesellschaftliche Räte* (social councils) and the *Sprecherräte* (spokespersons' councils), into union leadership bodies like the BGL and the *Vertrauensleute* assembly.[22]

Radical reformers also pushed unions to assume tasks they had not previously shouldered. For instance, radically reformed BGLs began to decide for themselves which sectoral union they would join, and some began to negotiate directly with plant management over wages and working conditions. As the survival of ever more GDR firms was called into question, reformed unions undertook the difficult task of protecting as many jobs as possible for as long as they could. For example, when a steel company manager tried to lay off 92 percent of the work force in a bid to reorganize, the union successfully resisted. "The union was very active during that period," explained a worker at the plant. "They drove all around and made phone calls getting support for the workers and creating opposition to the manager's plan."[23] Reformed unions also steadfastly refused to carry out certain functions they had previously performed, most notably the direction of socialist competitions and emulation campaigns.[24]

In attempting these and other changes, radically reformed unions sometimes behaved quite assertively, confronting management, party officials, and the union hierarchy in ways previously unheard of in the GDR. For example, they besieged the national FDGB leadership with demands for everything from the resignation of key union officers to changes in media policy and vacation scheduling to the institution of alternative military service and the forty-hour week.[25] One union, whose motto became "Union renewal from below to above," pressured the general director into an agreement guaranteeing its active presence, as part of the FDGB, in the firm.[26] Reformed unions tried to bolster their challenges by garnering support from workers' organizations outside the enterprise and outside the GDR. Meanwhile, revitalized unions from the Baltic Sea to Leipzig threatened, and occasionally carried out, strikes and work stoppages, with some success. An AGL chair in a Berlin electrical enterprise recalled the details of a one-hour warning strike called by AGL members and *Vertrauensleute,* in which fifteen hundred workers participated: "During the strike I was pleasantly surprised that our arguments were accepted by the people. When the enterprise says that we are destroying it with [our] demands, that simply isn't true. I pointed out to my fellow workers that enterprise contributions to the social fund had been suspended but that management already had their salary raises. Then they understood that we had to strike."[27]

Among the radical union reformers was a special group of worker activists—students from the Fritz Heckert union college.[28] At their campus in a forested setting northeast of Berlin, a number of these students, together with a handful of their professors, began meeting in small discussion groups. As the crisis escalated, their discussions rapidly became more critical, more open, and more frequent, until they were occurring almost daily. They culminated in October with the production of a discussion paper, which set forth their ideas for the radical reform of the GDR unions. After a struggle, the discussion paper was finally published in the FDGB newspaper, the *Tribüne,* beginning in late October. The document became the topic of a countrywide conversation, and its main ideas were at least partially implemented by radical reformers at some worksites.[29]

Four reform ideas were the backbone of this and other documents the students prepared during the *Wende*—union decentralization, union autonomy, union democracy, and workers' participation in decision making. The concepts of decentralization and autonomy were worked out in the most detail. Students supported decentralization through the strengthening of both the sectoral unions and the county and district levels of the union structure, proposals that sparked a great deal of debate over the course of the radical reform effort. They also called for union autonomy from state and party in certain areas of decision making, such as wage and salary policy, work norms, and merit evaluations. Some also supported the unions' right to veto the closing or dismantling of GDR enterprises and stressed the unions' need for independent research so they might develop their own stands on issues.[30] These four themes were worked out in fuller detail in sections of the controversial new GDR union law, approved at the Extraordinary FDGB Congress at the end of January 1990 and promulgated immediately before the March 1990 Volkskammer elections.[31] The provisions of this law guaranteed enterprise union leaders access to company records, granted them decision-making responsibility in personnel matters, expanded the decision-making rights of base-level union bodies, outlawed lockouts, and endorsed the right to strike.

As the pace of revolution quickened, the students' tactics became more assertive. For example, on December 6, they staged one of a number of demonstrations in front of FDGB headquarters in Berlin, demanding, among other things, the resignation of the FDGB executive committee, union participation in the round tables, and the continuation of a union confederation. Subsequently, the FDGB chair announced her intent to resign, and within hours, the FDGB gained representation at the national Round Table. About half the schools' students reportedly participated in this demonstration. The level of student activism stood in marked contrast to that of most professors from the union college. While some professors did participate in the discussion groups and the preparation of the discussion paper, according to one, "Until the day before the wall was opened, most of the professors and Ph.D.s were still only talking about strengthening the party." Responses to my inquires about the participation of union college professors in student-organized demonstrations ranged from "There was some, but it's hard to say how many professors took part" to "There was only one professor who participated—me."[32]

In their attempt to develop and realize their radical reform ideas, activist union college students made efforts to mobilize, consult, and represent rank-and-file workers.[33] Three or four times in the course of preparing the October discussion paper, they returned to their former workplaces and regions to gather workers' criticisms, demands, and suggestions. Ordinary workers and union leaders from all over the country also gathered at the college, where they became involved in ongoing reform discussions and in the production of position statements on a variety of union issues. In addition, some workers and grass-roots union leaders were invited to Fritz Heckert to work on preparations for the Extraordinary FDGB Congress. Students also organized workers to attend the demonstrations they staged, and in one case their calls were heeded by several hundred people. One such participant, a thirty-four-year-old laundry worker, recalled her involvement: "It was sometimes tense. Some people stood around and yelled at us and criticized us because we were demonstrating for the FDGB. I experienced a certain strength being part of the group though."[34]

Many actions the radical union reformers took, the positions they espoused, and the tactics they employed were very different from those of unionists in prerevolutionary times. Yet partly because radical union reformers judged elements of existing unions worth preserving, some working- and middle-class activists considered them too pro-government.[35] For example, their support for retaining some kind of umbrella union confederation, analogous to the FDGB, to which all sectoral unions would belong drew pointed criticism, as did the procedures for electing representatives to the Extraordinary FDGB Congress.[36] Union reformers were also impugned for their reluctance to forge links with the largely middle-class citizens' opposition groups, such as Demokratie Jetzt and Neues Forum. Yet attempting alliances with such oppositionists sometimes only meant that radical reformers found themselves targets of further censure. For example, an IUG activist who attended a union college meeting to help prepare for the Extraordinary FDGB Congress expressed displeasure in finding that 10 percent of the participants held district-level or higher union offices and that 35 percent were AGL or BGL chairs.[37]

The style of union reformers' appeals also identified them as old guard in the eyes of their critics. For instance, they frequently tried to legitimate reform ideas by emphasizing their compatibility with the legal and structural foundations of the old system—exactly the tack the government itself had often taken in forty years of attempts to promote changes from above. The October discussion paper thus reiterated the unions' close connection to "the party of the working class" (though it did not refer to it by name), and the flyers distributed by the committee preparing the Extraordinary FDGB Congress attempted to generate worker interest in the event by recalling that "Chapter 3, articles 44 and 45 of the GDR Constitution assure unions comprehensive participation in the state, economy, and society" and that "union rights to suggest, arrange, approve, control, and to get information are firmly established in the Labor Code."[38] Many workers encountering such appeals undoubtedly wondered at the extent to which radical union reformers really favored change. Surely it struck many as naive, at best, to link efforts at genuine union reform and worker empowerment to the foundations of a system that had so often discouraged them in the past.[39]

Original Forms of Worker Self-Representation

Another group of worker activists, instead of focusing their political energies on reviving pre-GDR forms of worker representation or on reforming ones that had functioned during the socialist period, boldly created their own organizations to advance their interests. From the perspective of these activists, the crisis demanded they follow an uncharted course, and the fruits of their efforts came to be known by a variety of labels—*Sprecherräte* (spokespersons' councils), *Gesellschaftliche Räte* (social councils), economic committees, editorial councils, independent unions, and so forth.[40] These revolutionary creations, however, did not ordinarily last much beyond the March 1990 elections, their formation and functioning were idiosyncratic, and their members had minimal contact across workplaces. They sometimes existed alongside old unions in various degrees of disintegration or revitalization, and their relations with these old unions varied tremendously. In different establishments, they replaced, worked alongside, or merged with old unions or even competed against them in dual power situations.[41] As with the *Betriebsräte*, middle-class activists from both inside and outside workplaces were integrally involved in the founding and functioning of some of these novel forms of worker self-representation.

One example of a *Sprecherrat* comes from a Berlin wire and cable factory with over a thousand employees.[42] This enterprise-level *Sprecherrat* was formed in January 1990, at a time when the workplace union continued to function, albeit in a severely weakened state. Ten older, male skilled workers from one department and a foreperson from another, all of whom knew one another well and were highly critical of the union's passive response to the crisis, initiated the *Sprecherrat*. "We said that if the union is so blind and deaf that it doesn't do anything even in times like these," one initiator recalled, "then at least within the *Betrieb* we could represent ourselves."[43] Most initiators had not previously been active in the union. This self-appointed group of eleven secured the right to attend meetings with management on an equal basis with the BGL. The *Sprecherrat* subsequently informed other workers about these proceedings, though this feedback was sporadic and dependent on personal social networks.

The spokespersons' council was not a militant body and, to some degree, worked to preserve the status quo at the firm. For example, when workers at the enterprise threatened to join a warning strike at a neighboring workplace, *Sprecherrat* members talked them out of it; when a group of workers demanded higher wages and refused to recognize the union, they persuaded them otherwise; when "the workers wanted to run out into the streets and climb over the wall," the *Sprecherrat* was able to neutralize the situation, enabling enterprise management to carry on normally.[44] Since the *Sprecherrat* was dedicated to keeping the peace and continuing production, made only limited demands, and had demonstrated influence over the work force, enterprise managers had no qualms about accepting it. Although its very existence was a clear challenge to the union, its members were decidedly uninterested in pursuing this challenge. When new union elections were eventually held in March 1990, only one of the "short-term activists" from the spokespersons' council was willing to be a candidate for the AGL or the BGL. As one *Sprecherrat* member explained, "I was more interested in my work than in struggling with some of the problems [the union would have had to deal with]. So I said to myself that as soon as a competent BGL was in place, one supported by the majority of workers, then I could leave the matter alone."[45]

A second example of an original form of workers' self-representation was the *Gesellschaftliche Rat*.[46] Following the suggestion of the author Stefan Heym, a well-known GDR intellectual, and a series of workplace gatherings, forums, and petitions, a social council was elected in a Berlin lighting enterprise of nearly five thousand workers in early 1990. Many of the successful council candidates had technical college or university degrees and came from lower administrative levels.[47] Employees from units likely to employ a high percentage of production-based intellectuals, such as administration and research and development, were especially influential members of the body.

The scope of *Gesellschaftliche Rat* functions in this factory was quite broad. The agreement it proposed for working with the enterprise director called for social council participation in decisions about major structural, financial, and ownership changes in the firm and about managerial personnel, investment plans, and employee remuneration, among other things. Participation by the *Gesellschaftliche Rat* was meaningful and expanded over time, and the body maintained a critical independence from management. The *Gesellschaftliche Rat* regularly reported its progress to its worker constituents through the enterprise newspaper and the distribution of flyers.

The social council's relationship with the enterprise union was complicated. The original paid BGL officers kept their distance from council members, but council members, along with several other BGL members and AGL chairs, staged a successful palace coup against these old BGL leaders. They surreptitiously organized a meeting of two representatives from every work collective (the *Vertrauenperson* plus one other) to gather suggestions for candidates for a new BGL. Confronted with this, the paid members of the BGL quit, and an interim leadership committee was formed that included former AGL and BGL functionaries, social council members, and other active employees. Both successful and unsuccessful candidates in the social council election eagerly ran for the unpaid BGL positions, and two were elected. After this March 1990 union election, the *Gesellschaftliche Rat* continued to function as it had, in addition to serving as a "brain trust" for the new BGL leadership.[48]

Spokespersons' councils and social councils, however, were only two of a variety of novel representational forms launched by worker activists during the revolution. An "employees' committee," for example, reportedly called the first strike in the GDR. Elsewhere, more than two hundred auxiliary workers, dissatisfied with their wages, unhappy with both enterprise management and the union, and condoning work stoppages as a means of securing their demands, formed their own "interest representation" group.[49] The group was recognized by the general director and pledged to keep workers informed, to communicate their demands upward, and to ensure that they were represented in the managerial decision-making process. With the blessing of all their peers, a subgroup of *Vertrauensleute,* which likely included a high proportion of intellectuals, formed an "economic committee" in an auto plant, after 81 percent of the workers had refused to take part in the election

for a new BGL.[50] Enterprise management recognized this economic committee, and it was granted veto power over economic questions.

A final original effort at worker self-representation involved the establishment of new unions from scratch. The activities of many workers involved
in this endeavor were, to some extent, organized and coordinated by the Initiative for Independent Unions (Initiative für unabhängige Gewerkschaf-
ten—IUG). The IUG was begun by ten to fifteen students, workers, and intellectuals in late September and early October 1989. Its philosophy was
grass-roots, radical democratic, and slightly anarchistic. IUG founders envisioned the group not as an independent union per se or as a group that
would organize unions for workers but as a resource for production workers and service workers who wanted to form their own independent unions.
On this point they were adamant:

> We had to tell workers all the time that we were not an organization they
> could join. They had to do something on their own. We didn't want to come
> from the outside, as some union that was 50 percent intellectuals, and in-
> vite workers to become members. That would be a joke. We didn't really
> want to go into companies too much. We wanted workers to organize them-
> selves, though we could inform them about what was happening in other
> companies. We also didn't want to be a service organization with member-
> ship fees and so on. And we didn't want full-time, paid functionaries who
> did all the work, because they would tend to represent their own interests.[51]

Consistent with this philosophy, the IUG embarked on a series of activities that managed to attract and activate some rank-and-file workers without thrusting the IUG into a prominent leadership role. It published a newsletter (*IUG*), which put out six issues between December 1989 and the March
1990 Volkskammer elections. *IUG* ran articles on independent union activities around the country, as well as features on the IUG itself. The IUG also
opened a small office in Dresden and another in Berlin, which was quite busy
with workers' letters, phone calls, and personal visits from late November
through early January. "Some visitors to the office were regulars, but there
were many new people all the time too. Some of them had little groups backing them and simply came to tell us that they had an initiative going and to
ask us questions," an IUG activist reported.[52] In addition, the IUG held regular local gatherings with up to 150 people in attendance, which one participant described as often "highly productive" and "relevant."[53] Sometimes
meeting participants came as individuals, but often they represented others
in their companies, whether small groups of activists, entire departments,
several hundred coworkers, or the majority of a firm's employees.[54] At these
meetings, people exchanged ideas and information about what was happen-

ing at their workplaces. Often discussions moved spontaneously to broader questions, such as the legal ramifications of organizing independent unions, pay inequities, whether white-collar workers should organize separately, and low-and middle-management eligibility for union membership. IUG enthusiasts also held regional meetings and, to some degree, were able to coordinate their activities at the county level. In February 1990, the IUG held its first and only national congress, which was attended by 150 representatives of workers' groups and received a great deal of attention in the GDR media. The congress considered a proposal for establishing an independent union at the national level, and it formed a nonpaid commission with representatives from Berlin, Dresden, and Neubrandenburg to analyze happenings around the country and to coordinate and prepare a second national congress, where this national independent union was to have been established.[55]

Most important of all, from the IUG perspective, were its appeals to workers to establish base groups for organizing independent unions at their workplaces. To facilitate this, the IUG sometimes accepted invitations from groups of workers to come into their enterprise to speak about IUG ideas, and it often encountered hostility from both management and other workers when it did so. It is impossible to know precisely how much success the IUG had in realizing its primary goal of fostering independent union development from the base. IUG activists I spoke with could not say how many of these unions were formally organized, how much they accomplished, or how long they lasted. Reportedly, however, worker base groups took the initial steps toward forming independent unions in about 170 enterprises throughout the GDR.[56] The workplaces in which these base groups were formed ran the gamut from heavy industries to service industries. Most were motivated by an explicit desire for the radical, grass-roots-led democratization of union life, by a distrust of both GDR and FRG unions, and by a will to fashion an alternative to these unions.[57]

Despite the positive responses of some workers, the IUG remained small and never developed into the grass-roots workers' movement its originators had hoped it would. The middle-class background of many of its most ardent enthusiasts was an important reason for this. IUG activists outside enterprises were usually cultural and scientific workers, whose prominence in the IUG grew over time. Inside firms, it was often the production-based intellectuals for whom independent unions held the most appeal. In a Berlin radio factory, for example, the only employees involved in the independent union initiative were engineers. "The [blue-collar] workers didn't do anything with it," one worker claimed.[58]

As a consequence of their class standing, many IUG activists were ill-prepared for the kind of work necessary to overcome such worker reticence.

For one thing, many had not worked in, had no contacts in, and were unfamiliar with production and service workplaces and were thus at a loss about how to begin the political and organizational task they had set for themselves. For another, most had only scant experience with unions, since unions in many intellectual workplaces were nearly nonentities before the revolution. Two IUG members lamented these points:

> We weren't experts in union work. We never had to deal with it until we started to organize the independent union initiative.

> I felt underqualified to be part of the IUG, because I knew it was necessary to know what was going on in the companies, but I really didn't have a clue. And in the beginning I had communication problems. You might say I wasn't even able to speak the workers' language.[59]

Many IUG activists thus found themselves in a predicament. Not only ill-prepared to work inside enterprises but also sensitive to, and sometimes embarrassed by, the class gap separating them from workers, many were hesitant to do anything that smacked of organizing workers from above. The elitist implications of such a venture were too distasteful. Although they were doubtless correct that unions organized for workers by intellectuals may not have survived, their reluctance to assume a more directive leadership role contributed to the failure of the independent union movement. The IUG, though not without much soul-searching, clung to its radical democratic philosophy until its February national congress—long after many of its allies, including its working-class supporters, had begun pleading with it to assume a more proactive political posture. Such appeals became more frequent and more urgent throughout December and January, as the collapse of the GDR began to look more possible, as support for the FDGB dwindled, and as FRG unions began aggressively to recruit GDR workers. One IUG activist recalled a poignant moment in mid-December: "A man got up at one of our meetings and said he would not leave the room until we had established an independent union." After a few hours of discussion, the group decided against this move and instead repeated its appeal to base groups to form such an organization. According to another activist, working-class pressure continued to mount through February as "workers from other cities and from the companies continued to ask us to establish independent union organizations." Even though it was clear the IUG was losing significant worker support, partly as a consequence of rejecting these appeals, it did not change its position: "We kept on telling them no. We kept trying to convince them that workers themselves needed to organize and that we could only try to combine different groups that had related interests. We didn't want to pick ten people per company from the outside and tell them to organize. Our whole approach was classic intellectual in that we wanted to give the workers a lot of space."[60]

Despite widespread agreement at the national congress that something had to happen fast, the IUG continued to balk, deciding to postpone the establishment of an independent national union until a second national congress one to two months later. Their inaction left their worker allies hanging. Not surprisingly, these workers were often among the first to respond to the overtures of FRG unions. As one IUG activist put it, "What else could they have done? They organized twenty or so people in their factory, got them to complain on a wall poster, and then they didn't have any organization to represent their interests. We [the IUG] didn't help them with that. They had to find someone to help them, so they joined unions from the West."[61] One IUG activist reflected on what she understood to have been the group's choices at the time: "Either we should have done what the workers wanted, that is, established a union and worked with them the way they were used to, instead of following our own dreams, or we should have had a union for intellectuals where we spent our time dealing with theoretical conflicts."[62]

The IUG, however, was ultimately unwilling to follow either path. Its strategic paralysis, rooted in the GDR class division of which most IUG activists were painfully aware, virtually ensured its demise.[63] Other types of activists committed to establishing entirely new forms of workers' self-representation also found that class undermined their efforts from the inside. The legacy of strained relations between workers and the GDR intelligentsia left their *Sprecherräte* and *Gesellschaftliche Räte* projects internally too weak to survive the FRG-dominated shift toward electoral politics. The radical union reform effort also succumbed to the growing momentum of this process. While class issues also figured in its failure, they did so in a different way. Less burdened internally by class divisions, this largely working-class movement encountered stiff external resistance from middle-class activists both supporting and challenging the status quo, and this opposition hampered the work of the radical union reformers. Of the three major strains of indigenous worker activism that blossomed during the *Wende,* only the *Betriebsräte,* the most moderate but internally plagued by class contradiction, survived the dissolution of GDR socialism. It was able to do so, however, only with considerable political, economic, and ideological support from outside the country.

Conclusion

Forty years of GDR socialism had neither inspired nor cultivated working-class involvement in the 1989–90 revolution. Nonetheless, we have seen that a minority of workers did enter the fray, creating *Betriebsräte,* radically re-forming existing unions, and inventing a variety of forms of self-representation unique to the crisis. Their efforts were diverse, serious, and imaginative, tackling political, economic, and social issues often neglected by middle-class activists. Although all three strains of worker activism were, to varying degrees, dependent on yet weakened by middle-class collaboration, their appearance begs an important question. Even while so many GDR workers withdrew from the epicenter of politics in the late twentieth century, why did a handful defy the norm, boldly attempting to influence the course of the revolution in directions of their own choosing? The answer to this question is the focus of the next chapter.

7   A Second Look at the Labor Process and Workplace Politics

In chapters 3 and 4, we saw how the labor process and workplace politics dissuaded many GDR workers from participating in the politics of the 1989–90 revolution. As prominent features of workers' day-to-day experience of socialism, both operated relentlessly and thoroughly to demobilize the working class. In the light of this, it might seem ill-advised to search workers' same daily experience of the labor process and workplace politics for explanations of working-class activism during the revolution. Must we now abandon this explanatory thread altogether? Must we turn to other aspects of workers' everyday lives or, as is more common, to less proximate phenomena, such as the country's economic performance or its political culture, to account for the activism of the few?

I would answer no to these questions. If we hold to the notion that to apprehend what people *as paid workers* did during the *Wende* we must scrutinize their experience of paid work, we begin to notice ways in which the labor process and workplace politics helped prepare and inspire some workers to become actively involved in the politics of the revolution. The GDR labor process did not just involve disorganization, lying, and failed remuneration and discipline systems, all of which suppressed political activism among workers. It also spawned three forms of workers' control over the immediate production process, all of which facilitated the active involvement of some in the politics of the *Wende*. Likewise, workplace politics did not just mean pre-chewed union leaders, union subordination to worksite party and management, minimal union involvement with economic and production matters, and hyperformalized and decentralized union political practice, all of which thwarted working-class activism. Workplace politics also allowed democratic selection of some union leaders, some notably independent union activity, demonstrable union successes in economic and production areas, and union political practice that was at once decentralized and agreeably personal. Together these alternate features of workplace politics represented a valuable base of experience on which some GDR workers were able to draw in their activist bids to influence revolutionary events. In the GDR, the dynamics of the labor process and workplace politics that advanced worker activism were less pronounced than those encouraging withdrawal from politics, but only by acknowledging them can we fully understand why a handful of workers appeared on the revolutionary stage in the fall and winter of 1989–90.

Activism and the Labor Process

We begin to unmask how the labor process impelled some workers toward activism if we reconsider shortages. Shortages, which lay behind many workers' withdrawal from revolutionary politics, also promoted activism among some workers because they spawned workers' control of production. Shortages induced working-class control of production in three interconnected ways. First, shortages continuously required producers to exercise their ingenuity and their spontaneous problem-solving and decision-making capabilities. Often work could not go forward unless they succeeded in making, repairing, inventing, or improving machinery and equipment without standard parts or preformulated plans, and often acceptable products and services could simply not be produced or delivered at all unless resourceful workers, lacking sufficient or proper production inputs, were able to invent a way to do so. Exercise of this positive and creative brand of workers' control, unlike the negative and restrictive sort many have highlighted in Soviet-type societies, varied by economic activity, job classification, and skill level.[1] Yet from what workers told me, jobs of all sorts, not merely those in the industrial sector, required this constant improvisation. White-collar workers, for instance, recounted "making everything from scratch" and "figuring out how to finish a report without the typewriter ribbon or the duplicating machine," just as blue-collar workers told of "making new things from old things or keeping old things going from new things."[2]

The pervasiveness of this first form of workers' control was evidenced in the Innovators' Movement and the rationalization workshops, which were attached to the *Kombinate* and large enterprises. The Innovators' Movement and the rationalization workshops represented substantial institutionalized efforts to reassert management control by organizing and monitoring rank-and-file inventiveness.[3] Both endeavors were large and grew rapidly. In 1987, 34 percent of GDR workers made some suggestions for innovations through the Innovators' Movement (the percentage realizing innovations outside this formal channel would have been far higher), and the monetary value of these suggestions, which had climbed steadily for decades, was placed at over 6 billion marks.[4] The value of output in the rationalization workshops was approximately 12.5 billion marks the same year, and production in rationalization workshops rose faster than total production in the industrial sector, climbing at an average annual rate of 22 percent in the first half of the decade. In the mid-1980s, over 70,000 workers were employed in these workshops, which by that time had been created in every industrial and construction *Kombinat* in the country, as well as in the majority of factories under them.[5]

The relentless dynamics of the shortage economy, however, meant that the Innovators' Movement and the rationalization workshops could never successfully bring this first form of workers' control under management supervision. Inga Markovits inadvertently underscored this point when she discovered that the most frequently litigated issue involving the rights of participants in the Innovators' Movement was whether their innovations were part of their regular work duties (and thus ineligible for a monetary reward) or they were not (and thus eligible for such prizes).[6] That this particular issue was so contentious, and not another, such as the financial value of the innovation (on which the size of the reward depended), suggests how ubiquitous and essential continuous worker innovation was to the GDR's economic success. If lines between compensable and noncompensable innovations had not been drawn somewhere, the rewards paid those who exercised this first kind of control on the job, which in fact most workers did all the time, would rapidly have gotten out of hand.

The second form of workers' control resulted from persistent pressures undermining any strict division of labor, which were themselves the consequence of the country's labor shortage. It is not possible to state the extent of the GDR labor shortage with certainty, though a professor at the most prestigious economics university in the country estimated that there were between 250,000 and 300,000 more jobs than workers in the GDR in the summer of 1989.[7] Under such circumstances, if each worker performed a greater variety of workplace tasks, fewer workers would be needed, while those remaining unavoidably extended their control over the production and service delivery process. As individual workers took over responsibility for more, and more varied, functions, which both required and enhanced their knowledge of the overall work process, management dependence on its work force as a whole deepened.

Labor shortage pressures counteracting a strict division of labor existed in varying degrees in different workplaces, and managers adopted various measures to counteract them. The strength these pressures could assume, however, is underscored by some well-known and favorably publicized cases in which managers, in an effort to turn necessity into a virtue, yielded to them. These managers heartily embraced despecialization, consciously ceding more control to workers in exchange for higher productivity and lower production costs. Rainer Deppe and Dietrich Hoß recounted one such example in which a top manager reorganized the work process so that machine workers handled practically all prep work themselves; secured most of their own supplies from within the factory; installed, serviced, repaired, and set up their machines; did most of the programming; had complete authority over quality control; and transported finished parts to the storage area and scrap heap.[8] Clearly, workers performing such a wide assortment of indispensable work tasks were neither easily replaced nor highly vulnerable to management attempts to assert its own diminished authority over production.

The third form of workers' control is suggested by a joke Peter Marcuse once heard: "'Why do you always go to work so early?' a woman asks her husband, a manager at a local factory. 'Do you think they can't get along without you?' 'No, I think they could,' the man replied, 'but I'm afraid someone will notice it!'"[9] As this GDR joke hints, arguably the most significant form of workers' control engendered by shortages was producers' organization of their own individual and collective labor. The closer researchers came to the actual workplace in socialist economies, the more impressed they were by the utter necessity of workers' self-management of production. Ulrich Voskamp and Volker Wittke, for example, were struck by the fact that "plant management in the GDR . . . suspected much but knew very little about how work was actually being organized in their factories."[10] Michael Burawoy and János Lukács were similarly impressed by the autonomy of shop floor organization in Hungary. "We did not notice," they wrote, "attempts by higher management to direct production on the shop floor."[11] There is little doubt that a notable by-product of shortage economies was, in Harry Braverman's familiar terminology, the recoupling of conception and execution in paid work.[12]

For workers with whom I spoke, self-management meant a variety of things. One machine worker, reminiscing about the changes in her work collective since the *Wende*, alluded to some of these:

> When you talk to people who are still there, they'll often say, "Oh, be glad you're staying home. It's not nice here at all anymore." That's because we all used to know about each other's jobs and we'd trade them when necessary. There were no divisions between us. One didn't think, "That's yours

and this is mine." If someone were missing some screws or something, I knew about it, and I knew how to do something about it, just like they did if I were missing my steel. But now there are strict divisions, and little co-operation, between workers. This is a loss.[13]

Besides formulating their own job classifications, concocting their own division and integration of tasks, and establishing and maintaining cooperation networks inside and outside the shop, as workers did at this woman's factory, there were additional ways in which they managed themselves on the job. They spoke, for example, of overseeing discipline, determining production speeds and job assignments, deciding on work hours and schedules, setting production and delivery deadlines, arranging production sequences, and determining the quality and mix of production. Because output targets could so often be adjusted ex post facto, GDR workers even exercised some control over the amount of goods they produced and services they delivered.[14] Confronted by such a list of decisions routinely made by management in most capitalist settings, one might indeed wonder whether GDR managers were missed when they were not at work.

The concurrent operation of these three forms of workers' control meant that by the time the revolution broke out, GDR workers had had years of collective daily experience successfully imagining and inventing, solving problems, and making complex judgments under pressure on the job. Many had also mastered multiple work tasks and thus possessed a sound knowledge of the overall production or service delivery process. Above all, GDR workers were used to organizing and managing themselves. This reservoir of skills, knowledge, and experience, and the sense of efficacy and confidence that were its by-products, helped generate an ability and willingness among some workers to intervene actively on the revolutionary political stage. In other words, every day for forty years paid work had been laying a partial foundation for activism, preparing workers to be able to establish work councils, to radically reform their unions, and to create entirely new organs of workers' representation.[15] Some GDR workers proved able to build, as Burawoy and Lukács have suggested they might,[16] on a positive legacy of the socialist labor process.

Activism and Workplace Politics

Just as GDR workers' day-to-day experience of the labor process was a double-edged phenomenon, so, too, was their experience of workplace politics. At the same time that selection procedures for union leadership, the imbalance of union tasks, union political process, and the union relationship with the worksite party and management conspired to demobilize many

GDR workers, each of these experiences displayed a flip side, which provided a few GDR workers with just enough evidence of the benefits of self-directed collective action to attempt it themselves when the *Wende* broke. As a general rule, workers' experiences with union activities, relationships, procedures, and leaders at the lowest organizational levels were the most likely to promote this activist outcome. My discussion in this section therefore most often focuses on workplace politics at the *Kollektiv* level, where the *Vertrauensperson* was the chief union officer.

Chewing, Not Pre-chewing

Vertrauensleute were the most likely of all union officers to be nominated, as well as elected, by rank-and-file workers.[17] The records of all *Kollektive* were by no means perfect on this score,[18] but the overwhelming majority of workers with whom I spoke described a *Vertrauensperson* selection process that in practice, not just in theory, gave them the power to choose who would represent them. *Vertrauensperson* selection, which took place every two-and-a-half years, was described in a similar and favorable way by most of those who talked about it. To identify candidates for the post, *Kollektiv* members first discussed potential nominees informally among themselves and lobbied on behalf of their favorites. The *Kollektiv* then convened a meeting, during which a formal consideration of candidates and the ultimate selection of the new officer took place. A child care worker described such a meeting in her *Kollektiv*: "Oral nominations are made. Someone says, 'I nominate *Kollegin* X because...' and then they give their reasons. 'She does her job well, she likes to help others. She is courteous.' Yes, even the personality characteristics of the nominees are introduced. There are usually two or three nominees, depending on the size of the *Kollektiv,* and after this discussion they are put to a hand vote." When I asked this woman how this two-stage process could be improved, she could think of nothing, adding, "The process leading up to the election is democratic." Another woman, responding to the same question, stressed the identical strength of the *Vertrauensperson* selection process: "It's a pretty neat thing when the *Kollektiv* itself can suggest and decide who the *Vertrauensperson* is. It would be very different if we just stood there and had somebody being placed in front of and above us."[19] Although other workers told me that only one nominee usually emerged from this process in their *Kollektive,*[20] quite a few expressed satisfaction with the procedure. A single nominee, they argued, was not always an indication of undemocratic process but could be the honest outcome of the informal politicking among a small group of well-acquainted workmates before the selection meeting.[21]

The relative absence of pre-chewing in *Vertrauensperson* selection procedures meant that workers afforded their lowest-level union leaders greater legitimacy than that conferred on most higher-level union officers. "When the *Kollektiv* can determine who the *Vertrauensperson* is, then there is already confidence in her or him," one woman explained. "If I really agree to having a certain person be my *Vertrauensperson*, I am also ready to go to them with my problems. And that's why this nominating in the *Kollektiv*, and the confirmation there too, is such a good thing."[22] This distinction was brought into sharp relief during the *Wende* when BGL elections failed because of low voter turnout, while *Vertrauensleute* elections in the same plant proceeded; *Vertrauensleute* were entrusted with heightened responsibilities, including the nomination of BGL candidates; and more *Vertrauensleute* than AGL or BGL officers won votes of confidence.[23]

The opportunity to engage in meaningful and self-directed political action through the selection of *Vertrauensleute* provided many ordinary GDR workers with some practical experience doing politics before the *Wende*.[24] Through this experience, denied them in so many other workplace political forums, workers became more practiced in the arts of negotiating, persuading, cooperating, strategizing, choosing battles, compromising, and challenging established union procedure, all of which furnished practical grounding for rank-and-file activism when the crisis began. The absence of pre-chewing also meant that *Vertrauensleute*, compared with their union superiors, enjoyed greater legitimacy and authority among ordinary workers, were less insulated from them, and were more knowledgeable about their concerns. When some of these *Vertrauensleute* became politically active during the *Wende*, they were able to capitalize on these positive attributes of their relationship with rank-and-file workers to convince some to become involved in politics alongside them. The suspension of pre-chewing in selecting its lowest-level leaders also helped the union counteract its lack of autonomy from state management and the party, partially neutralizing the negative impact this had on working-class activism during the revolution.

Challengers, Not Mascots

Vertrauensleute, however, could never have retained their legitimacy with *Kollektiv* members merely because they were often nominated and elected by the rank and file. *Vertrauensleute*, as well as some AGLs and the rare BGL officer, continually had to earn their rank-and-file support through independent advocacy of workers' interests and combative identification with their concerns. When this happened, it was no longer accurate to describe the workplace union as the mascot of management and the party.

Although not all *Vertrauensleute* matched such an autonomous profile, a good many of these *Kollektiv* leaders did. "What kind of person do you want as *Vertrauensperson* in your *Kollektiv*?" I often asked workers. "Whoever has the biggest mouth!" a petroleum worker responded emphatically.[25] "Why do you think the *Kollektiv* chose you to be *Vertrauensperson?*" I asked current and former holders of the position:

> Because when I saw things weren't alright for workers, I'd speak up. Ever since I was just an apprentice, I'd criticize things at meetings. The *Kollektiv* knew me as a critical person, one who stood up against management. A *Vertrauensperson* who's shy, a "yes person," is good for nothing. When I didn't feel I had enough information, I used to really dig deeply into things so I could have lots of arguments at hand. Harsh words are sometimes necessary.

> Because I don't have any inhibitions about speaking my mind in front of Herr Kraus [the boss] or the BGL. You have to do that sometimes as *Vertrauensperson.*

> Because if I know of a problem, I'll go to the top to fight it out. The job of a *Vertrauensperson* is asking the right question, to the right person, at the right time. It's even asking stupid questions at the right time, too.[26]

The combative, worker-grounded, and independent approach many *Vertrauensleute* adopted was one indication of the relative autonomy of grassroots union groups in the GDR. It was also the linchpin of the union's ability to carve out, maintain, and even expand an arena of union independence at GDR worksites.[27] It is therefore no surprise that before the *Wende,* workers sometimes referred to *Vertrauensleute* as the "motors" of their *Kollektive,* "the most important people in the union," and they frequently argued that *Vertrauensleute* deserved more recognition for their work.[28] During the *Wende,* it was often *Vertrauensleute,* together with any other workplace union officers with reputations for combative independence, who were elected to leadership posts by their work mates.[29] Nor is it a surprise that the impressions of some of the most careful students of work in the GDR suggested a qualitative difference in autonomy between union *Kollektive* headed by *Vertrauensleute* and the higher levels of workplace union organization.[30]

When I asked workers for concrete descriptions of *Vertrauensleute* and *Kollektiv* autonomy, they often described two general scenarios. In the first, individual workers or the *Kollektiv* broached a problem with their *Vertrauensperson,* who then took the issue "up the ladder," discussing it with department management, enterprise management, the AGL and the BGL, and, in rare cases, even management and union superiors outside the workplace.[31] *Kollektiv* members maintained these interchanges between *Vertrauensleute* and their union and management superiors were quite different from the prearranged, formal, BGL- or management-dominated meetings that many worksite union officers, including *Vertrauensleute,* were required to attend, and which workers ordinarily cited as examples of union leaders' upward focus and lack of autonomy. Workers saw the former parleys with superordinates as different, precisely because they were unplanned, informal, and direct, dealt with issues broached by the *Kollektiv,* and took place at the initiative of the *Vertrauensperson.* Moreover, the point of these meetings was not merely to report rank-and-file problems to higher-ups but also to resolve them. Workers perceived these meetings not as opportunities for grass-roots union leaders to schmooze with big shots but as demanding, delicate, and personally risky aspects of *Vertrauensleute* work, which required the officers' persistence, finesse, and steadfast commitment to and understanding of rank-and-file wants and needs.

The second scenario was the reverse. Here the *Vertrauensperson,* upon recognizing or being confronted with an individual or *Kollektiv* problem, tried to *avoid* taking the issue up with union, management, or party superiors and instead tried to solve it within the *Kollektiv.* Although this approach might be read as evidence of the timidity, fearfulness, or passivity of *Vertrauensleute* or as their attempt to protect themselves at the expense of advancing their constituents' interests, *Kollektiv* members usually did not evaluate it this way. Rather, workers read this scenario as a demonstration of the self-reliance, power, and gumption of both the *Vertrauensleute* and the *Kollektiv.* Workers also perceived it as the most democratic and participatory means of solving the problems of the *Kollektiv.* Moreover, workers consciously recognized the solution of problems within the *Kollektiv* as a way of staking out and developing an independent terrain of union work, one free from the oversight of superiors. This autonomous terrain only contracted, they argued, with each management, party, or higher-level union intervention in *Kollektiv* affairs.[32]

The relative autonomy of the union *Kollektiv,* of which *Vertrauensleute* were a primary symbol and promoter, made a major contribution to worker activism during the revolution. This contribution came in several ways. First, the *Kollektiv* was the principal site in which workers could elaborate their own goals and plans, where they could collectively begin to imagine and create alternative workplace arrangements and practices. In the *Kollektive,* in other words, visions of what could be were never totally overshadowed by what was. *Kollektiv* experiences thus emboldened some workers, even during the most disorienting moments of the *Wende,* to promote changes in their workplaces, many of which harbored the potential to alter social arrangements in the broader society as well.

But beyond nourishing their political imaginations, the *Kollektive* were the places where the widest assortment of workers were most likely to have had the ongoing experience of actually doing their *own* politics, of pursuing *their* collective agendas, rather than acting out political scripts written elsewhere. Previous political engagement of this sort is necessary grounding for future activism. It imparts various political and participatory skills and abilities, one of which, organizing people to work collectively, was especially important during the revolution. When the *Wende* broke, some workers were unwilling to wait passively for someone else to tell them what to do. They successfully organized themselves, building on both their past experience with autonomous, self-organization in the *Kollektive* and on the experience they had had jointly managing their own labor. Finally, the *Kollektiv* provided an environment in which genuine worker leaders could be nurtured. In the confusion of the *Wende*, as events unfolded at a dizzying pace, the presence of workers not only ready to act but also ready to assume leadership roles was key to the appearance of the activist efforts described in chapter 6.[33] It was from the ranks of the *Vertrauensleute*, those grass-roots union officers who had been tutored in the relatively independent haven of the *Kollektive*, that many of these working-class leaders often emerged.

Union Work Revisited

The relative independence of the lower levels of union organization would have had limited positive impact on worker activism during the *Wende* had it not been accompanied by concrete achievements. In other words, combative political engagement on the part of the union would have counted for little among workers—indeed it is hard to imagine it could have been sustained at all—if it had not produced some tangible results.

In chapter 4, we saw that workplace unions did enjoy some important successes, especially in the social and cultural spheres. Overall, however, their accomplishments in economic and production areas paled in comparison. Yet this distinction was not so clear-cut. On closer inspection, we see that GDR unions also registered some demonstrable achievements in these latter areas as well, and these were often realized outside formal institutional channels.[34] Many workers I spoke with praised such union accomplishments, for they had direct and positive effects on their daily work.

People were often energized and animated as they related examples of successful and informal proworker union interventions of this type. Take, for instance, the grass-roots union officer who told me he had "dropped everything" when management informed him that forty people in the sewage treatment plant where he worked would have to do their jobs without the proper footgear. He then proceeded to circumvent plant management, going directly to the *Kombinat* administration, where his simple but successful tactic had been to "just keep telling them we didn't have the right boots until they got us the right boots!" Or take an AGL officer in a furniture factory who recalled how he had gotten management to honor its promise to allow four workers three months off to attend job training courses. "It wasn't as easy as just writing this down in the collective agreement," he made sure I understood. "The reality was I had to fight about it before the workers were actually able to attend."[35] Or consider another worker's comments about her *Vertrauensmann:* "In the winter we had to work in the cold. Our *Vertrauensmann* began to monitor the temperature every day, and because of his diligence, things were improved."[36] Even though workplace-level unions were not involved in determining overall remuneration rates, as the following comments from women at two different establishments indicate, they were not always without influence over the amount workers actually took home:

> We had a problem here recently with overtime pay. Because the plan was mostly based on the amount of personal laundry we did, the manager proposed we be paid 40 marks per hour for the personal laundry we did on overtime, but only 20 marks per hour for the industrial laundry we did on overtime. The union said no. The difference was too large. We could just imagine the problems it would have caused to have had some people working the same amount of overtime and earning half as much as other people! The union submitted an alternative proposal and did not give up until management agreed to pay 40 marks per hour for both kinds of laundry.

> When the norms were changed there was, of course, quarreling. They wanted to run us over, and there were big fights. But we had one colleague on the AGL who sat down at home for days and figured everything out. This wasn't even his function. He really did that for the other workers. We were also lucky because the woman who works as a controller was also a BGL representative. And through these two, the best compromise for the workers was reached. The workers alone couldn't have done that, because, after all, you have to fulfill your output goals. I thought that was really great.[37]

Our look at union accomplishments would be incomplete without considering the *Konfliktkommissionen,* the centerpiece of the workplace grievance resolution system.[38] A grievance commission consisting of between four and fifteen people (eight or nine was average) existed in every workplace with over fifty employees. Since additional grievance commissions were to be formed where there were more than three hundred workers, the commissions operated, roughly speaking, at the department level. Members were elected in secret ballots every two-and-a-half years. Nominations were supposed to come from the *Kollektive* (union college figures indicated that 80 to 90 percent did originate there), and some workers told me this was what happened at their workplaces.[39] John Borneman, however, reported "general confusion about how the nominations [were] made."[40] In 1987, approximately 28,500 grievance commissions with 255,000 members existed in the GDR, and together they heard about 73,000 cases, up from 65,000 in 1981. The number of cases a commission heard varied markedly by economic sector.[41]

Grievance commissions were not union bodies, but the unions were involved in their operation in various ways. The first commissions were formed in April 1953, about two months after Stalin's death, and were one of several reforms intended to mollify a disgruntled working class.[42] Because some of workers' major complaints at the time concerned the unions, grievance commissions were explicitly structured as nonunion bodies. Many people I spoke with in the late 1980s still made a special point of distinguishing between the two.

Over subsequent decades, however, the unions and the grievance commissions became more intertwined, with no apparent decline in the status of the commissions. For some years prior to the *Wende,* for example, the enterprise-level union was responsible for organizing elections for members of the *Konfliktkommissionen,* ensuring that the commissions stuck to prescribed procedural timetables, and training grievance commission members in labor law and commission procedure.[43]

From most workers' point of view, however, the most crucial form of workplace union involvement with the *Konfliktkommissionen* was union service as workers' counselors and advocates when cases came before the commissions. Workers often sought, or were offered, union advice on the wisdom of pursuing their cases before the grievance commission or on the best course to follow when management had brought a case against them. Many workplaces had a union legal commission, sometimes including an attorney, to which employees could turn in such situations.[44] Similarly, if workers were dissatisfied with the *Konfliktkommission*'s resolution of their cases, they could seek union counsel on the advisability of filing an appeal.[45] Workers stressed the union's obligation to provide all such aid to workers, regardless of whether the union thought a worker was culpable.

Union involvement during actual *Konfliktkommission* hearings was especially important to workers. Most workers told me a union representative, often the *Vertrauensperson,* had to be present during such inquiries. A number also told me that when *Vertrauensleute* addressed the commissions, they did so not as individuals but, following a serious discussion in the *Kollektiv,* on behalf of the entire base-level work group.[46] Reports of the exact role of the union representative during commission proceedings, however, varied. At a minimum, union representatives participated by offering information. At a maximum, they came to defend the worker. When I asked whether the union was obliged or merely allowed to provide such support, some workers insisted the union had to furnish it. An important aspect of such assistance was the union's ability to put the case in proper context: "The *Konflikt-*

kommission not only deals with the specific incident but also with the general situation surrounding it, for example, a person's overall work record and their family situation. The union is there to see that all these circumstances are considered, not just the particular action or situation written up in the case."[47]

When speaking of the *Konfliktkommissionen,* as opposed to many other workplace political processes, no one complained of feeling frustrated by repeated yet futile attempts to get something accomplished. Grievance commissions appeared to have the authority to do what they were supposed to do in a reasonable amount of time.[48] Sessions, including both testimony and commission members' deliberations, were open to anyone from the workplace, and John Borneman related that all interested and involved parties were released from work to attend them.[49] The *Konfliktkommissionen* definitively resolved between 90 and 93 percent of all labor disputes they considered, meaning that less than 10 percent of all cases were appealed by the worker or the boss. Several GDR sociologists claimed that *Konfliktkommissionen* decided in favor of the worker, not management, 80 to 90 percent of the time.[50] Although most people I interviewed could not cite precise statistics, their observations of the *Konfliktkommissionen* did not refute reports of high success rates for workers. One man, for instance, recalled attending a labor law training session when he worked in the brown coal industry, during which a labor judge had impressed upon those assembled that "our first basic *Konfliktkommission* principle is that when there is doubt, one must decide in the worker's favor. Our second basic principle is that all conflicts are cases of doubt."[51]

As this discussion reveals, GDR workers' daily experience of workplace politics consisted of more than an ongoing string of discouraging failures. GDR workers had some opportunities not only to take part in politics at their workplaces but also to take part in politics that produced demonstrable payoffs. Through their experiences with successful *Konfliktkommission* proceedings and informal union bargaining, rank-and file workers acquired political savvy, refined their political skills, and gained a sense of political efficacy and empowerment, all of which proved good preparation for the risky road of revolutionary activism.[52] Grass-roots union leaders also spoke of how their successes invigorated them politically, how these helped counteract the powerful enervating tendencies of much of their union work—the "political burnout" to which so many fell victim in the years before the *Wende.*

Insofar as both the *Konfliktkommissionen* and the informal negotiations undertaken by the workplace union allowed them to grapple with production and economic concerns, workers also gained exposure to topics outside the purview of the workplace politics to which they were ordinarily privy. As a result, whether as grievance commission members or grass-roots union leaders, direct parties to or firsthand observers of conflicts handled through grievance commissions or informal union bargaining, workers sharpened and expanded their knowledge of many issues central to providing goods and services in a complex modern economy.

As examples, consider a few matters commonly the focus of *Konflikt-kommission* proceedings and informal union bargaining. In deliberations over pay, workers learned about the detailed workings of the remuneration system, workplace budgets and financing, comparative wage rates, and the use and calculation of overtime and bonuses. In disputes over transfers, they learned about not only specific regulations governing individual job changes but also labor allocation and skill needs in both individual firms and the economy, as well as how these related to technological change. In conflicts concerning job performance, they were exposed to the intricacies of employment contracts and labor coordination in large organizations. In disputes over alleged indiscipline, among the most acrimonious issues at many worksites, they digested contradictory information and opinions about work motivation, productivity, and, most of all, the distribution and negotiation of power, control, and responsibility at work. Familiarity with such controversial topics helped workers design and promote effective workplace restructurings in the midst of the *Wende*. The *Betriebsräte*, the radically reformed unions, and the original forms of worker representation that emerged during the crisis were all based on such knowledge and information about production and the economy that GDR workers had managed to acquire, albeit with difficulty, at workplaces across the country before the fall of 1989.

Personalized and Decentralized Union Political Practice

The experiences of workplace politics that induced some workers to assume active political roles during the *Wende* went beyond *Vertrauensleute* selection procedures, the relative autonomy of the *Kollektiv*, and the scope of issues unions successfully dealt with at the base level. Union political process also helped prepare the ground for activism. In the *Kollektive*, and to a lesser extent at the AGL level, the centralism and pretentious formalism so characteristic of political practice at higher workplace levels were much attenuated. Both were regularly supplanted by decentralized and personalized politics, which ultimately advanced working-class activism during the *Wende*.

The essential structural underpinning of this alternative brand of political practice was small size. The *Kollektive*, which emerged as the principal counterweight to the debilitating political practice workers endured elsewhere at their workplaces, usually grouped between twenty and thirty-five workers.[53] Commentators who consider size an important political variable have called attention to numerous procedural advantages associated with small groups, a number of which were apparent at the lowest union levels in the GDR. To begin with, small numbers limited the development and reproduction of rigid hierarchy and centralism, two marks of union political practice which, as we saw in chapter 4, meant that many workplace union leaders interacted largely with their organizational superiors and that their political energies were consumed by the interests of these same superiors, not those of ordinary workers.

By all accounts, however, *Kollektiv* politics were different. They transpired in the open, not behind closed office doors far removed from the shop floor, and all members of the *Kollektiv* were party to them. Certainly *Vertrauensleute* performed pivotal leadership roles in the *Kollektive,* but they customarily engaged in workplace politics alongside other collective members, not their union superiors. Nor did *Kollektiv* politics focus on the concerns of higher-ups. *Vertrauensleute* often explained that collective meetings were not called at the behest of superiors, and they were not devoted to external agendas. Instead, one told me, these meetings dealt with "anything *Kollektiv* members are interested in, their concerns, what's on their minds." "I never have a *Kollektiv* meeting just to have one," another remarked. "I only do it when I think there are special things of interest to the *Kollektiv* that we might discuss—not just the same old topic of plan fulfillment."[54] Many workers concurred: the agendas of *Kollektiv* meetings were theirs to decide, they could be changed in midstream, and ensuing discussions were inclusive and uncontrived.

The inclusivity of *Kollektiv* politics, together with their focus on rank-and-file issues, undermined the barriers between *Kollektiv* union leaders and their constituencies, so symptomatic of higher-level workplace politics. Workers could actually see what their union leaders were doing (and not doing) in the *Kollektiv,* because they were close to, indeed often part of, the action, instead of being shielded from it. Many *Vertrauensleute* applauded their visibility, their lack of isolation from *Kollektiv* members. "Of all the different union functions I've performed," one former *Vertrauensmann* told me, "I liked being a *Vertrauensmann* the best, because I was on the job in the middle of my colleagues, right there with them."[55] As a partial consequence, collective members only rarely lamented unresponsive *Vertrauensleute* or *Vertrauensleute* who had no handle on how workers were thinking and feeling. Nor did *Vertrauensleute* usually complain that collective members distrusted them or that their work went unappreciated. On the contrary, as a *Vertrauensfrau* in a laundry asserted, "I like this work because I feel acknowledged and my colleagues trust me." "The reason why I continued doing this work," recalled another blue-collar *Vertrauensperson*, "was because my coworkers trusted me."[56]

Small group politics also provided an antidote to the deadening formalism of so much workplace political practice. Despite the detailed codification of and slavish attention to every rule and regulation characteristic of higher-level union politics, spontaneity and flexibility survived at the lower levels. The recollections of a worker in a furniture factory, visibly pleased with the story he shared, suggested how this could be so: "The law is that women with kids and single mothers get one day off per month to care for sick children. But one man here had sick parents, so we decided to give him a half a day off for six months and then look into it again. It's very important not to treat all cases alike, but to treat people as individuals."[57]

Perhaps the biggest advantage of small group politics was that they allowed face-to-face, body-to-body communication among participants. Such direct and personal communication occurred among subgroups of workers in the *Kollektiv* and within the *Kollektiv* as a whole. It was also the hallmark of the interaction between *Vertrauensleute* and other members of the *Kollektiv,* so much so that nearly all the *Vertrauensleute* with whom I spoke emphasized the extent to which their jobs involved talking over issues personally with individuals or small groups from the *Kollektiv.* The method of union dues collection, for example, required a face-to-face exchange that many valued highly. Each month, as one worker explained, in the course of performing this important piece of union business, "the *Vertrauensperson* has a chance to speak with each *Kollektiv* member individually. The *Vertrauensperson* gets a lot of information that way. In fact, it's guaranteed they will, because they have to talk with each *Kollektiv* member. That's why personal dues collection is better than just deducting the money directly from the worker's paycheck."[58]

Many *Kollektiv* members credited face-to-face, body-to-body political communication, in contrast to the impersonal, indirect, and rule-bound variety typical of higher workplace levels, with additional advantages.[59] For example, people developed their active listening skills, along with their speaking and passive listening abilities. Communication could be direct yet subtle, cognitive yet affective, and there was a chance for participants to cultivate richer, deeper, more complete understandings of one another. In other words, politics occurred among whole people, with all their emotional, social, rational, and intellectual complexity. Politics also became more creative, and collective deliberation, common action, and outcome were more visibly linked in a closer temporal sequence. This in turn increased the possibility of more popular, and hence workable, political outcomes. From my conversations with both ordinary workers and low-level union officers, this last point should not be underestimated. Many of these people plainly yearned for the chance to concoct and implement practical solutions to the real-life workplace problems they understood so well.[60]

In addition, through face-to-face, personal politics in the *Kollektive,* many ingredients of friendship—compassion, commitment, empathy, respect—were nurtured rather than stunted, as they often are through the political practice of large groups and institutions. Many *Kollektiv* members spoke of one another not just as coworkers but also as friends, and research on miscellaneous GDR firms reported that between 33 and 53 percent of workers felt the same way.[61] Mutual help was one aspect of *Kollektiv* friendship that workers often discussed. I was told, for example, that collective members would sometimes take over their *Vertrauensperson*'s work station so she or he would not fall behind at the job when some union function had to be performed. Or, as one technician recalled of her *Kollektiv* after the *Wende,* "We were a good *Kollektiv.* Whenever I was having a hard time of it—we had quite a labor shortage so I was really doing more than one job—I could speak with any of seven people, and each one tried to help somehow. And when we had inventory, they all stayed longer to help me, so I could finish when everybody else did. There was a nice harmony about us. And we helped each other not only with work-related matters."[62] Displays of friendship, as this woman implied, were not confined to the job. They extended beyond work hours, blurring the separation, common in both East and West, between life outside of paid work and life on the job. *Kollektiv* members told of visiting their work mates at home when they fell ill and helping one other with household maintenance and improvement chores.

Much of this suggests, as feminists in particular have reminded us, that the face-to-face, body-to-body communication most possible in small groups allowed an expansion of the content of politics to include "private" life, feelings and emotions, and "personal" problems—"the new terrain of subjectivity," in Sheila Rowbotham's words.[63] Instead of being considered off limits, such matters could readily be woven into the fabric of small group politics alongside the threads of more standard political topics. People's conceptions of what constituted the legitimate focus of politics broadened, and the flavor of group politics changed. "Everyone [in my collective] knew exactly who had worries," explained an auxiliary worker in heavy industry. "That was quite normal for us. We would listen to each other talk about these over breakfast and at other times."[64] For many GDR workers, the politicization of the personal in the *Kollektiv* was highly prized and, as this woman expressed it, a "normal" experience of their paid work, so normal, that Marilyn Rueschemeyer pondered "whether the collective satisfies so many emotional needs that it acts as an extension of family relations—or takes the place of the family in some respects."[65] Although *Kollektive* that replaced families were undoubtedly the exception, I sensed that, at a minimum, the politicization of the personal increased workers' awareness of how their paid jobs and the rest of their lives were linked. Particularly for GDR women, who had one of the highest labor force participation rates in the world yet continued to do the largest share of unpaid labor in families, this possibility had special value, for it opened to public scrutiny and collective political consideration areas of life where their subordination was deeply rooted.[66]

It was clear that *Vertrauensleute* played a pivotal role in the politicization of the personal. When asked what kind of person was best for this job, workers often told me *Vertrauensleute* had to be people respected for their "human qualities," folks admired for their comportment in private, not just public, settings. Many *Vertrauensleute* also stressed the importance of this personal aspect of their union political work:

> *Kollektiv* members can turn to the *Vertrauensperson* with problems about their private life and get advice. The personal problems I hear about here involve child care, marriage, and housing. There are a lot of them. There are also problems that are even more private, where I can either say I can help or suggest we try to find a solution together. These are only between the *Vertrauensperson* and the worker. No one else. Otherwise, I lose the trust of my coworkers.

> I take care of people in the group. We establish a relationship, and I really come to know about *Kollektiv* members, about their home as well as their work life.

> I should be able to see in advance if someone is overworked or under too much pressure because something is wrong at home.[67]

An especially telling indication of their strong personal orientation was the label I sometimes heard grass-roots union officers use to refer to themselves: *die Betriebsmuttis* (the enterprise mommies). While clearly a commentary on the gendered division of labor in the GDR, the *Betriebsmutti* label also revealed a great deal about the nature of their union work in the *Kollektive*.[68]

In sum, everyday political practice at the lowest levels of the workplace, especially in the *Kollektive*, was distinct from that at higher union levels in numerous ways. To begin with, politics at the lowest levels occurred in the open where workers could scrutinize and take part in them, and these deliberations focused on rank-and-file concerns. Lower-level workplace union officers consequently were less isolated from their worker constituents than officers of BGL rank were, and this promoted worker trust of the union and its lowest-level leaders. As a result, there was a pre-*Wende* corps of grass-roots union leaders whose experience of workplace politics included positive reinforcement from an appreciative and respectful rank and file with whom they were in intimate daily contact. Thus, when some of these union leaders, such as those whose activities were recounted in the previous chapter, adopted active political roles during the crisis, there already existed groups of ordinary workers predisposed to join with them.

The political practice made possible by small size also helped inject some passion, vitality, and spontaneity into workplace politics, things that were continuously smothered by the rule-bound, preplanned, tightly controlled, and upward-focused nature of workplace politics above the grass-roots level. Small size also facilitated whole-person-to-whole-person political interactions through which workers broadened their assortment of political talents to include, for example, the ability to listen actively and to conduct affective and compassionate, while efficient, conversations. If usually undervalued, such skills are essential to successful grass-roots organizing anywhere. Small group political practice also nurtured friendships among coworkers. As a result, when the *Wende* began, solidarity did not need to be manufactured from scratch. It already existed within small pockets of workers across the GDR, and it provided the building block from which many worker activists launched their efforts for change. Finally, face-to-face, body-to-body politics permitted a host of "personal" issues, ordinarily not found on the workplace political agenda, to become a legitimate focus of politics. Many workers clearly cherished this feature of low-level union process, and it enhanced their overall experience with collective action through unions before the *Wende*. When the crisis broke, such positive pre-*Wende* experiences helped inspire some workers to engage in concerted worker-initiated political efforts both inside and outside the unions.

Conclusion

Echoing a recurrent theme of numerous prerevolutionary accounts, many who have written of the GDR since its demise have noticed little to commend. Jürgen Habermas, for example, likened GDR socialism to "forty years of disaster."[69] Similarly, Peter Marcuse characterized the history of GDR unions as "forty years in the service of power," describing them as "thoroughly integrated into the party" and "completely discredited" after October 1989.[70] From the perspective of workers' everyday experiences at paid work, however, such pronouncements appear overzealous in their condemnation and oversimplified in their analysis. From the vantage point of the social majority, both the labor process and workplace politics had been more than a forty-year string of unmitigated catastrophes.[71] As the politics of its demise have become better understood, our comprehension of GDR socialism has become more thorough, more nuanced, less monolithic, and less distorted.[72]

In reexamining workplace politics and the labor process, we have come to realize that both, despite their demobilizing outcomes, prepared some workers for active political involvement in the revolution. The labor process did this by enhancing workers' control over production in three ways: it dictated constant innovation and problem solving; it produced pressures undermining the strict division of labor; and it required producers to manage their own labor collectively. We also saw how, at the lowest levels of the workplace, union politics often did not resemble those simultaneously occurring at higher ones. At lower structural levels, especially in the *Kollektive,* many GDR workers participated in relatively autonomous union activity. They had demonstrable influence over selecting their union leaders, and they observed and were direct parties to successful union work around not only social and cultural issues but also economic and production matters. Moreover, the personalized and decentralized politics of the grass-roots level provided an antidote to political practice elsewhere in the workplace, which could accurately be described in opposite terms.

The working-class activists of chapter 6 owe a great deal to these invigorating political consequences of the labor process and workplace politics. Considered together, they help us understand how some rank-and-file workers came to swim against the tide of nonparticipation and emerged as activists during the revolution. They also help account for the grass-roots union leaders around the country who moved squarely onto the center of the political stage during the months of revolutionary turmoil. Finally, they help us grasp features of the relationship between these union leaders and the rank and file that had positive implications for working-class activism during the *Wende.*

8   Workers in the Wings: Passive Participants in Revolutionary Politics

Despite its mounting complexity, the story of working-class politics during the revolution told so far is still too simple. Activism and noninvolvement did not exhaust the range of worker responses during the crisis. Rather, they constituted opposite poles of a continuum of choices GDR workers made. Many workers, as we know, eschewed political participation almost entirely, while a few became actively engaged in the conflict. The more I discussed the revolution with GDR workers, however, the more it became clear that there was a third segment of the working class, likely the largest, which positioned itself in the wings, not in the gallery and not on stage, as the revolutionary drama played. These workers, who steered a middle course between activists and the uninvolved, could best be classified as passive participants in the politics of the day.

Passive participants can be distinguished from activists and from workers who eschewed political involvement on a number of counts. In contrast to many uninvolved workers, who reported few opinions on and took scant notice of revolutionary issues and events, passive participants were definitely partisan, though not fervently or unreservedly so. Unlike their uninvolved counterparts, who only discussed their opinions privately, passive participants were willing to speak out in public and semipublic forums. Yet in contrast to activist workers, passive participants were reluctant to act on their expressed opinions, and even when they did, their political deeds were of a different character. Passive participants ordinarily engaged in actions as individuals, and their activities were typically restrained and reactive, involved slight personal risk, exhibited little planning, organization, or coordination, and entailed minimal expenditures of time and energy.

Passive participants did not constitute a single homogenous group. Some workers could be counted as passive supporters of socialism as it had developed in the GDR, while others lent passive support to the antagonists of that system.[1] Both sides in the civil conflict, in other words, attracted some working-class support, albeit qualified. The most straightforward cases were workers who passively supported *either* the status quo *or* its challengers for the duration of the crisis. At least as common, however, were workers who lent passive support to each side *serially* (usually to the government first and later to its opponents) or to both sides *simultaneously.*[2]

In exploring passive worker participants of both ideological factions, this chapter devotes separate attention to working-class leaders. Worker leaders were workers who occupied largely unpaid positions in workplace union structures, especially *Vertrauensleute,* department-level AGL officers, and enterprise-level BGL officers, excluding the chair of this body. Workers who were party members but held no position of authority in the organization were also considered worker leaders. By virtue of their positions, these people were among the most politically seasoned members of the working class. Most had more leadership experience than their coworkers, and their personal and political networks inside and outside the workplace were more extensive. Their ability to shape working-class politics during the revolution was thus greater than that of most of their coworkers. A good number of these women and men chose the middle road of passive involvement during the revolution. Their choice to participate only passively, irrespective of the side to which they lent their support, had significant ramifications for the conduct of the revolution.

Workers' Passive Support of GDR Socialism

The evidence that some GDR workers passively supported the system under attack is varied.[3] I discovered it first in the newspapers of the period, not unexpectedly in such party publications as *Neues Deutschland* but also in smaller periodicals, such as factory newspapers, which had severed all ties to the party.[4] In such accounts, some workers came out against the weekly street demonstrations. "I don't understand those on the street who are shouting around saying 'Gorbie, Gorbie' or 'SED, It Hurts.' I would like to see how these people behave in their enterprises," wrote a Leipzig worker in his factory newspaper.[5] Sometimes workers even went so far as to support the use of force to break up these gatherings.[6] Other workers rose to the public defense of the party and its leaders. "Egon Krenz has caused me to hope," wrote a turner from Leipzig. "It's clear to me we can trust the SED," concluded a foreperson in a ceramics factory in the south of the country.[7] Still others proclaimed their general support for socialism. "We don't want to get rid of socialism: We want to improve it," stressed a foreperson in a steelworks. "It's time to remember the virtues and powers of our society," echoed a worker in a synthetics factory.[8]

Additional evidence of workers' passive support for the status quo surfaced in the stance some adopted toward both top management at their workplaces and fellow workers who identified with the opposition. As examples of the latter, in one factory I visited, disapproving workers "hassled" coworkers who resigned from the party, and night-shift workers in an electronics firm reported a colleague to their superior (who then called the police) after the activist hung an opposition manifesto on a company wall.[9]

Prior to the revolution, top-level GDR managers were closely identified with the supraworksite party and state apparatus. For decades before the crisis, top managers at all but the least important workplaces were nearly always members, and often leaders, of the party; they were chosen, and could be removed, at the behest of state and party officials; their day-to-day work was dictated by the state plan and by those outside the worksite responsible for its implementation; and managers' authority could be overridden by supraworksite party and state leaders. Despite their position as obvious, logical, and accessible targets of worker dissatisfaction, there were few reports of workers' making moves to oust or replace top management during the *Wende*. In the fall of 1990, a sociologist of work at Humboldt University told me that the same managers continued to be in charge at most workplaces, and well into 1991 the situation still had not changed in many enterprises.[10]

This assessment is consistent with my own. In a widespread display suggesting passive support for the status quo, workers avoided any challenge to top management in most places with which I was familiar. In some they went a step further in their passive support of "in-factory" representatives of state and party authority. For example, twenty-eight workers from a Leipzig transport factory made it publicly clear they felt the director of the firm should stay. In a farm equipment factory, the top manager (an eighteen-year party veteran) said, and workers confirmed, that when he called for a vote of confidence, 88 percent of the employees supported his continued tenure. Even in a workplace where top management was ousted, not every worker agreed with the action. "All of a sudden," one worker recounted, "I found out that Herr Meier was dismissed. He was always nice to us. We had a good relationship with the director here. Well, I thought it was sad what became of him."[11]

Workers' passive support for the status quo can also be read in the unwillingness of many to challenge workplace unions during the crisis. Interpreting this stance, however, is tricky, for we know from earlier chapters that workers perceived and experienced unions in at least two ways. At the lowest levels, while plainly part of a larger labyrinthine organization closely identified with the state and the party, unions and their leaders exhibited some degree of combativeness and independence from the regime. Workers' reluctance to challenge unions might therefore have signified halting support for those opposing GDR socialism. At higher levels, however, the unions and their leaders merged with the country's political elite to such an extent that workers saw no difference between them. Insofar as this was the case, workers' unwillingness to challenge the unions should be understood as a straightforward, albeit passive, sign of their support for at least some elements of the status quo.[12]

Thus, partly because workers took no actions and voiced no demands to jettison them, prerevolutionary union structures and leaders rode out the crisis fundamentally unscathed in many GDR workplaces.[13] In others, the original unions existed alongside *Betriebsräte* or some new organ of worker representation, though sometimes their most discredited functionaries were replaced. Elsewhere only part of the workplace union organization remained intact, typically the shop floor structures headed by the *Vertrauensleute*. Regardless of the details of union survival or partial survival, workers often expressed their support for the existing unions as confidence in particular union leaders. A laundry worker, for example, told me, "We didn't even try to dismiss our *Vertrauensfrau*. We had always been pretty satisfied with Katya, even though she decided a lot of things without asking us and tried to convince us of her opinion. But we always told her she couldn't do that, that she had to ask us when something was going on. She was a strong believer in the SED. But no, we *never* said that we didn't want her anymore."[14]

Even after numerous union leaders at various levels had resigned in disgrace, many GDR workers showed little sign of giving up on the existing unions. Many remained willing to take part in union elections at various points throughout late 1989 and early 1990. Brigit Grabsch, Karel Kschischan, and Lutz Kirschner, for example, reported on enterprises in which one-half to three-quarters of the work force was motivated to cast ballots in such elections.[15] Many workers also maintained their union memberships throughout the *Wende*. Others, who had disaffiliated from the old unions once the crisis erupted, reenrolled before it was over.[16] This occurred in a Berlin cable firm, where only 50 percent of the employees were paying dues in December and January but 77 percent again showed up on union rolls in March 1990.[17]

The high frequency with which old plant-level union leaders won open elections or votes of confidence during the crisis is an additional indicator of passive rank-and-file support for the status quo. Astrid Segert, for instance, reported that 50 percent of the *Vertrauensleute,* 80 percent of the AGL chairs, and 75 percent of the BGL members won votes of confidence in a large steelworks in Brandenburg.[18] In a Baltic shipyard, a new BGL was chosen at the beginning of 1990. Many of its old members were reelected, including the previous chair, described as a "very critical and militant woman who was held in high esteem throughout the company."[19] Not only did I learn of other such occurrences through interviews, so too did Kirschner in both enterprises he studied and Grabsch and Kschischan in five of the six firms they researched.[20] Undoubtedly, some old union leaders were retained because they had posed insider challenges to the status quo prior to the revolution. But given the frequency with which the very people who had held offices in the prerevolutionary unions were reelected or won votes of confidence, I doubt this is the whole story. At the very least, these votes suggested that leaders' identification with the prerevolutionary unions did not damage them much in many workers' eyes. At most, the reelections signaled workers' affirmation of the prerevolutionary unions, which had shown some inclination to tolerate, if not encourage and protect, workplace union officers in whom the rank and file had confidence.

Many worker leaders in the GDR also showed passive support of the existing system through their public pronouncements and strategic inaction. Their public pronouncements appeared, not unexpectedly, in both *Neues Deutschland* and the *Tribüne* ("We want a good socialism, not the wolf's law of capitalism," argued a *Vertrauensperson* from Gera).[21] Plant-level union officers also echoed such sentiments in letters to the higher echelons of the FDGB and in their enterprise newspapers.[22] Some worker-members of the party likewise expressed passive support for the status quo in these enterprise publications. In Leipzig, for instance, an office worker and future member of the SED complained of the "hateful campaign of West Germany to raise doubts about socialism" and condemned both emigration and street demonstrations as actions benefiting the enemies of socialism. Some I interviewed recalled the early appearance of deep splits in worksite party groups between reformers and those who publicly insisted on "maintaining old ways."[23]

All over the GDR worker leaders also showed passive support of the existing system through their strategic inaction. Shying from deeds that would have demonstrated unequivocal support of the regime, these worker leaders instead chose not to act in specific situations. Such behavior would come as no surprise to Michael Kennedy, for it was indicative of those he dubs vassals in Soviet-type societies. Although GDR worker leaders were not prototypical vassals by Kennedy's definition, their structural position closely resembled that of vassals, whose hallmark behavior was passivity.[24]

Strategic inaction, like nondecisions,[25] whether adopted for tactical or opportunistic reasons, can be an effective method of forestalling change. Worker leaders' calculated decisions not to act thus often prolonged the life of workplace union structures, sometimes even in the face of rank-and-file opposition and after union officers had announced their wish to step down. Worker leaders' inactions included postponing or delaying new union elections, refusing to allow votes of confidence, and skipping meetings where they expected to be criticized. Other worker leaders simply refused to respond to any demands or challenges, defiantly continuing to conduct business as usual. In one factory, for example, the BGL successfully neutralized pressures for the resignation of some of its members by insisting that if any of its number were asked to leave, all would abdicate their posts.[26] Elsewhere worker leaders went to even greater lengths of strategic inaction in their passive support of the old guard and its practices. As the political situation became more tense, an extraordinary number of workplace-level union officers either fell "ill" or took their vacations.[27] Their disappearing acts often spelled temporary union withdrawal from workplace politics, allowing some unions, which might have been dismantled had they remained engaged in worksite struggles, to weather the most dangerous moments of the crisis intact.

Workers' Passive Support of the Opposition

Numerous workers also lent passive support to those challenging GDR-style socialism in ways that did not deviate sharply from common pre-*Wende* patterns of protest.[28] At a minimum, these workers discussed their oppositional opinions informally and semipublicly. Such discussions could be intense and protracted, but many participants preferred not to translate their opinions into concrete actions and often not even to share them outside a small circle:

> I was in quiet agreement with these [citizens' opposition] groups. But I wasn't directly a part of any of them, nor were my coworkers. There was a wish to start something new, but there wasn't any clarity about what. There were no protests or walk-outs. There were thoughts of them, but they never came to anything. If we'd have done something, instead of just talked, we could have gotten some publicity. If we had sabotaged a concert or something, we would have caused some trouble. But we never did.

> In my department, we sat around and discussed things in the smoking corner most of some days. Much of the talk was critical of the government. But it really didn't spread to other departments. Even though people in my department knew some people in the other departments, they really didn't talk to each other about political things.[29]

Many workers who passively supported the opposition, however, went beyond semipublic, informal expressions of their views, airing them, often spontaneously, in the numerous meetings, forums, and dialogues held at many workplaces; through the print and broadcast media; in petitions; and in wall newspapers, which cropped up at workplaces and other public gathering spots and attracted large crowds of readers.[30] Many of these expressions of support for the opposition came indirectly, as criticisms of the existing system.[31] As time went on, they assumed an increasingly political flavor, condemning travel restrictions, the continued tenure of state leaders judged responsible for the country's failures, and unsatisfactory media reporting ("It does not correspond in the least to the convictions and perceptions of the majority of our co-workers if the media, after an embarrassing silence, now attempts to explain the exit of so many of our people as the work exclusively of the class enemy.") and backing street demonstrators ("Would anything have changed or happened at all if people had not gone out on the street? We don't think so, as harsh as that sounds.") and eventually unification on FRG terms ("I want to earn D marks, not buy them. I plead for a united German fatherland!").[32]

State managers and the party also came under fire, and, as the following examples demonstrate, many workers minced few words in their attacks. Workers in a large Berlin factory censured Egon Krenz as "the Emperor of China,"[33] and members of a transport collective, outraged at their party secretary's duplicitous attempts to paint himself as an opposition supporter all along, wrote their factory newspaper:

> We are annoyed that he seems to want to give the impression, since the *Wende,* that the *Wende* could never have happened without him. What did he do before October 1989 anyway? Didn't he praise precisely those whose strict punishment he now loudly calls for? We are especially outraged about such *Wendehälse* [political opportunists], because until quite recently they forbade themselves any criticisms of state leadership and the SED. Now some leave the party and run around making a big fuss about what they've done. In our opinion the SED has now finally ruined its claim to be the basic organization in our enterprise in the future.[34]

Eleven workers in a Berlin furniture factory were equally piqued by management at their worksite: "After numerous fruitless attempts to get the management, of whom there are many, to follow a new path of progressive forms of production, we are of the opinion that management either didn't understand or doesn't want to understand. Management attempts to shove its incompetence onto the workers by not hesitating to scold them whenever a catastrophic situation arises. Blaming us workers for the poor condition of the factory is outrageous and no longer acceptable."[35]

Unions and their leaders likewise became targets of scathing worker critiques. Already by late October, the *Tribüne* alone had received "hundreds of letters" lambasting Harry Tisch, chair of the FDGB,[36] and enterprise-level leaders were receiving their share of criticism as well ("The BGL chair has lost our trust. While in office he represented workers' interests in a very inadequate manner").[37] The substance of many of these criticisms is predictable. The union was taken to task for deferring to the party and state management, ignoring workers' problems and suggestions after being repeatedly informed of them, being passive before the *Wende,* and refusing to adopt an active oppositional stance during the crisis. Workers denounced union leaders' special privileges, called for revamped union electoral procedures and a reduction in the number of BGL functionaries, and insisted that the practice of importing people from outside the factory to serve on the BGL be halted.[38]

Some workers moved beyond public and semipublic expressions of their views to engage in limited action on behalf of regime adversaries. Severing their ties with government-associated organizations was the quintessential example. For instance, after workers' militias were instructed to prepare for riots in August, many workers simply left the groups. The union, too, lost members. Some workers merely stopped paying their monthly dues, while others chose to disaffiliate more dramatically, returning their membership booklets to the union, sometimes accompanied by an explanatory letter. Altogether, one million workers (approximately 11 percent of all FDGB members) reportedly took this action in October and November 1989. Scattered reports indicate that the percentage of employees who demonstrated their passive support of the opposition through union disaffiliation ranged between 7 and approximately 80 percent at different worksites.[39]

At times, workers' passive support of the opposition involved a somewhat higher level of political activity. In some workplaces, producers' public and semipublic criticisms of the union prompted the resignation of workplace union leaders and the organization of elections for new officers. Despite workers' varied roles in advancing such elections and the victories of critical and independent candidates in many of them, these working-class political challenges were actually fairly limited. For one thing, workers repeatedly showed extreme reluctance to run for union office in the elections they had demanded. In both the enterprises Lutz Kirschner studied, for example, there were serious difficulties getting candidates for BGL and AGL races, and in some contests not a single worker would agree to run.[40] In others, the prerevolutionary practice of running one candidate per position remained the norm.[41] Many workers even hesitated to vote in these contests. Between 28 and 50 percent of the workers in the eight enterprises included in Kirschner's and in Grabsch and Kschischan's research did not cast ballots, and in an auto plant in the southwestern corner of the country, only 19 percent of the employees showed up to elect a new BGL, a percentage Theo Pirker and his cohorts judged typical.[42]

Like many ordinary workers, some worker leaders publicly voiced their criticism of the existing system either at workplace meetings, in print, or in letters to top-level union officers. As early as the end of October 1989, the executive committee of the FDGB reported receiving thousands of such statements from *Vertrauensleute,* AGL, and BGL members,[43] and the party hierarchy was also besieged by "demands not suggestions" from its members. Worker leaders expressed many of the same criticisms that rank-and-file workers had.[44] In addition, they exposed the continual pressures to present their superiors with overly rosy assessments of everything, as well as the intense frustration of having honest reports of problems fall on perpetually deaf ears: "In thousands of base organizations, the members continuously asked critical questions, pointed out problems, and demanded answers. Every great once in awhile, a party higher-up would come and say that they had made note of what had been said and that they were passing it on to higher levels. However, they would also tell us, 'You have to understand, blah, blah, blah ...' And in the end, it was clear everything would continue as before."[45] The upward focus of fellow union leaders, both a cause and a symptom of the hypercentralization of GDR unions, likewise came under attack. "The BGL chairs should be seen more in the factory itself," complained a thirty-year unpaid union functionary, "and not waste their time with higher union levels like the *Kreisvorstand* [district union executive committee]."[46] As time went on, some called for open dialogue with citizens' opposition groups and spoke in favor of the formation of *Betriebsräte,* other worker-initiated representative structures that competed with the unions, and the radical union reformers.

Worker leaders also resigned from the party and the union. Many *Vertrauensleute,* AGL functionaries, and BGL committee members, for example, left the union once the corruption in its high ranks became public.[47] Alternatively, some base-level union leaders unilaterally stopped forwarding workers' dues to higher union levels. Worker members of the party also resigned. For instance, the party secretary of a yarn factory in Leipzig reported that about 5 percent of the party nucleus left or was dropped near the end of October, and a Berlin worker recalled that "almost everyone" left the party in December.[48] All told, party membership losses were catastrophic, much larger than those suffered by the unions. By October and November, 22 percent of the party's members had already departed, and the figure stood at 83 percent by May 1990.[49] Upon taking this action, a thirteen-year party veteran at a steelworks submitted the following to his enterprise newspaper: "Until a few days ago I was still of the opinion that the renewal of the party was necessary for the future development of our socialist state. But in the process of the revolution only democratic citizens who were not party members stood on the front line. They were the ones who reawakened democracy. So far only empty words and promises have been heard from my party."[50]

Like the rank and file, some worker leaders evinced passive support for the opposition that went a step beyond merely expressing their opinions or leaving the union or the party. Their activities, however, were largely one-shot efforts taken on the initiative of individual worker leaders, without the involvement of the rank and file. For example, the union officers of a large Berlin enterprise telephoned Harry Tisch and summoned him, on a moment's notice, to a meeting at their factory called to discuss their problems.[51] In a Brandenburg steelworks, the BGL abolished censorship procedures that had previously blunted discussion in the *Vertrauensleute* meetings, and party members refused to stand behind top party leaders in a 3,000-person worksite gathering in October.[52] Other worker leaders went further, spearheading the removal of old union officers and calling for new elections. Like many rank-and-file workers, however, worker leaders were often averse to becoming candidates in these new union contests.

In conclusion, let us consider the significance of the fact that many worker leaders of *both* political inclinations chose neither activism nor noninvolvement in revolutionary politics. Prompted by complex motives, these men and women instead opted to steer the middle course of passive participation. In declining to put their political experience, resources, and influence to the task of mobilizing and organizing workers on behalf of the status quo, some of these worker leaders helped ensure that the old order could never emerge victorious from the political maelstrom. The same can, of course, be said of the worker leaders who lent passive support to the opposition. They also failed to use their political advantages, abilities, and experience to motivate workers to join and strengthen the challenge. At the same time, the fact that these same worker leaders offered some endorsement of the opposition, albeit hesitant, made it much more difficult for the regime to muster working-class backing in many workplaces. Of course, the challengers, both inside and outside the enterprises, were likewise stymied by those worker leaders who sided with the regime, however quietly.

The political consequences of worker leaders' passive support for both the status quo and the opposition were far-reaching. That a visible segment of worker leaders on both sides of the political divide opted for passive participation in the revolution weakened both sides in the civil struggle. Both saw their ability to attract political champions from the working-class severely curtailed, and neither ended up with a social base broad enough or deep enough to prevail over the other. Nor was the social base of either side sufficient to stay the political intervention of powerful FRG interests, which, as was soon apparent, were left virtually free to determine the course of the GDR revolution.

Explaining Workers' Passive Involvement in the GDR Revolution

A final group of GDR workers judged neither activism nor withdrawal their best political option during the *Wende*. These were the passive participants in revolutionary politics, some of whom engaged in passive participation on behalf of those supporting the status quo and others of whom did so on behalf of the challengers. The passive support many such workers lent to both sides was neither unwavering nor exclusive. Rather, it was common to find many who offered passive support to either side *successively* or to both sides *simultaneously*. How can we explain the inconsistent and equivocal political involvement of this large group of GDR workers?

In chapters 3 and 7, we saw how workers' daily experience of the socialist labor process was double-edged, leading many workers to eschew political involvement while steering a handful toward activism. The GDR labor process, in other words, was both empowering and enervating. To understand why such a large number of GDR workers participated, but only passively, in the revolution, we need to appreciate how their daily experiences of the labor process were *neither* one *nor* the other of these things, but *both* one *and* the other, at the same time. Workers could observe firsthand the economic costs of a shortage economy. They also knew how the economic system failed them as producers on a direct and daily basis. They saw their hard work mocked by the lying endemic to the labor process, obscured by the disciplinary and remuneration systems, and subverted by the disorganization that reigned at their workplaces, all experiences that contributed to their withdrawal from politics and their dissatisfaction with the system that gave rise to these experiences. Yet simultaneously—and the word *simultaneously* is key—the same labor process challenged workers to innovate, to develop a range of mental and manual skills, to grasp the entirety of the production process, and to organize and control their own labor collectively, all politically enabling outcomes they hoped could be preserved. In other words, the GDR labor process was two things to workers. As a result, many workers were both for *and* against the system they associated with such a labor process, which in its turn had left them both prepared *and* unprepared for political activism. Said another way, many GDR workers found themselves in a position that translated easily and logically into faltering support for both groups in the civil struggle.

Chapters 4 and 7 revealed that workers' daily experience of workplace politics was similarly dichotomous. Workers saw unions shy away from a host of economic and production issues of special concern to them. They found the formalization and centralization of union political practice both deadening and exasperating. They observed the union play third fiddle at their workplaces, and they were aware of how many union leaders were in the hip pockets of party and management, partly because workers had so little say in selecting candidates for these positions. Yet all the while workers were buffeted by such negative experiences of workplace politics, which dulled their taste for activism, the unions that engaged in this brand of politics, and the wider system that encouraged it, something else was happening. Especially in their union *Kollektive*, often headed by *Vertrauensleute* they had chosen and whom they respected, workers collectively created unions that acted autonomously on their behalf and that extracted gains and protected rights they both valued and knew were exceptional. Finally, many workers thrived in the personalized and decentralized political atmosphere of their *Kollektive*, refining their political skills, developing solidarity, making friends, and finding their "private" needs a serious focus of union political work.[53] GDR workers, as a consequence of their daily experiences of workplace politics through the unions, came to lack *and* possess the potential for political activism. Moreover, they came to judge unions, and by extension the larger socioeconomic and political system of which they were a part, to be in need of drastic overhaul, even while they appreciated certain of their aspects. Of two minds about this system and these unions and simultaneously able yet unable to assume activist political roles, many GDR workers offered equivocal support to both those who would dismantle and those who would protect GDR socialism.[54]

GDR workers had lived two contradictory experiences of the labor process and workplaces politics in the years leading up to the revolution. They thus found themselves pulled in opposing directions when it came to deciding which side in the civil conflict to support and when it came to their ability to evidence that support. Coupled with the fact that many working-class leaders themselves chose the route of passive political involvement instead of mobilizing workers to participate actively in politics, it is no wonder that so many rank-and-file workers remained in the wings, probably none too comfortably, as the GDR disintegrated.

9 Class, the Labor Process, and Workplace Politics in Comparative Perspective: Poland and the GDR

Socialist societies around the globe have been engulfed in crisis during the last quarter of the twentieth century. Yet the wrenching changes each country has undergone in the course of these crises have been dissimilar in many ways, including the role workers played in these historic events. Chapters 2, 6, and 8 focused on what workers did and did not do during the short civil struggle that preceded the dissolution of the German Democratic Republic in 1990. As it turns out, the nature of working-class involvement in this struggle was not uniform. A handful of workers participated quite actively in the politics of the *Wende*, and, in the judgment of many of these workers, their most significant political efforts were expended at their workplaces. In the GDR, however, activist workers were the distinct minority. More commonly, GDR workers chose to absent themselves from the contest entirely or to offer their hesitant support to the government, its adversaries, or both.

Despite these variations in workers' political involvement, the *Wende* was not a working-class revolution. GDR workers did not begin it, they did not lead it, and they were never the most visible players during any period between the late summer of 1989 and the late winter of 1990. This workers' state crumbled as most workers either watched from the gallery or offered their passive support to both protagonists from the wings.

Across the placid Oder River, within clear sight of Frankfurt Oder, a city where I conducted a number of interviews and made several worksite visits, lies Poland. Poland was also a workers' state but one in which the working class played a dramatically different part in the events that ultimately overturned socialism. The year 1980 marked the definitive beginning of the end for Polish socialism, and the Poles who set this process in motion and for a while charted its course were not of the intelligentsia, as was the case in the GDR, but of the working class.

Polish workers burst onto the stage of world consciousness in the Gdańsk strikes of mid-August 1980. Observers were in awe of their militancy, their discipline, their determination, their sophistication, their democracy, the coherency of their goals, and the sophistication of their tactics. Within two weeks, the government had accepted their demands, the centerpiece of which was the right to form independent unions, and a mere month after they first struck, Polish workers had created a national structure for this already world-renowned independent union, which they called Solidarity. Intellectuals were involved in these dramatic events, but workers were the dynamic agents of Poland's transformation.[1] Solidarity developed from below; it was grass-roots and workplace-based; workers led it; its structure, tactics, and demands were endogenous creations of the Polish working class. In short, the revolutionary stage belonged to workers, not the intelligentsia, in Poland.

Chapters 3, 4, 5, and parts of 1 and 8 were devoted to explorations of how the labor process, workplace politics, and class helped explain the reluctance of the majority of GDR workers to become actively involved in the events that overturned socialism in their country. But if the dynamics of the labor process, workplace politics, and class were able to shed light on workers' politics in the GDR, might they not also have figured in workers' very different political involvement in the Polish crisis at the dawn of the 1980s?

Workplace Politics and Working-Class Activism in Poland

If anything, Polish workers appeared to have had a more debilitating experience of workplace politics through the unions than did GDR workers. On a general level, one might conclude this from the numerous references in Polish studies to increasing worker dissatisfaction with union performance; from commentators' assertions of the weakness and ineffectiveness of Polish unions;[2] from workers' own assessments ("The unions are a cancer on the body of the working class");[3] and from their actions ("With bars and hooks, the front doors [of the union building] are beaten apart, and the crowd piles in. From all the windows on all the floors, furnishings start flying out onto the street").[4] Focusing on the four specific aspects of workplace union politics considered in chapter 4 reinforces this conclusion.

First, workplace unions in Poland were burdened with an unreasonable number of tasks. Yet, just as in the GDR, unions opted to ignore their production and economic responsibilities, even though, from workers' point of view, these were among the most important.[5] My fieldwork in the GDR, however, revealed that, especially at the lowest level of the workplace, unions did sometimes attend to such matters, and their interventions were sometimes successful.[6] There is virtually no indication that this was the case in Poland, however. To the contrary, unions at Polish workplaces reportedly had little influence over working conditions, bonuses, or pay for special conditions; they had no role in negotiating worksite collective agreements; and they were not especially effective in disputes over workplace safety.[7]

In the GDR, workplace unions sometimes prevailed in conflicts over such issues through informal and direct bargaining with management. Even though informal bargaining between workers and managers took place in Poland, unions did not seem to have been party to the process.[8] *Konflikt-kommissionen* were the formal and institutionalized avenue through which GDR workplace unions fought to exert control over the most contentious production and economic issues. Disciplinary cases were often referred to these bodies, and here again the contrast to Poland is suggestive. In Poland, firm-level and worker-elected grievance committees were reinstated after 1956.[9] By the 1970s, however, management and unions were apparently choosing their members. Moreover, the 1975 labor code, which broadened the scope of arbitrary dismissal, made it clear that the manager also had the unilateral right to fine insubordinate workers and to fire them for disciplinary reasons.[10]

Second, also reminiscent of the GDR, Polish unions had come under frequent criticism for their formalized and centralized political practice since the 1950s. Union operations at Polish workplaces were evasive, inflexible, deceptive, aloof, and closed. There is little evidence that any of these negative attributes of union political practice were tempered at the lowest level of union organization, as they often were in GDR *Kollektive*. Accounts of Polish unions make no specific mention of open, participatory, rank-and-file focused, flexible, or personalized union political practice at this level. Union dues collection procedures provide one example. GDR workers praised union dues collection as an example of regular, face-to-face interaction between the *Vertrauensleute* and the rank and file. In contrast, at least during some pre-Solidarity decades, Polish union dues were apparently just deducted from workers' pay; no personal contact between union leadership and the rank and file was necessary.[11]

Third, Polish workers regarded union electoral procedures even more deficient than GDR workers did. If a Polish worker Lawrence Goodwyn quoted is any indication, this was true as far back as the 1950s: the trade union apparatus "was like a theater, like a mock democracy. . . . It's just a satire, those seemingly democratic elections of [union] representatives." At the factory level, the party nominated candidates, who usually won.[12] Given all this, it appears that many Polish workers had concluded long before 1980 that they could not trust their union leaders, even those at the lowest level, and by the early 1970s the demand for open elections to replace union officers had already become common during worker protests.[13] In contrast, while workplace union electoral procedures were far from perfectly democratic in the GDR, at the *Kollektiv* level, GDR workers were fairly content with them. As a result, many conferred a certain legitimacy on their low-level union leaders, who went on to earn that confidence through their active defense of workers' interests. In Poland, such a situation rarely, if ever, existed.

A final contrast between Polish workplace unions and those in the GDR is the degree of union dependence on worksite party and management. In Poland, independent unions ranked high on the lists of workers' demands during the protests of 1970, 1971, and, of course, 1980.[14] This demand did not come out of the blue. Years of experience with official unions had brought it to the fore and kept it prominent.

Since the latter half of the 1940s, Polish workers had watched with disdain as workplace unions labored under the yoke of two masters, the party and management. By the 1970s, as Alex Pravda put it, "the great majority of workers saw unions as not just *subordinate to* but *as part of* factory management."[15] The party was said to have such a "stranglehold" on union activities that all aspects of factory union work were seriously undermined.[16] If day-to-day evidence of union subservience were not enough, workers also found it confirmed by union behavior during crisis periods. Unions played little role in the political tumult of June 1956. Fourteen years later, a worker leader at the Lenin Shipyard in Gdańsk reported "the flight of the entire management, along with the party secretary and the chairman of the trade unions" on the very first day of the strike.[17]

For decades prior to the *Wende,* it would not, of course, have been difficult to find GDR workers who also disparaged union spinelessness before factory management and the party, as well as union leaders who fawned before representatives of both. Nonetheless, this comparison reveals how the overall lack of enterprise-level union autonomy in both countries was tempered in the GDR by workers' experience in their *Kollektive.* In these smallest of union bodies, many GDR workers had a taste of independent union work, and they witnessed and benefited from the emergence and development of grass-roots union leaders who fought hard for workers' rights, despite opposition from party and management. I found little to indicate that this degree of union autonomy, however limited, was a feature of base-level union operations in Poland.[18]

So far I have suggested that unions at Polish workplaces were at least as unconcerned with economic and production matters, hyperformalized and rigidly hierarchical, undemocratic in their electoral procedures, and dependent on the party and management as workplace unions in the GDR were. In chapter 4, I argued that these four union characteristics contributed to the political demobilization of the GDR working class. But if I am correct in my assessment of workplace unions in Poland, how was it that Polish workers, instead of retreating to the sidelines, initiated and led the 1980 revolution? Perhaps the GDR was idiosyncratic. Perhaps the militancy of the Polish working class bore no connection to its experiences of workplace politics in the decades leading up to the appearance of Solidarity.

I would, however, argue otherwise. This seeming contradiction is easily resolved if we recall from chapter 7 the second side of workplace union politics in the GDR, which, among other things, provided a handful of workers with enough actual practice *doing* workplace politics that they were prepared for activism when the *Wende* broke. From the 1950s on, many Polish workers had also lived this second, politically instructive and invigorating brand of workplace politics, and they experienced it in far larger and more powerful doses than GDR workers had in their union *Kollektive*. In Poland, however, workers' experience of this second brand of workplace politics came not through the official unions but far outside, indeed often in direct opposition to, them. It came through decades of political struggle organized by the working class at worksites throughout the country.

The history of the working class in socialist Poland reads as a nonstop litany of strikes, demonstrations, negotiations, independent organizing attempts, and protests, sparked by workers' astute appraisals that one government move or the other was contrary to their best interests. In 1945–46, independent and socialist unions clashed with the communist authorities then struggling to solidify their power. In 1947, workers in one Łódź plant boycotted attempts to require work on unpaid labor days and later carried out a sit-down strike as well. In 1951, miners used the same tactic, as Stalinism "wore itself out" in the midst of continuous strife on the shop floor.[19] In 1956, 15,000 workers at a Poznań machine works, after independent worker representatives had unsuccessfully tried to negotiate with authorities up to the national level, went on strike and marched through the city, eventually engaging in a pitched battle with security forces.

Approximately fourteen years later, workers in Gdańsk struck and took part in street protests lasting one full week, during which selected public buildings and other properties were destroyed or damaged. Following by one month a confrontation over layoffs in a Warsaw plant,[20] the actions were prompted by a surprise announcement of price hikes. Protests quickly shut down the port at Gdańsk, extended through the remainder of the city, spread to the neighboring port of Gdynia, moved to additional Baltic Coast workplaces (including ninety-four in Szczecin, the other principal shipbuilding province on the Baltic cost), and erupted in industrial areas elsewhere in Poland. "There is every reason to believe," wrote Jan De Weydenthal, "that within a week or so there was no large city, nor important industry, left unaffected by work stoppages, protest meetings, or other form of manifestations of workers' discontent."[21] Then, during the first two months of 1971, textile workers in Łódź struck several times at both the factory and citywide level, and the northern coast once again became engulfed in a "rolling wave of strikes."[22]

The remainder of the decade was punctuated by hundreds of workplace disturbances of various sorts,[23] the most celebrated of which occurred in 1976. That year, workers in a metal products factory in central Poland, again angered over price hikes, struck and took to the streets, and workers in a tractor plant near Warsaw struck and dismantled a vital east-west railway connection. Around the nation, over a hundred major industrial plants organized support strikes, many occupying their worksites, and women at the strike center near Warsaw protested before party headquarters waving empty shopping bags. Thereafter, the road to Solidarity was paved with work stoppages and additional strikes, including 177 alone in July 1980, the month before the Gdańsk shipyards once again exploded in protests that sent shudders through the authority structures of East and Central Europe.[24]

All such actions provided Polish workers with almost continuous opportunities to engage in cumulatively empowering workplace politics. Again my logic follows that of chapter 7, in which I demonstrated how the practice some GDR workers had had doing workplace politics prepared them to step onto the activist stage when the revolution broke. Simply put, doing politics demands knowledge and skill, and, much like portrait painting, parenting, nursing, teaching, or welding, it requires practice to be done well. Moreover, for the socially disadvantaged who lack the material, ideological, and educational resources their opponents can bring to the struggle, political skill and knowledge are crucial. By 1980, Polish workers had had many years of practice doing workplace politics, albeit outside the unions, in the course of which their political knowledge and abilities had multiplied and matured. The practice GDR workers had doing workplace politics, largely in their union *Kollektive,* while motivating a few, quite simply paled in comparison.

Polish workers amassed a tremendous, varied, and interconnected store of political knowledge and skill as they did workplace politics over the decades before 1980. Among the most visible lessons they learned were organizational ones. They learned quite well how to pull off round-the-clock sit-down or occupation strikes at their workplaces. Moreover, at these times, during which workers secured total control over the productive process and apparatus, they had to arrange to feed and shelter themselves, secure the premises, defend themselves, and care for the ill and injured. Workers also practiced choosing their own representatives democratically. They envisioned the interfactory strike committee and then turned it into an organizational reality, which linked worker delegates from multiple workplaces who planned and coordinated efforts across large geographical areas. They learned how to construct their own communication networks within and among groups of workers by printing posters, flyers, and leaflets, by utilizing workplace public address systems, and by organizing a latticework of messengers and couriers within workplaces and throughout the country.[25] Key to all of this, workers learned how and where to recruit other workers, without getting fired or worse.

Aside from these organizational lessons, Polish workers absorbed other equally important lessons about political process. For instance, they learned how, where, when, and with which management and party personages to negotiate, and they discovered that sometimes talking with the other side was less effective than breaking dialogue.[26] They learned the value of good timing and the importance of being able to back up demands and proposals with sound technical knowledge of production and economic issues. They learned how both traditional and self-invented symbols, for example Gate #2 at the Lenin Shipyards in Gdańsk where fifteen workers were killed or wounded in 1970, had the power to motivate others to join their cause, even at the risk of their own lives. Workers also became aware of the importance of forging good relations with other sectors of the population. They thus appealed to the army to recognize workers' patriotism and thanked the general population for its support and advised it to keep children safely off the streets at tense moments. They also practiced bringing their struggles to the attention of foreigners and the international media. They perfected the art of crafting an agreement among themselves and formulating it in writing. They learned to prioritize their demands and to push for the most important, including the demand for independent unions, which required them to envision something that did not yet exist and that the authorities would view as extremely threatening.

Workers' years of experience doing workplace politics also imparted useful, though sometimes costly, lessons about their adversaries and about themselves. Authorities either passed the buck or lied. They said, promised, and intimated one thing but then did another. They offered repeated proof that they considered workers' lives less valuable than the retention of their own power.[27] At the same time, Polish workers periodically rediscovered that collective activity paid off, even when the gains turned out to be less permanent and less significant than they had hoped. As the decades marched inexorably toward the showdown of 1980, Polish workers saw price hikes rescinded, the country's top leadership overturned, unions temporarily reformed, layoffs retracted, and the enactment of new policies that bettered their wages and their working and living conditions. But beyond this, workers learned some more subtle lessons about one another as individuals, upon which the success of their next action sometimes hinged—who did what well and not so well, who could be counted on for what, who had the personality for which tasks.[28] Workers also learned who they most trusted to lead them. Thus, as occurred on a much smaller scale in many GDR *Kollektive,* a working-class counter-leadership was developing in the decades before Solidarity. By 1980, some of these worker leaders were veterans in this role, having emerged decades earlier in self- rather than party- or union-identified shop floor actions.[29]

In sum, even though Polish workers did not have practice doing workplace politics through established unions, as GDR workers often did in their *Kollektive,* this did not mean that they lacked such experience altogether. Quite the contrary. The political practice Polish workers obtained through independent actions spanning decades was quite extensive. Each time Polish workers took on their superiors, they became more confident both as individuals and as a collective, more politically skilled, better organized and informed, clearer about what they wanted and more determined to get it, more inspired by their previous successes, better led, and at once stronger, more united, and less innocent about the use and abuse of power. This is not to say that Polish workers acquired this impressive array of knowledge and abilities uniformly, quickly, easily, in logical order, or without interruption.[30] Nonetheless, their experience doing workplace politics before 1980 was quantitatively and qualitatively different from that of workers in the GDR, and as a consequence, so was their level of political activism in 1980.

Middle-Class Homogeneity, Interclass Contact, and Working-Class Activism in Poland

Polish workers' more extensive practice doing workplace politics cannot alone account for their far greater activism. The nature of their relationship with the Polish intelligentsia also contributed to their higher level of involvement in the political crisis that eventually brought socialism to its knees. The story here is a complex and, at times, a subtle one.

In chapters 1 and 5, I argued that the relationship between the working class and the intelligentsia in the GDR had long been characterized by three features that acted to dampen working-class predilections to activism. Two of these—workers' perception of the intelligentsia as homogenous and the paucity of contact between workers and intellectuals—are the focus of this section. Since the Polish working class displayed a far greater penchant for activism, could this be partially explained by differences in these two characteristics of class relations? As it turns out the answer to this question is both yes and no. In some respects, the relationship between workers and intellectuals in Poland was very much like that in the GDR along these two dimensions. It was not identical, however, and the difference not only was enough to neutralize some of the deactivating impacts of class on workers' politics that we observed in the GDR but also directly and indirectly helped sustain and strengthen working-class activism in Poland at decisive moments and in particular ways.

Let us begin with interclass contact. I argued in chapter 5 that GDR workers and intellectuals had little contact with one another before the *Wende*. They simply did not live much of their lives in one another's company. In the GDR, many of the networks and organizations of civil society, from the most to the least state-controlled, provided specific and consequential examples of how this was so. A good number of these networks and organizations were dominated by the middle class, and few workers had much to do with their activities.

Pre-1980 Poland looked fairly similar. Many authors have referred to the fact that ties between the two classes were not plentiful. Michael Kennedy cited studies claiming informal contacts were class endogenous; George Kolankiewicz and George Gömöri suggested interaction between the managerial and cultural intelligentsia and workers was limited; Marc Weinstein noted that even those who disagreed on the importance of intellectuals for the events of 1980 concurred that the two classes "moved in different social orbits" before that time; and Lawrence Goodwyn likewise insisted that twenty-five years before Solidarity, intellectuals of opposite political persuasion "shared an enormous distance from the realities of life in the working class."[31] Just as in the GDR, another indication of the want of contact between the classes was that many civil society networks and organizations were dominated by the middle class.[32] As an example of how extensive these were, a document regarding censorship, authored by opposition intellectuals, listed no less than sixteen groupings of largely intellectual membership, sometimes in the thousands, to which the document could be forwarded.[33] Also reminiscent of the GDR, and partly an outgrowth of these types of class-homogenous involvements, many intellectuals forged dense, cohesive, and class-exclusive friendship networks in pre-1980 Poland.[34]

Despite these similarities, there was one important difference between the two countries in terms of interclass contact. In the GDR, the two classes lived largely segregated lives at the same time that members of the intelligentsia occupied a variety of social spaces where they engaged in regular, sustained, and often intimate contact with their class peers. In Poland, this was also true, but something else was also going on. Not only intellectuals but also workers inhabited social spaces in which they passed hours in one another's exclusive presence. These spaces could not be described as formal groups, but that does not mean they were unorganized or haphazard. It only means their existence is harder to uncover and to depict. These were the very spaces workers invented or appropriated in the course of doing politics alongside their class peers for the more than three decades before they actually formed a national independent union. The significant point here is that these were Polish workers' own spaces. They did not share them with intellectuals. In fact, they expended a good deal of effort making sure they did not have to share them. They were class-homogenous spaces that were not duplicated in either extent or kind on the west bank of the Oder, where working-class history before the *Wende* had not been one of widespread working-class political engagement.

Glimpses of these working-class social spaces dot the works of many interested in Polish workers' politics in the decades preceding 1980. From these accounts, spaces of working-class interaction and activity begin to assume some tangible form. We learn, for example, that for years they were as inchoate as workers' kitchen tables, where long before many "actions" had been taken, family members, neighbors, friends, and workmates mumbled and gesticulated as they related their grievances, talked about their goals, and shared their ideas for achieving them.[35] They were the working-class high-rise apartments and neighborhoods across Poland, such as Stogi, which Lawrence Goodwyn described as "Wałęsa's terrain" and where largely workers peopled the sidewalks, stairwells, and open areas.[36] Here, in the course of everyday encounters, small groups of workers shared feelings and ideas about what they wanted and what needed to be done, without attracting much attention. In Gdańsk, they were the trams and buses crowded with workers going back and forth between their jobs and their neighborhoods, where conversations occurred and where later on even leafletting took place, once it was certain the conductor was sympathetic. Beyond all else, they were the workplaces, where workers conversed, argued, planned, and imagined with one another. During the thousands of ordinary workdays before August 1980, only parts of the workplace at certain times could actually be said to be "intellectual-free" zones—locker rooms and meal breaks, for instance. Yet during the extraordinary workdays when Polish workers staged occupation strikes, of which there were more than a few before 1980, workplaces could truly be described as working-class spaces. During these periods in these places, hour upon hour, sometimes day after day, workers made their own decisions and their own mistakes, organized and amused themselves, and did the work they decided needed doing. Intellectuals of all stripes, whether bosses, writers, party figures, professors, economic planners, or priests, were largely absent.

The decades-long creation and utilization of these working-class social spaces, which again were comparatively absent in the GDR, fueled working-class activism in Poland in various ways. These class-homogenous social spaces were the ones in which Polish workers could best discover and then develop their own strengths, reinforce one another's confidence, refine their own priorities, recognize and work through their own conflicts, and forge a successful solidarity in spite of them. Outside these socially segregated places, it was far more difficult to do many of these things well. In the company of members of the intelligentsia, who, whether consciously or not, ordered them about, patronized them, reminded them of their inadequacies, and questioned their goals and tactics,[37] workers found their attention continuously diverted from such pursuits, to the detriment of their activist politics.

Subordinate social groups in many places at many times—African Americans, Indians in Guatemala, women in the United States—have cherished and protected such socially homogenous spaces as sites of renewal, political creativity, and healing, and they have recognized them to be essential underpinnings of the social movements they have built. Those outside these spaces the nonprivileged create or appropriate as their own are often bewildered, distressed, and angered at their exclusion. Be this as it may, for the Polish working class, as for many other disadvantaged groups, political activism flourished within, because of, and alongside such segregated spaces. When these spaces are few or nonexistent, as in the GDR, noninvolvement or passive involvement is a more common political response among the nonprivileged.

Ironically, when we turn to a second element of the class relationship, we are confronted with the fact that while segregated working-class spaces proved a boon to workers' activism in Poland, working-class activism also benefited from collaboration with intellectuals. By collaboration, I do not refer to a situation in which intellectuals led and workers played a subordinate political role. Nor do I allude to one in which workers and intellectuals became equal partners in a joint political endeavor. Instead, I mean that working-class activism developed and thrived in Poland because workers remained in charge of the movement, at the same time they were able successfully to solicit and reject aid from the intelligentsia. That is to say, working-class activism in Poland was strengthened to the extent that it could draw on valuable skills and resources of the intelligentsia. Polish workers were able to do this in 1980 because they did not view the intelligentsia, whether managers, artists, party authorities, oppositionists, engineers, or doctors, as uniform. In other words, while their GDR counterparts perceived the intelligentsia as largely homogenous, Polish workers were able to discern cracks in the intellectual facade.

Had they been unable to do so, their level of activism probably would have been less pronounced and their success less phenomenal.

But why were Polish workers' perceptions of the intelligentsia different from those of GDR workers in this regard? After all, when we scrutinize the boundaries between the political and other segments of the intelligentsia in Poland, we see numerous reasons why Polish and GDR workers might have shared the view of middle-class homogeneity. Considering the relationship between the technical intelligentsia and the political elite, Michael Kennedy described the 1970s as a period of "professionalization" of the latter group. To enhance its own waning legitimacy, the political elite welcomed professionals into the policy-making and governance fold, and some even began to boast scientific degrees, whether they had earned them or not. In return for "mingling with the authorities and acknowledging their professionalism," the technical intelligentsia was awarded substantial material privileges, thereby heightening its dependence on the political elite.[38] In short, the distinction between "expert" and "Red" became nearly meaningless in 1970s Poland,[39] which many of the country's increasingly politicized workers surely understood.

It would have been equally difficult for Polish workers to detect much of a difference between the country's managerial elite and its political elite. For one thing, the majority of Polish managers, especially those at the highest levels, had also been party members throughout the 1950s, 1960s, and 1970s.[40] Even those managers who were not outright party members were beholden to the party for their appointment, retention, and advancement. Again, this was especially the case at higher levels of management. Yet Michael Kennedy noted regular gift exchanges between political authorities and managers; Jean Woodall dismissed the notion that many managers were eager to challenge the party; and Roman Laba reported that workers in 1970 called for taking the enterprise director and the party committee hostage in the same breath,[41] all observations that suggest it was hard for workers to distinguish between political and managerial intellectuals, regardless of the latter's position in the workplace hierarchy.

Even though I could uncover no reason why Polish workers would not also have viewed the relationship between the political elite and additional subgroups of the intelligentsia in a similar fashion, there was one group of intellectuals who did appear to have been cut from a different mold. These were the oppositional intellectuals. I have no intention of arguing that Polish oppositional intellectuals saw eye-to-eye with workers on all matters, that they ever fully understood what workers needed and preferred, or that they shared those needs and preferences. Nor do I want to leave the impression that they never patronized workers, that they never gave workers poor advice, or that they never put their class interests before those of workers. The scholarship of Roman Laba and Lawrence Goodwyn,[42] as well as even a surface familiarity with the history of worker-intellectual relations in Poland after 1980, quickly disabuses one of such ideas. Nonetheless, in the five years preceding the events of 1980, opposition intellectuals cooperated with the working class in a number of ways and on a variety of occasions. In so doing, Poland's oppositional intellectuals distinguished themselves from other segments of the intelligentsia, and Polish workers took note of this. In other words, many Polish workers had been unable, for at least five years before 1980, to consider all intellectuals exactly alike, and, as they cautiously began to accept the presence of some of these relatively privileged citizens alongside them in their struggles, their movement benefited, even as their view of intellectual homogeneity was further diluted.

Most observers trace the beginning of the story of interclass political cooperation in Poland to the period immediately following the 1976 strikes. The intelligentsia was absent from the strikes themselves, but when workers began to be arrested and imprisoned for their participation in them, a small group of ideologically diverse intellectuals founded KOR (Committee for the Defense of Workers), which eventually included hundreds of people. Until amnesty was declared approximately one year later, KOR devoted itself to ending the persecution of workers involved in the 1976 disturbances. It attempted this using a variety of tactics, including staging hunger strikes, organizing national and international appeals campaigns, providing legal assistance and child care, showing up at workers' trials, writing and circulating informational bulletins that publicized the deceptive conduct of the state in these proceedings, and providing medical aid to people who had been beaten. KOR also raised money to support families of workers who were unemployable because of their political activity. Within four months after the strikes, KOR was regularly supporting ninety-eight such families, and several hundred families were being aided throughout 1977. Intellectuals also came forward with financial support for Lech Wałęsa's family, allowing him to devote himself to full-time organizing, and they provided him legal support when he got into trouble for doing so.[43]

In 1976 intellectuals, particularly those associated with KOR, also began publicizing workers' actions to the international media and human rights groups and, just as important, throughout Poland itself. "Thin as it was," wrote Lawrence Goodwyn, "[KOR's] network of activists across Poland had now been placed in the service of the working-class movement."[44] Later, KOR helped start several dozen publications, targeting various sectors of the Polish population, among these *Robotnik*. Directed to workers, *Robotnik* appeared bimonthly, beginning in 1977. Within a year of its appearance, it had a printed circulation of twenty thousand, and presumably many more than that number read it.[45] Among other things, *Robotnik* spread information about workplace protest actions across the country.

Through some of these activities, intellectuals also helped keep workers' fight for independent unions alive between 1976 and 1980. Then, between 1977 and 1979, small independent union groups were actually formed in at least five different locations, and these included intellectuals, as well as some worker members who had been important leaders in 1970 or would emerge as prominent leaders in 1980. Wałęsa, for one, was inspired by an intellectual publication to take this step, and the Baltic Coast independent union group he joined soon issued its own publication, the *Coastal Worker*, a useful recruiting device. Worker-intellectual cooperation continued right up to the events of mid-August 1980. At least one intellectual, who had worked closely with workers for some time, helped plan these protests, and the editors of *Robotnik* and the independent union group from the Baltic cosigned the leaflet that appeared on the buses and trams carrying workers to their jobs on Thursday, August 14, the first day of strike action.[46]

Cross-class political activities such as these of the late 1970s facilitated working-class activism in 1980 in a number of ways. At the intellectual level, the multiple writing and publishing activities of opposition intellectuals, as well as their increasingly frequent personal conversations with workers, helped workers clarify the complex connections between their daily work lives, firm economic realities, and the broader political and economic system in People's Poland.[47] On the psychological plane, the direct aid middle-class people provided workers and the role a few intellectuals played in urging the formation of independent unions boosted workers' spirits at discouraging junctures. Lawrence Goodwyn was especially clear about this. The 1978 formation of a free trade union on the coast, he wrote, was "a genuine shot in the arm" for Wałęsa. "After years of going it alone," it presented Wałęsa with what he called "my first taste of genuine human solidarity."[48] One can not quantify what such moral support meant to Wałęsa or other less famous Polish workers. Yet in whatever ways it helped counteract the fear, self-doubt, and despair that are the constant companions of those facing the political odds they did, it was of great benefit.

There was also a practical and strategic facet of the assistance Polish oppositional intellectuals lent worker activists in the late 1970s. The material aid they provided persecuted workers and their families, including Wałęsa himself, protected and encouraged worker activists, permitting them to continue their political activity, despite the periodic repression they faced. The hours intellectuals devoted to helping organize independent union committees kept these worker-inspired organizations alive as more than mere ideas. Their publications, as well as their ability and willingness to spread information about workers' actions in person, opened fissures in the state-erected barriers separating workers in different parts of Poland, allowing those in one location to gain inspiration from what those in others were doing. Finally, their work at the beginning of August helped ensure that the August 14 strike came off successfully. Had it failed, Solidarity may well have been a much longer time in coming.

Workers themselves, of course, were the primary generators of their own activism in 1980. They recruited one another to the movement, they organized their own actions, they formulated their own goals, and their revolutionary consciousness was a product of their own reflections on their own life experiences. Nonetheless, in the latter half of the 1970s, oppositional intellectuals of many ideological and organizational affiliations provided repeated evidence that they were serious about political cooperation with workers and that they were willing to risk a good deal to bring it about. Joint class action never came easily in Poland. It was hard to overcome the distrust and animosity bred of the huge gap in social standing, experience, and understanding separating workers from intellectuals. But whenever during the late 1970s this could be accomplished, whenever the abilities and resources oppositional intellectuals had acquired by virtue of their privileged position could be marshaled in the service of the social majority, working-class activism, present and future, was the winner. Viewed another way, Polish workers and oppositional intellectuals, unlike their GDR counterparts, had constructed a joint history of political cooperation in the years before 1980. This common history, however abbreviated, was both the cause and the effect of Polish workers' readiness to judge specific intellectuals by their actions instead of lumping all intellectuals together in the company of the political elite, as GDR workers were wont to do.

The imprint of this prior history together was clear in mid-August 1980. Opposition intellectuals supported the workers' movement in many ways once it arose. They were elected to the Interfactory Strike Committee and to its leadership; they published a strike information bulletin; they accepted posts as expert advisers; and they helped secure food for the strikers. Intellectuals were also trusted in the dangerous but essential courier role, shuttling messages and back and forth across the country. Electronics engineers devised an apparatus allowing shipyard workers to eavesdrop on police communications; an artist created the Solidarity logo; intellectuals wrote and delivered manifestos of support to the workers; they drafted union statutes for the Baltic Coast region;[49] some largely intellectual workplaces (administration, commerce, education, health) actively joined the strike. Intellectuals also kept Polish workers' struggles in the international limelight.

Throughout the late 1970s, working-class activism had received periodic infusions of strength from joint worker-intellectual engagement, paving the way for this historically rare level of interclass cooperation in 1980. For all its frailty and for all the immediate and subsequent difficulties that can be traced to it, this 1980 alliance helped workers seize the political reins and hold onto them well into the following year. As they had been able to for several years, Polish workers in 1980 and 1981 were successfully able to solicit aid from the intelligentsia and to accept or reject such aid on their own terms and according to their own calculations of its strategic value. As I have said before, this advantageous position was both a cause and an effect of Polish workers' unwillingness to view all intellectuals uniformly. The contrast with the GDR in 1989–90 could not be more pronounced. There, few workers joined the intellectual challenge to socialism, few responded to intellectuals who encouraged them to become politically active on their own, and few sought help from intellectuals when they did initiate their own actions. Workers' overriding experience of the GDR intelligentsia as homogenous in the years leading up to the *Wende* helped prevent most from doing so.

The Labor Process, the Class Divide, and Working-Class Activism in Poland

The two final elements of my explanation for GDR workers' politics during the *Wende* concerned the labor process and workers' perception of a difference between their lives and those of the intelligentsia. In the final pages of this chapter, I examine how these two elements also affected the political behavior of the Polish working class approximately ten years earlier. In so doing, I underscore the following point: in both places, forces that were politically enervating and forces that were politically invigorating emanated simultaneously from the labor process and from workers' perception of the class divide. Both elements thus harbored the *potential* to encourage and to discourage working-class activism. Their actual impact therefore depended on the complex of other influences on workers' politics alongside which they operated in both countries.

Consider first the labor process and how it hampered working-class activism. Shortage was an endemic feature of the economy of Poland as well as the GDR. Largely as a consequence, hard work was also a feature of Polish, as well as GDR, workers' experience of the labor process. In Poland, the normal work week remained six days throughout the 1970s; long overtime hours were clearly mandatory (it was common for about 80 percent of shipyard workers to clock overtime); and storming regularly left workers in drastic need of "rest and repair."[50]

Just as in the GDR, hard work occurred in the context of a horribly disorganized labor process. At the Baltic shipyards, for example, completed jobs had to be redone several times, and by management's own estimates, "Forty to 60 hours of every workers' monthly work time was routinely spent looking for or waiting for material, parts, and tools. The shipyard was a traffic jam of workers searching and bargaining for needed materials."[51] Elsewhere, such production inputs routinely arrived so late or in such insufficient quantity that work operations were severely disrupted. As a result, Polish workers, like those in the GDR, harbored feelings of deep frustration and ineffectiveness, which in turn thwarted their activist inclinations.

Hard work also transpired in the context of pervasive dishonesty, in which Polish workers, like GDR workers, were sometimes complicit. Boastful proclamations of record production therefore contrasted sharply with what workers knew was happening at their workplaces; whatever the original impetus, the multiple forums set up to encourage workers' participation in management (production meetings, workers' councils, conferences on workers' self-management) soon came to be viewed as charades;[52] and the informal bargains management commonly struck with workers, some of which went so far as to allow petty pilfering in exchange for meeting production quotas,[53] only added to the web of fabrications encircling the workplace. Such experiences mocked and obscured Polish workers' hard-won accomplishments, thereby helping squelch activist tendencies in their ranks.

Finally, as in the GDR, the Polish remuneration and discipline systems went a long way toward uncoupling reward, effort, and outcome. Egregious cases of indiscipline went unsanctioned, which was a very sore spot for Polish workers;[54] remuneration calculations were so complex and bonuses awarded so automatically that they bore no discernible connection to effort; piece rates were described as ad hoc; and norms, with overfulfillment rates averaging 140 percent and sometimes reaching 300 percent, were nonsensical as indicators of good work justly rewarded.[55] This situation demoralized Polish workers, as it did GDR workers, fostering a paralyzing indifference and cynicism antithetical to activism.

At the same time, however, the labor process also functioned to promote activism in the Polish working class. Students of paid work in Poland have provided little direct evidence for this labor process outcome. This is not surprising, however, since most people who have written of paid work in socialist countries have spent too little time at the point of production to be able to recognize this second product of shortage.[56] Nonetheless, shortages were, if anything, more severe in the Polish economy than in the GDR's. If my analysis of how the labor process helped motivate some GDR workers to become politically active is correct, there is no reason to think it would not also have done so in Poland. After all, many of the most active workers in Poland, those on the Baltic Coast, had a decade before 1980 produced enough ocean-going vessels to move Poland to tenth place in the world in tonnage of ships produced, second place in the production of fishing vessels, and fifth place in foreign ship sales.[57] Would it be reasonable to assume Polish workers could have accomplished all this, and much more, given the extreme shortage conditions under which they labored, had they not consistently exercised remarkable resourcefulness and problem-solving capabilities, had they not been multiskilled and possessed a sound knowledge of the entire production process, and, above all, had they not organized and controlled their own labor? In other words, would any of this have been possible if Polish workers had not lived, probably more intensely, the very shortage-induced outcomes of the labor process that would later prove an incentive to political activism for a handful of GDR workers?

Because the labor process made simultaneous contributions to working-class activism and noninvolvement in Poland and the GDR, one might conclude that its overall effect on workers' politics was neutral in both places. But we need to be clear that in neither country did these labor process effects appear in isolation. Rather, they operated within an overall context of mobilizing and demobilizing factors that was quite different in each country. In the GDR, they existed alongside a host of other elements associated with class and workplace politics that *retarded* working-class activism during the *Wende*. In this situation, the labor process outcomes channeling workers toward political withdrawal magnified (and were magnified by) these outcomes of class and workplace politics. The political consequences of the labor process that fostered working-class activism were rendered largely impotent by this powerful combination. Yet in Poland, because of the powerful mix of workplace political and class factors *promoting* activism, the opposite occurred. The invigorating outcomes of the labor process, class, and workplace politics were mutually reinforcing, overwhelming those effects of the labor process that induced workers to turn their backs on activist politics.

In chapter 5, I maintained that GDR workers were acutely aware of the different and more privileged lives led by the intelligentsia. The literature on pre-1980 Poland gives us every reason to think Polish workers were confronted with at least an equal, if not a greater, amount of evidence of a class divide in their country.[58] As in the GDR, this evidence surfaced both at their workplaces and outside of them. For example, reports on the 1970s noted substantial earnings gaps between workers and both the managerial and the technical intelligentsia, and surveys between 1955 and 1980 indicated that Polish workers perceived such gaps to be far too large.[59] Working conditions also exemplified the distance between the two classes. Workers, for example, received fewer vacation days and poorer sick pay, they labored in far more uncomfortable environments (70 percent of the work at the Lenin Shipyards was conducted outside all year long), and working-class participation in workplace decision-making bodies compared badly with that of the intelligentsia.[60] Moreover, Polish workers seemingly were subjected to particularly harsh control strategies at their jobs. "High-handed" and "autocratic," Polish managers, according to George Kolankiewicz, rode "rough-shod over their employees."[61]

Outside the workplace, the contrast between the lives of workers and intellectuals was also stark. In fact, some have singled out the ostentatious consumption and materialistic style of the highest social stratum as the defining feature of the Polish class divide in the 1970s.[62] As examples, members of the Polish intelligentsia resided in better and more spacious quarters, and they shopped in well-stocked stores offering specialty items at artificially low prices, some conveniently located at intellectual workplaces and accepting only hard currency. Polish intellectuals were also the disproportionate beneficiaries of certain categories of social spending. Some received special housing and transportation subsidies; others had access to drugs and health care facilities unavailable to workers; and their children partook of reserved spots in the best educational institutions. Moreover, in the early 1970s, high-ranking government, party, and trade union officials were awarded unlimited retirement benefits that could even be collected by distant kin.[63]

Polish and GDR workers' recognition of the gulf of privilege separating them from the intelligentsia had a two-pronged effect on their politics. On the one hand, the recognition of their own relative deprivation wore workers down. It led to disabling doubts about their own self-worth and paralytic feelings of inferiority, powerlessness, and resignation, in short, to a state of being that was incompatible with political activism. On the other hand, class inequality incensed workers, arousing them to resist it through active political engagement. In other words, anger over class inequality could be a politically constructive passion. Recall that even in the GDR, where working-class activists were relatively few, the imprint of workers' indignation over class difference could be seen in the goals and creations of working-class activists and in the complaints of those passively involved in challenging the status quo as well. They were even more obvious in the working-class protests that racked socialist Poland throughout its history, when, for example, workers demanded income differentials be limited to 2:1; complained to the premier that his wife loaded "ham on her sandwiches, while [their] children [ate] dry bread"; and gleefully watched as the woman whose dismissal precipitated the events of mid-August 1980 was returned to the shipyard in the *director's* car.[64]

As with the labor process, whether the invigorating or the enervating out-

comes of workers' recognition of the class divide surfaced as the more prominent depended on the overall balance of forces affecting workers' politics in
each country. In Poland, workers' extensive practice doing workplace politics, the existence of socially segregated spaces in which they could interact
beyond the watchful eye of intellectuals, and the joint involvement of workers and intellectuals in opposition politics during the last half of the 1970s
all served to advance working-class activism in the summer of 1980. Under
this set of historical circumstances, workers' recognition of class difference
weighed in on the proactivist side of the equation, in the process dwarfing
the ways in which this awareness promoted political inertia. In the pre-1989
GDR, however, workplace politics served, on balance, to dampen working-
class activism. Moreover, the particular form that the absence of class contact assumed left workers without the segregated social spaces conducive to
activism among the socially subordinate. Finally, many GDR workers had
come to view all sectors of the intelligentsia as similar, thereby curtailing their
desire to support strongly any version of middle-class activism during the
Wende. Under this set of very dissimilar conditions, it was the deactivating
outcomes of workers' recognition of the class divide that emerged as the more
powerful, while those encouraging workers to pursue an activist path were
smothered under a thickly layered blanket of political apathy.

Conclusion

The foregoing comparison of Poland and the GDR shows how cross-currents
impelled workers simultaneously toward both activism and political withdrawal. These crosscurrents had three principal, though indiscrete, sources:
the labor process, workplace politics, and class relations. I suspect that an
analogous situation existed in other socialist countries as well. We should
therefore expect levels of political activity (withdrawal, passive participation,
and active engagement) to vary among subsets of workers throughout the
socialist world, just as they did in the GDR and as a closer examination of
Poland would surely reveal. At the same time, the overall balance of mobilizing and demobilizing outcomes of the labor process, workplace politics,
and class is not identical across cases. As a result and as the cases of the GDR
and Poland illustrate, working-class politics in socialist settings will display
substantial variation across time and space.

As I argued in the introduction, the political stories of the GDR and the
Polish working class are relevant beyond the geographic boundaries of each
country and even beyond the borders of the past and current socialist world.
From these stories, activists everywhere who are working to further peace,
equality, democracy, and justice in the broadest sense of these terms can learn

or be reminded of several things useful to their own struggles: doing politics in local everyday worlds, such as workplaces, provides the socially disadvantaged with political skills and experiences indispensable to their political success outside these local arenas; socially segregated spaces, free from the manipulations and distractions of the powerful, strengthen the ability of the socially disadvantaged to begin their challenge and to sustain it over what often turns out to be a very long time; and selective cultivation of particular sectors of the socially privileged and active political engagement alongside them expand the strategic, material, and ideological resources that popular movements have at their command. These resources are only useful, however, so long as these privileged allies do not assume control of movement politics.

Practice doing politics in local worlds, socially segregated spaces, and selective political cooperation with the more privileged are never givens. They are accomplishments realized against long structural and historical odds. Nor is the popular activism that they sustain permanent. The story of Poland after 1981 is bleak testimony to this. Yet even when, as in the GDR, the socially subordinated lack local and everyday political practice, do not inhabit their own socially segregated spaces, are unable and unwilling to cooperate with those among the privileged who might be of genuine assistance, and therefore withdraw from politics, we should not expect this situation to be permanent either. In other words, neither activism nor noninvolvement is the immutable condition of those who have suffered most under current social arrangements and who must be at the forefront of any efforts to alter them in significant ways. This is the lesson, at once hopeful and sobering, that both GDR and Polish workers leave those who would try to promote meaningful social change. The obstacles to success are daunting, yet the hope that it will nonetheless be attempted is not futile.

Appendix: Doing Research in the GDR and the Former GDR

Three major sources of primary data ground this study—face-to-face in-depth interviews, visits to worksites, and documentary evidence published by unions, a variety of groups politically active during the *Wende,* and national, regional, and factory newspapers.

The in-depth interviews, averaging several hours in length, were conducted on three trips to the GDR, two before the revolution (spring/summer 1988 and 1989), and one afterward (fall 1990).[1] Two GDR research assistants conducted additional interviews through the middle of 1991. In all, 112 interviews were completed. The majority of these were conducted with individuals, though occasionally I interviewed several members of a BGL or two workers together. The interviewees, some of whom I reinterviewed on subsequent trips, were workers, union officers, managers, and other members of the intelligentsia. Fifty-eight respondents were men, and thirty-nine were women. On my postrevolutionary trip, I sought to conduct interviews with as many of the people I had originally interviewed, and in as many of the worksites I had previously visited, as possible, but I was only partially successful. Only about half my post-*Wende* interviews were conducted with an individual I had interviewed or at a worksite I had visited before the *Wende.* Post-*Wende* interviews also included some with intellectuals active in the 1989–90 opposition. In all, I visited fifteen GDR worksites, located in Frankfurt Oder, Bernau, Apolda, Berlin, Leipzig, and semirural areas near these cities and towns. I spent between half a day and five days at each site, revisiting four of the fifteen after the *Wende.*

Kran, the newspaper of a transport equipment factory in Leipzig, was among the most useful of the primary written materials I consulted. Forty years old with a readership of forty-five hundred, *Kran* was the only weekly factory newspaper in Leipzig. It appeared throughout the *Wende,* though in late 1989 it ceased being published by the party group in the factory and became the responsibility of the factory administration.[2] About six hundred factory newspapers, with a circulation of approximately 2.5 million, were being published in the GDR immediately before the *Wende.* I was told that even before the *Wende,* factory newspapers attracted the GDR's best journalism students, who had greater editorial freedom in these forums than did reporters in the general circulation press with larger readerships.

As a North American researcher conducting fieldwork in the GDR, I confronted a number of obstacles. The first was repression. Would GDR citizens really speak candidly or act normally if they feared retaliation from the security apparatus or the party? I do not doubt this was a serious consideration for some people I interviewed in 1988 and 1989,[3] just as I also suspect that after the *Wende,* in the prevailing climate of euphoria over the collapse of Communism, some people overestimated their oppositional activism during the revolution, as well as their dissatisfaction with the previous regime.[4]

The fear of repression, whether subtle or overt, posed less difficulty for my research than three other things—ignorance, regimentation, and chaos. The GDR was firmly situated on the "other side" of the cold war chasm separating capitalism and socialism, which has profoundly influenced twentieth-century history in ways that will take years to recognize. As a result, U.S. researchers of the GDR unavoidably began their fieldwork in a state of relative ignorance, for information on the GDR was scant compared with that available on most places on the capitalist side of the divide. I and others like me were simply not prepared to begin our fieldwork the way we would have been had we chosen to do research in France or even the FRG, for instance. As is so often the case, estrangement and ignorance bred arrogance, prejudice, and hostility. Despite notable exceptions, such Western and capitalist hostility, prejudice, and arrogance had permeated too much of the research on the GDR too deeply for it to be of great value in educating me for my fieldwork.[5]

Once in the field, I found the pre-*Wende* regimentation, or hyperformalism and organizational rigidity of the GDR, and the chaos of social life after the revolution the sources of my biggest data-gathering problems. In 1988 and 1989, the tangle of bureaucratic red tape I had to maneuver through before worksite visits, living arrangements, and traveling plans were approved was more than exasperating and slowed my research considerably. Of course, with the right contacts, on which I increasingly relied as I discovered them, and plenty of luck, there were ways to circumvent some of this. But it was not always possible or even desirable to do so. More than once, I learned I had to endure the demands of bureaucratic gatekeepers to put simple requests in writing, to follow cumbersome regulations precisely, to travel across town to have something cross-checked by someone's boss, or to meet with people of peripheral interest to my project, before I was left alone to talk with whomever I wanted or to wander unaccompanied wherever I pleased around a work center.

In 1990, the biggest problem I encountered in my fieldwork was in some ways the reverse of the stifling regimentation with which I had to reckon before the *Wende*. Social chaos reigned in the GDR in October and November 1990. As a consequence, I had tremendous difficulty locating most of the people I had previously interviewed, since many had lost their jobs and had dispersed hither and yon around the country. Worksites I had visited were shut permanently or temporarily, and work force and management turnover was extremely high. Worst of all, the sudden and near total disintegration of familiar GDR social, political, and economic institutions and arrangements produced in many a deep fear and insecurity about their own, their family's, and their community's welfare.[6] Pervasive fear and insecurity were tied, I became convinced, to the startling number of physical ailments and accidental injuries among the people I interviewed, which in several instances interfered with my interviews. Many people, including some I had known and interviewed previously, also seemed depressed. They spoke less and more quietly, and it was often harder to engage their energy and attention during interviews than it had been before the *Wende*. In the most extreme instance, I discovered one man bedridden in a darkened room, where he had lain since late spring 1990, with no detectable physical problem. An interview under such circumstances was clearly out of the question.

There is no doubt that ignorance, regimentation, social chaos, and the fear of repression negatively affected my ability to collect some data, and they should surely heighten concerns over the validity of the data I was able to gather.[7] There was no magic solution to these problems, largely because they were the product of forces far from my control. My major recourse turned out to be patience and persistence, as well as the time necessary to exercise both. If I was patient and persistent, some people trusted me enough to decide that speaking to a North American researcher was worth the risk it could entail. Patience and persistence were required to uncover that rare documentary source, which, though infrequently cited, offered revealing glimpses into the lives of GDR workers relatively undistorted by the ideological fallout of the cold war. Patience and persistence were also necessary to endure more easily the (to me) unreasonable demands of bureaucratic gatekeepers and to be allowed to pursue my research as I saw fit. Finally, patience and persistence helped me try harder and longer to engage people who were socially and emotionally adrift, thereby acquiring a deeper appreciation of the intersection of their personal biographies with the tumultuous slice of history through which they had lived.

Notes

Introduction

1. On the extent to which these events caught the world off guard, see Kuran (1991:7–13).

2. See the appendix for details of my methodology.

3. Dorothy Smith (1987), whose work I discuss in chapter 1; Harding (1986, 1991); and Collins (1990) are important examples.

4. Discussions of the centrality or potential centrality of the working class to social change in socialist societies run the gamut from ones that entirely discounted workers' importance to ones that argued progressive change would not occur unless workers were at the forefront of the process. For examples, see Bahro (1978:149, 327–28); Burawoy and Lukács quoting Adam Michnik (1992:111); Connor (1981:159–61); Offe (1991:26); Reißig (1992:34); Lewin (1988:124); Kennedy (1991:191–97, 286–89, 337–48); and Konrád and Szelényi (1979:220, 232, 246).

5. Slavs and other minorities constituted only 0.3 percent of the population (Keefe [1982:xx]). A few thousand guest workers lived in the country (McFalls [1992a:21]). Between 48.0 percent and 50.1 percent of the labor force was female during the two decades preceding the revolution (Staatliche Zentralverwaltung für Statistik [1988: 17]). Although the GDR working class was predictably heterogeneous along other axes, such as age, skill level, and economic sector of employment, the logic of this paragraph applies to these differentiations as well.

6. For discussion of the history of this term, see Philipsen (1993:5–6). Although there is debate over whether the *Wende* should be thought of as a revolution, I use the two terms synonymously to connote a forcible process through which a complete change in a political, social, and economic system is realized.

7. Over the course of the *Wende,* some individual workers moved between these three groups.

8. The most significant of these included the CDU (Christian Democratic Union), the LDPD (Liberal Democratic Party of Germany), the DA (Democratic Awakening), the DSU (German Social Union), the SPD-DDR (Social Democratic Party of Germany in the GDR), and the PDS (Party of Democratic Socialism). The CDU was one of the GDR's Block parties, which had all been financed by the ruling SED (Socialist Unity Party of Germany) and guaranteed a percentage of the seats in the national legislature. The CDU left the Block in December 1989, as did the LDPD. DA grew out of church protests in the summer of 1989 and organized itself as a political party in December 1989. The DSU, closely allied with the CSU (Christian Social Union) in the FRG, held its first party congress in February 1990. The SPD-DDR was founded in October 1989. The PDS, successor of the SED, was formed in December 1989.

9. Neugebauer (1990b:29). See also Greenwald's (1993:282) anecdotal recollection of this shift.

10. Together the SPD and the CDU/DA/DSU alliance polled 70 percent of the vote. The PDS ran alone and polled 16 percent. The LDPD joined other smaller parties in the campaign, eventually garnering 5 percent of the vote. Neues Forum and Demokratie Jetzt ran in alliance with another citizens' opposition group and received 3 percent of the vote. Vereinigte Linke, allied with an independent Marxist group, received less than 1 percent (Hanhardt [1990:appendix 2]). See also Neugebauer (1990b:30).

Chapter 1: Everyday Worlds of Work and Class

1. Dennis (1991:12) quoting Irene Böhme. See also Belwe and Klinger (1986:62); Keefe (1982:88); Frowen (1985:34); Rueschemeyer and Scharf (1986:76); and Wierling (1996:54).

2. Dorothy Smith (1987:82). I substituted the sentences "Here she is bored." through "Here she cooperates with others and makes fast friends." for "Here she gives birth. It is a place she dies in." in Smith's original text.

3. Ibid., 56. See also ibid., 2, 3, and 109. Does Smith's emphasis on beginning sociology from the everyday, from where people actually are instead of from the perspective of the extralocal ruling apparatus, really boil down to an argument that researchers can profitably study only people socially like themselves? I think not, even though social congruence between researcher and researched is in many ways advantageous and in some research situations even essential. Social congruence with those being studied does not necessarily prevent researchers from beginning from the perspective of the extralocal ruling apparatus, nor does the absence of such congruence ensure their inability to begin from the everyday world in which those they are studying exist. In any case, it is not easy to do sociology as Smith advises, and although I know I have not always succeeded, I have tried to keep her counsel in the forefront of my mind through the conceptualization, fieldwork, analysis, and writing stages of this project.

4. Ibid., 90, 111, 134. The phrases in square brackets are mine but, in my reading of Smith, true to her overall argument.

5. Ibid., 94.

6. I refer to workers who were members but not leaders of the SED, together with low-level union officers, as worker leaders (see chapter 8). A frequently noted problem with official GDR class categorizations was that people were often designated as workers, no matter what their current job or position, merely because they were from a working-class background. In contrast, my class categorization scheme is based on current activity alone. For some discussion of the elasticity of official working-class categorizations, see Baylis (1978:89); Klier (1990:160–61); Neugebauer (1990a:8); and Konrád and Szelényi (1979:176–78).

7. Meier (1987b:16) noted that 15–20 percent of the posts requiring a university degree were occupied by those without higher education.

8. Class assignment is also difficult because Marx's original conception of class pertained largely to capitalist societies.

9. Figures calculated from Staatliche Zentralverwaltung für Statistik (1988:6, 17). For further information, see Erbe (1979b:416–17). In 1987, 15 percent of those employed in industry, 14 percent of those in construction, and 9 percent of those in agriculture had technical college or university degrees (Staatliche Zentralverwaltung für Statistik [1988:23, 33, 186]). These percentages varied at the plant level as well. One estimate of the proportion of "managers, economists, engineers, and the like" at a Baltic shipyard at the time of the *Wende* was 33 percent (interview in Berlin, fall 1990). According to another calculation, almost 50 percent of employees in GDR industry were white-collar workers (*Angestellten*) (*IUG*, February 1, 1990, 11). Wierling (1996:54) noted that at the end of the 1980s, about 40 percent of workers worked primarily with their hands, not at machines.

10. See, for example, Glaeßner (1988:6); Glaeßner (1986:19), and Scharf (1984:147).

11. Some of the people Zierke (1993:11–12) identified as members of the alternative political subculture in Brandenburg would be examples.

12. On the superelite, see Scharf (1984:154–55); Gleye (1991:197); and Dennis (1988: 54–55). On the party or party-related elite, see Minnerup (1982:15); Keefe (1982:81, 82); and Weber (1988:99).

13. Quoted in Hancock (1978:134). See also Dennis (1991:3, 4, 8).

14. Bahro (1978:200). More research began to be conducted, particularly in the last decades of the GDR's existence, that discriminated among different social strata. Much of it called attention to the intelligentsia, which came to be seen by some as a distinguishable social stratum, though not a separate class. As one GDR academic told me, "Class relations became more complex as socialism developed. Stratification deepened in various ways. That was a surprise to us, because we had assumed the opposite" (interview in Berlin, summer 1988). On the ongoing refinement of GDR research on social structure, as well as the debates accompanying it, see Scharf (1984:146–47); Dennis (1988:48–49, 51–53); Dennis (1991:6–11); Zimmermann (1978: 18); Glaeßner (1986); and Glaeßner (1988). Despite what Glaeßner (1986:19) termed a "long and unresolved debate" over whether class or stratification models could best

describe GDR society, the value of much GDR research on social structure was diminished by the tendency to classify as many people as possible, and many more than was usually sensible, as workers.

15. Opp, Voss, and Gern (1995:184) appear to fall in this camp. Kornai (1992:40–1) made a comparable distinction, though he preferred the terms *apparatus* and *bureaucracy* to *ruling elite*. See also Ticktin's (1992:64–65) discussion. Some of Philipsen's (1993:172, 251) interviews with middle-class revolutionary activists revealed that they, too, were partial to this model.

16. Bahro (1978:esp. chap. 6); Ticktin (1992:84). Others have also used the content of labor performed to differentiate classes but have focused on job titles or positions, levels of skill or training, or economic sector of employment. See, for example, Teckenberg (1990).

17. Bahro (1978:esp. chap. 7, 320).

18. Ibid., 326–27.

19. Ticktin (1992:61).

20. Bourdieu (1991) seemed to concur on this point.

21. Konrád and Szelényi (1979:222). In a later publication, Szelényi (1986–87) said that their earlier contention that the political elite was merging with the rest of the intelligentsia, something they called the "New Class Project," had suffered "significant setbacks" after the mid-1970s, partly because the political elite resisted joining forces with the rest of the intelligentsia more forcefully than they had predicted. Despite this reformulation, Szelényi (1986–87:140, 141) concluded that the New Class Project "is still not altogether impossible" and that it may indeed "be in the making in Eastern Europe."

22. Kennedy (1991). My discussion does not pretend to include all the important work dealing with class or class-like differentiations in socialist societies. For related discussions of interest, see Keefe (1982); and Staniszkis (1992). Income, one common indicator of class and status differences under capitalism, is occasionally mentioned as a criterion for differentiating social groupings under socialism. Likewise, though more work is being done that distinguishes classes under capitalism on the basis of such things as culture, lifestyle, consciousness, communication, values, and belief systems (e.g., Lamont [1992] and Huspek [1994]), this approach to the study of the social structures of the countries of East and Central Europe was not highly developed by the late 1980s. Bahro's (1978) discussion of consciousness and surplus consciousness was an exception. See also Rakovski (1978:esp. chap. 3), for whom the intellectuals of interest in one section were defined as those intellectual workers who "are in regular contact with the process of cultural and scientific creation" and who are thus able to participate in a web of relatively institutionalized communication spheres. In contrast, workers were those "not linked by a network of communication comparable to that which makes the intelligentsia a coherent cultural entity . . ." (Rakovski [1978:43, 65]). Kennedy (1991:esp. chap. 5) was also relevant here.

23. My focus is the ongoing reproduction of class rather than the sometimes, though not necessarily, related topic of social mobility, that is, the movement or lack of movement of individuals back and forth across class boundaries. For information

on social mobility in the GDR, see Dennis (1988:53); Keefe (1982:83); and Krejci (1976:95–118).

24. These four do not exhaust the list of the nodal points implicated in class reproduction. For example, both Bahro (1978) and Haas (1988) suggested that the labor process itself, as distinct from the occupational structure, was an important site in and from which class was reproduced in the GDR. Other authors have assigned the following a role in class reproduction: ideology and principles (Burawoy and Lukás [1992:82–83, 147–48]; Kennedy [1991:202–7]); internally and externally imposed coercion and self-censorship (Konrád and Szelényi [1979:189, 246, 248]; Minnerup [1982:22, 24]; Kennedy [1991:198, 222, 359]); selective use of incentives to divide and weaken various social groups and to reward political loyalty (Konrád and Szelényi [1979:217–18]; Kennedy [1991:226–28]); and economic growth, efficiency, and reforms (Ticktin [1992:62]; Altvater [1981:5, 7, 8, 9]).

25. Glaeßner (1986:20).

26. For details of these programs, see Steele (1977:176); Baylis (1974:45, 47, 48); Glaeßner (1984); Zimmermann (1978:29); Minnerup (1982:23); Scharf (1984:109–10); Page (1985); and Keefe (1982:92–95).

27. Steele (1977:176); Page (1985:60). Klier (1990:161–62), however, argued that the figures for the 1970s were the partial result of gross distortions in the determination of students' class.

28. For example, see Scharf (1984:157); Steele (1977:176); Grote (1979:192); and Fulbrook (1991:231).

29. Kornai (1992:329). At the same time, Jugel, Spangenberg, and Stollberg (1978:59–60) found that high school achievement was significantly poorer among students with two parents engaged in shift work. Most people doing shift work in the GDR were from the working class.

30. Haas (1988:33). On some of these issues, see also Bahro (1978:178–82); Zimmermann (1978:29); G. E. Edwards (1985:26–29); Scharf (1984:152, 156); Scharf (1989:18); Klier (1990); and Erbe (1979b:420).

31. On these points, see Page (1985:55); Klier (1990:150–57); Steele (1977:177); and G. E. Edwards (1985:8–12).

32. Klier (1990:153–66). Recall that only 21 percent of the GDR population had technical college or university degrees.

33. Baylis (1995:246).

34. See also Bahro (1978:212); Keefe (1982:83, 170); Scharf (1984:140); Zimmermann (1984:30); Zierke (1993:11); Bourdieu (1991:37); and Joppke (1995:52). For how politics played out in school admission processes for artists, see Rueschemeyer (1991:39). Page (1985:61) also noted that SED members dominated class and school parent-teacher associations.

35. Klier (1990:152, 160, 165).

36. Scharf (1984:42) reported, "More than fifty percent of SED recruits have just graduated from a university or technical college." See also ibid., 43.

37. See Neugebauer (1990a:9); Neugebauer (1991:5); Erbe (1979b:419); Keefe (1982:170); Zimmermann (1984:17, 30–31); and Weber (1985:8–9, 79).

38. Zimmermann (1984:93–94). See also Schröter (1992:6).

39. Scharf (1984:47). Klier (1990:165) reported that people were especially likely to make the nomenclature if both their parents had earned university degrees.

40. Kennedy (1991:385); Weber (1988:99). Other individuals besides party members could also be listed, but they were the exceptions.

41. Bahro (1978:215); Konrád and Szelényi (1979:150–51). See also Granick (1975:166); Fulbrook (1991:224); Schröter (1992:6); Meier (1987b:1); Haas (1988); Konrád and Szelényi (1979:26); and Erbe (1979b:414). The family was also implicated in the job-education loop. College credentials served as a proxy for ensuring that holders of certain positions possessed not only particular intellectual and technical abilities but also, under the guise of merit and universalism, a complex of distinctly middle-class cultural traits inculcated through the family long before a person's college days.

42. Konrád and Szelényi (1979:151 [quotes], 224).

43. Schröter (1992:8); Granick (1975:457–59). In earlier years, before it was the norm for top managers to have university or technical college degrees, it was possible for such people to earn these credentials while serving in their managerial posts. Granick (1975:458–59) was also impressed with the extensive career planning, which included a formal educational component, from which some top managers in the GDR benefited.

44. It seemed to have for McFalls's (1995:171–72) respondents, a substantial group of whom cited the desire for career advancement as the reason they joined a GDR political party. Many have suggested that the connection between politics and occupational position varied by class. Scharf (1984:149) argued that some form of organizational participation was especially important for workers' career success; McCauley (1981:7) said college graduates, but not production workers, needed to join the party if they were to be successful; Konrád and Szelényi (1979:190–92, 222), though not focusing specifically on the GDR, noted the centrality of party membership for the careers of both intellectuals and workers. For the situation in the arts, see Rueschemeyer (1991:39). See also Fulbrook (1991:224); Schnibben (1990:30); Rakovski (1978:57); Kornai (1992:325); Kennedy (1991:276); Haas (1988:esp. part 4); Klier (1990:152); and Konrád and Szelényi (1979:182, 217–18). The linkage between family background and politics has also elicited comment. For example, being from a middle-class family could facilitate party membership. The party's cadre selection criteria included "moral behavior" and "personal appearance," both quite likely to have been related to family upbringing (Weber [1988:79]). Nor was one's family background independent of one's position in the occupational structure. For relevant comments, see Scharf (1984:42); Erbe (1979b:420); Haas (1988:32); and Konrád and Szelényi (1979:208–9).

45. Kennedy (1991:esp. 215–32). See chapter 8 herein for how vassalage affected workers' politics during the *Wende.*

46. See Haraszti's (1978:71–72) sterling description of "them" in Hungary. He argued that this perception was especially pronounced among factory workers.

47. I use the word *understand* to connote both perception and knowledge based on concrete experiences and interactions. I view both perceptions and concrete ex-

periences and interactions as inseparable aspects of social relationships. The perceptions that people carry to their concrete interactions and experiences affect what these interactions and experiences are like. Just as important, these interactions and experiences affect perceptions, changing, reinforcing, erasing, confounding, and complicating them.

48. Glaeßner (1986:25).

49. For a small sampling of discussions that highlight distinctions within the socialist intelligentsia, see Bourdieu (1991); Keefe (1982:81–85); Erbe (1979b:414ff); Dennis (1988:51); Kennedy (1991:215–21, 238–43, 250, 386–87); Lewin (1988:50–52); Ticktin (1992:48–50, 66); Szelényi (1986–87:110–18); Klier (1990:150–53, 161–66); Rakovski (1978:51–52); Singer (1991:212–16); Zeman (1991:299–300); Musch (1990); Minnerup (1982:25–26); and Glaeßner (1986). Some have also tried to link differing political predilections within the intelligentsia to their various structural locations, though they have not always done this in the same way. See, for example, Hancock (1978:145–46); Rakovski (1978:51–52, 58–62, 90–91); Staniszkis (1991:14–16); Keefe (1982:100); and Glaeßner (1986:25).

50. For a good example, see Philipsen (1993:88).

51. It is not surprising that my review of the literature on socialist countries uncovered far fewer accounts of divisions in the working class than in the middle class. One working-class division that has been mentioned is between "core" workers (highly skilled, stably employed, and often male workers in key economic sectors) and "periphery" workers (less highly skilled, less stably employed, and often female workers in peripheral economic sectors). See, for example, Burawoy and Lukács (1992:76); Cox (1991:178–81); and Konrád and Szelényi (1979:217). See also my discussion in the introduction.

52. Although research objectives unavoidably bear the social imprint of whoever conducts the research, there is no simple, precise correspondence between the two.

53. Szelényi (1986–87:106). See also Konrád and Szelényi (1979:xiv–xv). The following discussion focuses on classes' generalized perceptions of and interactions with each other. Individuals from different classes could and did have perceptions of and interactions with one anther that did not fit this overarching pattern.

54. See, for instance, Singer (1991:211, paraphrasing Alexander Zinoviev); Connor (1991:228); Galtung (1992:83); Rakovski (1978:86, 101); Bahro (1978:215, 320); Klier (1990:165); Meuschel (1992:148); Staniszkis (1992:101); Ticktin (1992:74); Konrád and Szelényi (1979:82, 202, 247); and Szelényi (1979:190).

55. Hancock (1978:150).

56. On these matters, see McCauley (1981:7); Zimmermann (1984:29, 30); and Scharf (1984:42). In a post-*Wende* interview, a former party member told Philipsen (1993:276) that only about 42 percent of the SED membership was workers. Much of the remaining 58 percent were likely from the intelligentsia.

57. Interview in Berlin, fall 1991.

58. Joppke (1995:224). The Buddenbrook reference is to a Thomas Mann novel. For additional commentary on the intellectualization of the SED, see Minnerup (1990:5); Keefe (1982:82, 170); Erbe (1979b:419); and Hancock (1978:150).

59. See, for example, Heller (1990:7); Staniszkis (1991:14); Konrád and Szelényi (1979:179–80, 182); and Kennedy (1991:264).

60. Konrád and Szelényi (1979:191–92).

61. See Erbe (1979b:416–17); Konrád and Szelényi (1979:207); Feffer (1992); and Sodaro (1983:86).

62. Grote (1979:189–90); Sodaro (1983:89); Fulbrook (1991:251, 360, 380). For further discussion, see Konrád and Szelényi (1979:216); Woods (1986:23); Keefe (1982:84–85); and Scharf (1990:9).

63. Interviews in Bernau and Berlin, fall 1990.

64. See, for example, *Kran,* November 9, 1989, 5. The closeness of management and the political intelligentsia in the eyes of GDR workers parallels that noted in other socialist societies. Kornai (1992:325), for instance, called managers soldiers of the party, whose appointments ultimately depended on that organization and whose career paths often led not to a higher management post but to an appointment in the party hierarchy. Pravda (1979:233) spoke of the "close involvement" of management and the party, including managerial domination of party executive bodies. "The proximity of outlook and the overlap in personnel between management and party," he continued, "often creates the impression among workers that the two are in partnership."

65. In terms of workers' inability to perceive any difference between the oppositional intelligentsia and the political intelligentsia, it did not help that some members of the literary-artistic cohort were stalwart public supporters of the political elite.

66. Here I distance myself from the intellectual bashing, especially directed against oppositional intellectuals, that has become something of a public sport in Germany since the *Wende.* See the interesting comments of Baier (1990) and Baylis (1994). My point is not to pass judgment on the pre-*Wende* political philosophies of the oppositional intellectuals or their tactics, which definitely included contact and compromise with the political intelligentsia. Rather, it is to argue that, from outside the class boundaries of the intelligentsia, these philosophies and tactics often worked to reinforce workers' perception that the oppositional intelligentsia and the political intelligentsia were similar.

67. The chronology of this thawing process has been chracterized differently, partly because relations between the two groups never warmed completely. They could more accurately be described as having undergone a gradual warming punctuated by dramatic, though temporary, freezes, usually precipitated by actions of specific oppositional individuals.

68. On these matters, see Hancock (1978:149–50); Süß (1989:175); Scharf (1984:129, 139, 156); Hanke (1984:233); Rueschemeyer (1991:49); Wallace (1992); Duncan Smith (1988:153); Keefe (1982:100, 178); Woods (1986:21); Greenwald (1993:141); and Philipsen (1993:262–64).

69. Joppke (1995:72); Rueschemeyer (1991:48); Philipsen (1993:44); Goeckel (1990:237); Reißig (1991:15). See also Woods (1986:18, 21–22); and Mushaben (1984:133).

70. Philipsen's (1993:55, 82, 131, 135, 140–60, 163–64, 168, 171, 228, 238, 258, 283, 294, 296) interviews were filled with comments on the regularity with which the church aligned itself with the political leadership before and during the *Wende.*

71. Ibid., 391.

72. Biermann (1990:44). For another example, see Rein (1989:27, 29). See also Kramer (1991:80); Joppke (1995:143); Herminghouse (1991); and Wallace (1992:105–7).

73. Joppke (1995:142) quoting Lutz Rathenow. Volkmer (1979:114) suggested the applicability of the expression might have been long-standing.

74. Konrád and Szelényi (1979:221). See also Bahro (1978:329); and Konrád and Szelényi (1979:234, 239).

75. Interview near Bernau, summer 1989.

76. Burawoy and Lukács (1992:128). See also Schnibben (1990:30); and *Kran*, February 15, 1990, 2. Other observers of East and Central European workplaces have commented on analogous working-class critiques of the intelligentsia. See, for example, Burawoy (1985:196–97); and especially Connor (1991:228–29). Bahro (1978:168, 209, 212) judged such complaints well founded, arguing that higher-level employees were less productive in state socialist economies and that there were too many of them. See also Baylis (1974:99, 107).

77. See also Meuschel (1989–90:5); Wierling (1996:55); Parmalee (1994:307); Philipsen (1993:172–73, 250–51, 376–77); Woods (1986:44); and Musch (1990:97). In response to assertions of workers' lack of interest in democracy and politics, Belwe (1982) found that GDR workers often left their workplaces in the 1970s because they were not involved enough in the decision-making process. The comments GDR intellectuals made about workers are reminiscent of the cultural excluders Lamont (1992:esp. chap. 4) identified in her study of French and U.S. upper-middle-class men. That the same opinions about workers were widespread elsewhere in East and Central Europe is evident in Pravda (1981:47); Connor (1981:170); Pravda (1979:215); Konrád and Szelényi (1979:247); Connor (1991:227–28); and Ticktin (1992:74, 96), who noted that "cattle" was a favorite Soviet epithet for workers.

78. André Brie quoted in Philipsen (1993:177). See also ibid., 274.

79. Overall, I found intellectuals more inclined than workers to voice negative assessments of the other group. This was probably because they saw me as "one of them" and therefore assumed I would sympathize with their views. Although I did not fit neatly into workers' understanding of the GDR class schema, they sensed differences between us reminiscent of those separating them from the intelligentsia and therefore were more circumspect.

80. Baylis (1974:100ff). See also Steele (1977:136); and Harman (1983:68–69). Both Baylis (1974:71) and Leonhard (1958:379) commented on workers' resentment of middle-class material privilege in earlier years.

81. Scharf (1984:154); Gann (1992:106); Darnton (1991:173); Feffer (1992:81); Woods (1986:44–45); Parmalee (1994:304); Lötsch (1992:52). It is easy to find accounts of other East and Central European countries that painted similar pictures. See, for example, Bahro (1978:324); Rakovski (1978:66); Ticktin (1992:96); Connor (1991:227–29); Urnov (1990:25); and Burawoy and Lukács (1992:159).

82. Scharf (1984:118); Michalsky (1984:252).

83. See also Philipsen (1993:116–20, 288); Opp, Voss, and Gern (1995:9); and Wierling

(1996:58). For mention of analogous forms of resistance in other East and Central European countries, see Connor (1991:229); Bahro (1978:325); and Szelényi (1979:188–89).

84. There is still much we do not know about pre-*Wende* public protest in the GDR, including its class character, since the government went to great lengths to conceal it.

85. Gleye (1991:197).

86. Volkmer (1979:119–20).

87. Ibid., 119. For relevant information, see Darnton (1991:189); McFalls (1992b:17); Woods (1986:44); Baylis (1974:71); Zimmermann (1978:32, 38, 39); and *Kran,* October 26, 1989, 4.

88. See, for example, Baring (1972); and Joppke (1995:57–61). A conflicting account, which downplayed the role of workers, was published by the FRG government on the tenth anniversary of the uprising. See "'Umgeschult'" (1963).

89. Baring (1972:52–53, 70).

90. Joppke (1995:61–65); Minnerup (1982:9). The single-class character of overt protest activities seemed to have been common elsewhere in East and Central Europe prior to the late 1980s. See, for example, Connor (1991:227); and Singer (1991:217).

Chapter 2: Workers in the Gallery

1. The issue is not whether the majority of each class was politically active but from which class most activists hailed. McFalls's (1995:185, 186) random sample of 202 people from around the country revealed that before November 9, 1989, 56 percent either thought demonstrations stupid or held some positive views of demonstrators but did not participate in the demonstrations themselves. After that date, 81 percent said they did not participate in any demonstration. See also Opp Voss, and Gern (1995:257–58), who maintained that in Leipzig, a center of revolutionary activism, between 61 and 76 percent of the populace did not participate in demonstrations.

2. Ash (1990:136).

3. I expect little disagreement with my characterization of activists supporting the status quo as relatively privileged, even from those who disagree with my definition of the intelligentsia. This chapter therefore concentrates on the social composition of those who challenged the existing regime.

4. Interviews in Berlin, fall 1990, fall 1991, and winter 1991; near Bernau, fall 1990; and in Frankfurt Oder, fall 1990. See also Kirschner (1990:25). Connelly (1990:71, 83–84, 86) suggested that workers were quite active in public protests in Plauen (population 80,000) but that this was the only city where "the East German upheaval was from its inception a *mass* affair."

5. Interview in Berlin, spring 1991.

6. Ibid., winter 1991 and fall 1990.

7. This jibes with Opp and Gern's (1993:670) findings on the gender of demonstration participants in Leipzig.

8. Interview in Bernau, fall 1990. Workers Philipsen (1993:127, 344, 375) interviewed offered another reason for their nonparticipation: some were basically satisfied with many, especially economic and social, aspects of their lives in the GDR.

9. I thank Ilka Cohen for sharing this recollection with me.

10. Interview in Berlin, fall 1990. Kirschner's (1989:27–28) discussion of why some people declined to participate in his survey is relevant here. See also *Kran*, November 9, 1989, 5.

11. This characterization may have been more accurate in some regions of the country than in others. See, for example, Philipsen (1993:212–13).

12. Lötsch (1992:52).

13. Hanhardt (1990:19–22); Greenwald (1993:141); Philipsen (1993:299). See also Knabe (1990:26–27); Greenwald (1993:130, 252–53, 267); and Musch (1990:96).

14. Greenwald (1993:196).

15. Interview in Berlin, spring 1991.

16. See chapter 5.

17. Opp, Voss, and Gern (1995:158–59); interview in Berlin, fall 1990. See, however, Opp, Voss, and Gern's (1995:163–65) discussion of class-related variables and activism in Leipzig.

18. Hanhardt (1990:13–14).

19. Interviews in Berlin, winter 1990 and spring 1991. See also Rein (1989:28–29).

20. Interviews in Apolda, fall 1990, and Berlin, spring 1991.

21. See chapter 5.

22. Scharf (1984:134). Åslund (1983:184) reported that in 1982 the LDPD, the CDU, and the NDPD (National Democratic Party of Germany) together organized approximately half the private entrepreneurs in the country.

23. Interviews in Berlin, fall 1990 and summer 1989.

24. Philipsen (1993:172).

25. Interview in Berlin, fall 1991.

26. Minnerup (1990:5). See also Minnerup (1989:8); and Greenwald (1993:267).

27. For some miscellaneous information reinforcing the view of the major parties as havens of the intelligentsia, see Marcuse (1991:197); Neugebauer (1990a:23); and Heller (1990:7). For more on the role of the SPD during this period, see Philipsen (1993:316, 317, 325, 326, 335).

Chapter 3: The Socialist Labor Process

1. In particular, see Kornai (1986, 1992); and Maier (1987).

2. A ritualized 2 percent was standard in the GDR (Maier [1987:83]).

3. Maier (1987:56–57). Maier (1987:56) reported that between 1971 and 1985 the national consumption and accumulation rose 80 percent, while the stock of goods and materials grew 184 percent. Maier (1987:83) also noted how GDR firms bargained to make acceptance of additional plan tasks contingent on the receipt of more inputs.

4. The center therefore attempted tight supervision of production and service delivery units through a plethora of detailed standards, calculations, rules, rates, and so forth, to which work centers had to make documented efforts to subscribe. Edeling (1990:6–7) had some interesting comments on how central directives created multiple layers of administration in enterprises. As one economist put it, "Centraliza-

tion creates shortages, and shortages then produce greater centralization" (interview in Berlin, summer 1988). See also Maier (1987:84); and Baylis (1974:255–56).

5. Quoted in Opp, Voss, and Gern (1995:57).

6. Interviews in Leipzig, summer 1988, and Berlin, summer 1989.

7. *Kran*, October 26, 1989, 5; *Leipziger Volkszeitung*, October 20, 1989, 3.

8. Machine tool operators, for example, routinely worked several machines (in one case four) simultaneously, and other production workers reported attending up to seven machines at once (Deppe and Hoß [1989:181–82]; Kirschner [1990:20]). Or, as a *Vertrauensmann* remarked to Philipsen (1993:287) soon after the *Wende*, though GDR workers knew they would be paid "three or four times as much," they "now figure that a job in the West certainly could not be much harder."

9. See Burawoy and Lukács (1992:66) on the issue of hard work under socialism. Clarke (1993:21) discussed variations in the intensity of labor required of different kinds of workers in Soviet enterprises.

10. Lasky (1991:22), for example, wrote that after the *Wende*, the "grim prospect of competitive hard work was daunting" to GDR workers. Connor (1991:147) reported that workers in the Soviet Union judged it their "social right" not to work hard. According to Ticktin (1992:88), there was a period before 1988 when Gorbachev hardly made a speech in which he did not criticize workers for not working hard enough.

11. Interviews in Bernau, summer 1989; Schnibben (1990:31).

12. Philipsen (1993:287); interview in Bernau, fall 1990. See also Greenwald (1993:60).

13. Voskamp and Wittke (1991:360). The work week had been 42 hours since 1977, down from 45 or more in 1960 (Ludz [1981:277–78]). A 40-hour week was a common worker demand during the *Wende*. See, for example, *IUG*, December 1989, 4.

14. Kirschner (1989:19–20).

15. Greenwald (1993:91). Cabaret performances composed of a series of humorous political skits were well attended in the GDR. There were cabaret theaters, and many workplaces had their own amateur troupes as well. Overtime was one of the topics that generated the most heated exchanges between workers and managers during GDR planning discussions (interview in Berlin, summer 1988). See also Kirschner (1989:109).

16. See, for example *Kran*, October 26, 1989, 2. Here the storming period lasted half of every month. See also Burawoy (1985:163); and Stark (1986:494).

17. In the Hungarian machine shop where Burawoy worked, female mill operators made the coffee. The woman who attended the speed drills was apparently on permanent coffee duty. "How she makes her rates I never understand," Burawoy and Lukács (1992:46) commented.

18. That GDR workers recognized both idleness and hard work as parts of their paid labor experience is not contradictory. I found that Clarke's (1993:20) description of the Soviet Union held for the GDR too: "The co-existence of overwork and idleness, which under capitalism separates the employed from the unemployed, exists within the Soviet enterprise."

19. Interview near Leipzig, summer 1988.

20. Two union college professors told me of a survey study they had conducted in which the majority of workers said they worked primarily because "they wanted to contribute to society," not for the money. They also reported that many respondents said they did not like "just hanging around" at work (interview in Bernau, summer 1989). As Burawoy and Lukács (1992:44) discovered, idleness and sporadic activity were much more exhausting than working at a steady clip throughout the day.

21. Interview in Berlin, winter 1991. See also Marcuse (1991:55); *Kran,* October 26, 1989, 2; and Schnibben (1990:30, 31).

22. Interviews in Leipzig, summer 1988.

23. Interview in Berlin, winter 1991.

24. Interview in Bernau, summer 1989, and Berlin, winter 1991.

25. Interview in Berlin, winter 1991; Kirschner (1990:21). For additional examples, see *Kran,* January 18, 1990, 4, October 26, 1989, 2, and November 23, 1989, 4, 5; Scharf (1984:72); and Deppe and Hoß (1989:184–85). Scharf (1984:75) cited several antecedents of worksite management error on which workers did not comment: frequent major structural reforms and endless changes in plan indicator and incentive systems.

26. Philipsen (1993:128).

27. *Kran,* December 14, 1989, 4; interview in Leipzig, summer 1988. See also Kirschner (1989:20, 102); and *Kran,* January 18, 1990, 4. So long as workers did not suffer monetarily, GDR managers could legally reassign them for up to one month.

28. Interview in Berlin, winter 1991.

29. The following discussion is reminiscent of what Burawoy and Lukács (1992:esp. part 2) referred to as "rituals of affirmation" or "painting socialism." The difference in our emphases, however, suggests that deceptions in the labor process had plural, yet simultaneous, outcomes. Burawoy and Lukács wrote mostly of the critical political potential of "painting socialism," whereas I emphasize how the process contributed to the demobilization of the GDR working class.

30. Interview near Bernau, summer 1989. For other discussions of union involvement in lying at work, see *Kran,* November 30, 1989, 4; Kirschner (1990:21); and Philipsen (1993:116).

31. Interview in Bernau, summer 1989.

32. Interview in Apolda, fall 1990; Philipsen (1993:121). See also Philipsen (1993:284–85). Accounts of ordinary workers who were also party members reveal that precisely the same kind of misrepresentation occurred in the party as well (Philipsen [1993:291]; Parmalee [1994:300]). Kirschner (1989:28) noted one reason some people gave for declining to be interviewed for his project was that since there weren't any problems, there was no reason to study them.

33. *Kran,* November 2, 1989, 4, October 29, 1989, 2, and October 26, 1989, 5. See also *Leipziger Volkszeitung,* October 20, 1989, 3. Maier (1987:176) described another lie regarding economic performance: firms claimed high innovation rates by making minuscule or pseudo changes in their products, thus justifying higher sales prices. Sometimes this also made it possible to report higher productivity, profits, and production and lower input levels, thereby entitling firms to larger bonuses.

34. *Kran,* November 2, 1989, 5; Maier (1987:91).

35. See, for example, Burawoy and Lukács's (1992:124–26) firsthand account of preparations for the prime minister's visit to a Hungarian steel mill.

36. *Kran,* November 30, 1989, 3.

37. Interview in Bernau, summer 1989. See also Segert (1992:11). For a comparison of workers' participation in planning in Cuba and the GDR, see Fuller (1990:84–87).

38. Interview in Bernau, summer 1989. See also Kirschner (1989:109–10) on this point.

39. Interview in Leipzig, summer 1988. See also Kirschner (1989:109–10); and Baylis (1974:146–47).

40. For another example, see the discussion of union elections in chapter 4.

41. For information on housing, see Krisch (1985:95–97); and *Kran,* October 12, 1989, 4. As one worker exclaimed, "We work a lot and well. So where are the things we produce?" (interview in Bernau, summer 1989). In a letter to *Kran* (October 26, 1989, 4), one *Kollektiv* asked rhetorically, "What can one get in the shops after 4 P.M., after the end of the shift? What goods and services can one still get at that hour?" Workers also complained to *Kran* about the lack of hot water, winterized work buildings, proper lighting, and good ventilation. See also chapter 5.

42. See, for example, Scharf (1984:71); Meier (1987a:13–14); Voskamp and Wittke (1991:359); and Philipsen (1993:128, 291).

43. Interview near Leipzig, summer 1988.

44. Interview in Berlin, fall 1991. See also *Kran,* November 2, 1989, 2. Stollberg (1988:150) cited an interview study in which "an open and critical atmosphere regarding indiscipline and bad work" was the second most important factor influencing *Kollektiv* members' relation to their work. For related discussion, see Stollberg (1988:157–58).

45. Interview in Berlin, summer 1988.

46. Kirschner (1990:22). This sentiment was also captured by an AGL (department-level union committee) chair in a transport factory who, in announcing his readiness to work well and more, stipulated, "The requisite for this must be payment that corresponds to achievement. This is the complete realization of the performance principle. In the future, work time must also truly be achievement time" (*Kran,* November 9, 1989, 5). See also Schnibben (1990:28); Musch (1990:104); and *Kran,* February 1, 1990, 3. In Bahro's (1978:209) words, "The principle of payment according to work has a very attenuated application. Once the plan targets and salaries are fixed and settled, the sun shines equally on the righteous and the unrighteous." Belwe and Klinger's (1986:63) research also highlighted the lack of a clear connection between income and achievement in the GDR.

47. Note the difference between workers' concerns and how Opp, Voss, and Gern (1995:55) described the problem with the GDR remuneration system, which unselfconsciously confounded job title with achievement: "Particularly disturbing was the permanent wage leveling of skilled and unskilled labor as well as of employees with and without leadership positions. This situation hampered the introduction principle that wages depend on achievements." Bahro (1978:208) was excellent on this

point. See also Bahro (1978:209, 397). Szelényi (1978:75) suggested what GDR workers may also have been thinking when he wrote of the "quite questionable and certainly unsustained assumption that skilled labour is producing more value than simple [labor] and is therefore better rewarded."

48. Zimmermann (1978:5). See also Kirschner (1990:22); and Zimmermann (1977:115). Bonuses were often distributed in complex combinations of annual and monthly allotments, which added to the confusion.

49. Overtime, which was almost guaranteed to some workers, was also an issue. It was sometimes collectable just for showing up. Voskamp and Wittke (1991:361–63) reported not only that overtime was remunerated with little eye to effort or results but also that some workers received overtime pay by arranging "fictive" overtime, that is, they accumulated inventory during regular work hours, which they used to complete overtime targets in fewer hours than they were paid for. See also Kirschner (1989:19, 99, 111); and Kirschner (1990:22).

50. That training and educational credentials became increasingly important criteria for assignment to a higher base wage bracket, especially after the 1976 wage reform, only exacerbated workers' perceptions that the correspondence between reward, effort, and result was awry. To a large degree, the base wage mirrored the country's economic, political, and social priorities, none of which could be equated with performance or effort.

51. Scharf (1984:98); Zimmermann (1977:115, 116).

52. On these points, see Scharf (1989:13); Scharf (1984:99); and Markovits (1982:567–68, 581).

53. Interview in Berlin, winter 1991. This is, of course, a variation in the dishonesty theme discussed in the previous section.

54. Many workers argued that, under prevailing circumstances, the thirteenth-month bonus should be paid automatically. Workers, they argued, were not often to blame when plan goals were not met, and, in any case, plans were revised so often that it was usually impossible to ascertain whether targets had been fulfilled.

55. Interview in Bernau, summer 1989. This worker went on to explain, "It works that way with general directors too. They receive a bonus when the plan is fulfilled. The ministry proposes what it should be to the BGL. If the BGL doesn't think the general director has done that good a job, it's possible they could lower the director's bonus. That doesn't happen often though."

56. Interview in Berlin, winter 1991.

57. Scharf (1989:14).

58. *Kran,* February 15, 1990, 1–2.

59. Interview near Bernau, summer 1989. See also Philipsen (1993:286–87).

60. Interview in Bernau, summer 1989.

61. Literally, *Wasserkopf* means hydrocephalus. In other words, the organization had too much head (administrators and bosses).

62. Bahro (1978:209). See also ibid., 212. Konrád and Szelényi (1979:227–28) advanced a similar argument, though they apparently included administrative personnel from lower levels in their critique. The 1976 wage reform also proposed to link

the wages of some college- and university-educated personnel and forepersons more closely to achievement (Zimmermann [1977:116]).

Chapter 4: Workplace Politics

1. The *Kollektive* I knew firsthand had between 9 and 52 members, with 22 the average. Each *Kollektiv* was headed by a *Vertrauensperson*. The BGL (*Betriebsgewerkschaftsleitung*) was organized at the enterprise level. Between the *Kollektiv* and the BGL was the AGL (*Abteilungsgewerkschaftsleitung*), or department-level union committee. The AGLs with which I was most familiar had between 95 and 203 members. Scharf (1974:130) noted a great deal of variation in AGL size, some incorporating nearly 300 workers. Workers sometimes considered AGL-level politics more akin to politics at the *Kollektiv* level than at the BGL level. This was more likely in smaller work establishments. Outside the enterprise, union structures existed at the 219 *Kreis* (district), the 15 *Bezirk* (county), and the national levels. On the idea of multiple union experiences, see Segert (1992:10).

2. Interviews in Bernau, summer 1989.

3. Kirschner (1989:112) made the same point. Konrád and Szelényi's (1979:174) comments suggested this situation had been common to all socialist countries for some time.

4. Interviews in Bernau, Apolda, and Berlin, fall 1990; the final response was elicited by Kirschner (1990:32). See also *Kran,* November 16, 1989, 1, and November 30, 1989, 4; and Kirschner (1990:21, 22).

5. Interviews in Leipzig, summer 1988, Apolda, fall 1990, and Bernau, summer 1989. More than two decades ago, Scharf (1974:250) noted this "convenient division of labor" in planning as one of the major difficulties surrounding union participation in the enterprise planning process. See also Scharf (1974:246); and Rueschemeyer and Scharf (1986:73).

6. Interview in Leipzig, summer 1988.

7. Kirschner (1990:38) and Pirker et al. (1990:78) noted one argument for the continuation of the old unions advanced during the crisis was that union social work efforts would be jeopardized if unions were allowed to collapse. The following information conveys some sense of the scale of the unions' cultural and social work before the *Wende*. The enterprise union retained 25 percent of the dues it collected, and of that percentage 25 percent was devoted to cultural and educational work. Overall the GDR unions operated around 400 culture houses and 600 large and 2,000 smaller libraries throughout the country. *Kollektive* first prepared their own cultural and education plans in 1960, and 98 percent were doing so by the late 1980s. Most collectives had a union officer who was specifically responsible for this area of union work. So did most BGLs. In the mid-1980s, nearly 334,000 people served as union culture officers (Lehrstuhl Gewerkschaftsaufbau [1989:6]). Over twenty years ago, Scharf (1974:129) wrote that the culture officer probably ranked second in importance to the *Vertrauensperson* in the *Kollektiv*. For the 1989 union financial report for a Leipzig transport factory, see *Kran,* February 1, 1990, 6. Approximately 65 percent of this enterprise union's budget of close to 300,000 marks went toward cultural and

social expenditures. Dennis (1988:107) reported that the FDGB (Freier Deutscher Gewerkschafsbund [the Confederation of Free German Trade Unions, which linked the various sectoral unions in the GDR]) arranged holiday tours for more than 1.8 million people in 1984. Union members paid only about 30 percent of the cost of their vacation stays in the more than 1,600 holiday places the FDGB distributed. For a description of one FDGB vacation hotel, see Duncan Smith (1988:100–101). For information on social insurance, see Michalsky (1984:249–54). Nearly 78 billion marks were expended on the FDGB-administered social insurance system between 1971 and 1975, and in the mid-1980s, over 331,000 people served as social insurance officers in the unions. In addition, there were 290,000 union sports organizers and over 318,000 health and safety officers at this time (Lehrstuhl Gewerkschaftsaufbau [1989:6, 7]). Despite the demands to rebalance the substantive focus of union work once the *Wende* began, workers were also clear they did not want the unions to stop attending to cultural and social issues. See, for example, *Kran*, November 9, 1989, 2, and November 30, 1989, 5; Kirschner (1990:31); and Pirker et al. (1990:78). For generally positive evaluations of social and cultural union work at two different times, see Kirschner (1989:98, 107–8, 110–11); and Scharf (1974:269–78).

8. Interview near Bernau, fall 1989.

9. Interviews in Berlin, summer 1988, winter 1991, and spring 1991; in Leipzig, summer 1988; Kirschner (1990:26 [last quote]). Many students of GDR unions during different periods would concur with these comments. See, for example, Lohr (1990:1); Scharf (1974:260–64); Dennis (1988:161); and Kirschner (1989:69–70, 98, 105, 102, 106, 118–20, 122). When Kirschner (1989:74–75) asked *Vertrauensleute* and AGL/BGL functionaries in a large enterprise what areas they thought the union *should* have influence over, both groups thought the unions' main concern should be social rather than economic tasks. For example, 87 percent of the *Vertrauensleute* and 82 percent of the AGL/BGL officers thought such issues as sanitation, breaks, and vacations should be a principal union focus. Yet only 26 percent of the *Vertrauensleute* and 30 percent of the AGL/BGL officers thought working out a realistic enterprise plan should be a principal union focus, and only 9 percent of both groups thought questions of work organization should be. In the midst of the *Wende*, some union members called for a rebalancing of union work, urging, for example, that the organizations drop their involvement with socialist emulation (a large part of which concerned the fulfillment of cultural and educational tasks) and pay more attention to economic questions. See, for example, Kirschner (1990:8); *IUG*, December 1989, 3; and *Kran*, November 9, 1989, 2.

10. Autonomy and independence are slippery concepts that have been used carelessly in analyses of unions in socialist societies. Implicit in many such analyses is the view that the unions' relation to management and the party could take but one of two forms: either unions were autonomous and independent of party and management or they were not. Reality, however, is not that simple. Unions everywhere fall somewhere between these polar extremes in terms of in their relationship with other organized political players. Autonomy and independence are therefore best conceived as relative, not absolute, concepts.

11. Interviews in Bernau, summer 1989, and Berlin, winter 1990.

12. Rueschemeyer and Scharf (1986:61) emphasized an increase in union autonomy in the GDR, describing it as "an active junior partner" in the 1980s. Several people I interviewed mentioned that the party sometimes sided with the union against the state administration, helping it devise arguments to support its case during a conflict with management, for example. Others reported that if management ignored or did not please the union, then the union would go straight to the party for help.

13. Interviews in Bernau, summer 1989.

14. Interviews in Berlin and Leipzig, summer 1988.

15. Interviews in Berlin, summer 1988 and fall 1990, and in and near Bernau, summer 1989 and fall 1990. See also Kirschner (1990:31, 27).

16. For other GDR workers who concur with the analysis presented in this section, see Kirschner (1990:28, 32, 38, 45); *Kran*, November 16, 1989, 3, and February 1, 1989, 5; *Tribüne*, February 5, 1990, 1; and Segert (1992:10). See also Neugebauer (1990b:10); *IUG*, February 1, 1990, 10; and Kirschner (1989:59, 63, 101, 116, and esp. 82 and 83). For information on the lack of union autonomy at the time of the 1953 June uprising, see Baring (1972).

17. In Kirschner's (1989:116) study of one factory, managers held the majority of unpaid union leadership posts. See also Kirschner (1989:56–58). In the GDR, managers and workers from the same economic sector were all members of the same union.

18. Interviews in Bernau, summer 1989, and Leipzig, summer 1988. See also *Kran*, November 16, 1989, 1. Just as the unions' focus on social and cultural tasks attracted and produced leaders able and willing to do this type of work, union dependence on management and the party attracted and produced union leaders disposed to accede to the wishes of these other two bodies and unwilling to chart a more independent union course.

19. Rueschemeyer and Scharf (1986:60) reported that "virtually all paid union officials, as well as a great many volunteer union officials, are members of the SED." See also Kirschner (1990:27); and Scharf (1984:138).

20. Kirschner (1989:56) noted that in the factory he studied the percentage of SED members was the same for both the *Vertrauensleute* and the union membership as a whole.

21. Interviews in Bernau, summer 1989, and Berlin, summer 1988.

22. Interview in Berlin, fall 1990. See also *Kran*, November 9, 1989; and Kirschner (1989:56). Philipsen (1993:113, 127) also recorded interesting worker comments on the party-union leadership overlap.

23. Scharf (1974:145) discovered this was true more than two decades earlier as well.

24. Interview in Berlin, winter 1990. See also *IUG*, February 1, 1990, 10; and Kirschner (1990:38).

25. Segert (1992:10) called this a "forced marriage." Zimmermann (1984:21) noted this was often true in the previous decade.

26. Interview in Bernau, fall 1990.

27. For example, an enterprise with about a thousand workers elected approximately eighteen members to its BGL alone. Lehrstuhl Gewerkschaftsaufbau (1989:1)

reported that in 1989, 2.6 million people were elected to "union leadership, *Vertrauens-person*, and group functionary positions." Rueschemeyer and Scharf (1986:67) reported that in the early 1980s, more than 25 percent of union members held at least voluntary positions in the workplace union. See also Rueschemeyer and Scharf (1986:168, n. 39).

28. These percentages were similar to those Radcliffe (1972:100) reported for the late 1960s.

29. Interview in Leipzig, summer 1988.

30. Some people I interviewed, however, reported hearing of workplaces where BGL members received as little as 70 percent of the vote, and I also heard there had been a downward trend in the percent of affirmative votes received by BGL members throughout the country.

31. Lehrstuhl Gewerkschaftsaufbau (1989:2).

32. The depth of workers' disgruntlement with union electoral procedures was illustrated by the frequency with which reforms in the process were demanded and implemented once the crisis broke. See, for example, *Kran*, November 9, 1989, 4–5, November 16, 1989, 5, and March 1, 1990. 2; Kirschner (1990:16); *IUG*, December 1989, 3, and January 1990, 5; and Segert (1992:20, 21). See also chapters 6 and 8 herein.

33. Interviews in Bernau, summer 1989, and Leipzig, summer 1988. The discrepancy between the union's formal and actual commitment to democracy was also noted by Scharf (1974:308). Kirschner (1989:50–51) heard that in union elections in the plant where he did his fieldwork, a few workers merely checked every fifth name on the ballot. "Apparently an election process that [workers] experienced as simply a ritual was countered with a ritual of their own."

34. For example, I was told that BGL elections could be annulled and then recalled by higher union levels and that, while votes were tallied in public, the tallies might be manipulated since no workers ever went to witness the counts.

35. Gleye (1991:chap. 8). A union college professor's comments are pertinent here. "People who are eventually elected to union office," he told me, "need to be analyzed and trained and educated in how to perform their functions *before* they are approved as candidates" (interview in Bernau, summer 1989). See also Ratsch (1984:20).

36. Interview in Berlin, summer 1988.

37. Kirschner (1989:52).

38. For additional commentary on the role of supraworksite union bodies in selecting candidates for worksite union office, see *Kran*, November 9, 1989, 4; *IUG*, February 1, 1990, 10; and Rueschemeyer and Scharf (1986:60, 67). The practice was long-standing. See Scharf (1974:183, 184).

39. Interview in Bernau, summer 1989. This man, one of the most independent-minded of the *Vertrauensleute* I interviewed, criticized the party and local governments for also trying to recruit such workers. He was adamant that such people were most needed in workplace-level union positions. "Other groups should only get a minimum," he declared.

40. Interview in Frankfurt Oder, fall 1990. I was told candidates were sometimes recruited with an eye toward age, gender, and SED representativeness as well.

41. Interview near Bernau, fall 1990.

42. Interviews in Bernau and Frankfurt Oder, summer 1989. The content of these reports is a related matter, which was discussed in chapter 3. The reports were often contrived, embellished, and inaccurate. From Scharf's work (1974:134, 249), we see this was not new.

43. Interview near Bernau, summer 1989.

44. Interviews in Berlin, summer 1989, and Frankfurt Oder, fall 1990. For other critical comments on the quality of *Vertrauensleute* and BGL meetings, see Kirschner (1989:96); and Segert (1992:10).

45. Zimmermann's (1984:27) observations suggest this cabaret skit would also have struck a responsive chord some years earlier: "It is thus hardly surprising that no-one speaks off the cuff in GDR political life. Presentations, and even discussion contributions in decision-making bodies and all GDR organization meetings, are always in document form before they are delivered; the speaker reads out a text that has been formulated and agreed to in advance." See also Rueschemeyer and Scharf (1986:76).

46. Interviews in Berlin, summer 1989, Berlin, winter 1990, Bernau, fall 1990, and Berlin, winter 1991; Kirschner (1990:25). See also Kirschner (1990:8). The estrangement of union officers from the rank and file increased at each rung of the union hierarchy. At the top sat FDGB chair Harry Tisch, of whom one worker said, "He doesn't seem to live on the same planet we do. The things he says are so incredible! He has no grasp of our reality" (interview in Apolda, fall 1990).

47. Interview in Bernau, fall 1990.

48. Interview in Apolda, fall 1990. See also *Kran,* November 9, 1989, 4–5; and Gleye's (1991:47) succinct description of how democratic centralism functioned in the GDR.

49. These included the FDGB and one of the sixteen sectoral unions, both of which usually staffed offices outside the enterprise at the national, the *Bezirk,* and the *Kreis* levels.

50. Kirschner (1989:111).

51. Interview in Frankfurt Oder, summer 1989. See also Zimmermann (1984:63). Kirschner (1989:120) concluded that making worksite discussion processes "transparent" would be an important improvement in union work.

52. Kirschner (1990:28).

53. Interview near Bernau, summer 1989.

54. The experience of workplace union leaders is important because a large number of workers held or had held such positions. My best estimate is that the year before the revolution, when there were about 9.6 million union members, between 2 and 3 million workers held some sort of leadership post in the workplace, which is equivalent to approximately one-quarter to one-third of the union membership. This range matches that which workers gave me for individual sites I visited, as well as Segert's (1992:17) report and Scharf's (1974:144) from two decades earlier. If the number of workers who had *ever* held union office were considered as well, the number of GDR workers to which this discussion is applicable would be substantially larger than 2 to 3 million.

55. Interview in Bernau, summer 1989.

56. Interviews in Bernau and Berlin, fall 1990; Philipsen (1993:127 [last quote]). See also *Kran,* November 9, 1989, 4; and Kirschner (1989:109–10).

Chapter 5: The Class Relationship Revisited

1. Lewin (1988:80).

2. I am convinced this pattern was generally true elsewhere in society as well. For relevant comments, see note 28.

3. Staatliche Zentralverwaltung für Statistik (1988:409). Zimmermann's (1984:40, 41) analogous percentages from elections in the late 1970s were nearly all lower.

4. Staatliche Zentralverwaltung für Statistik (1988:410). See also Scharf (1984:135–36). Other government bodies were probably also dominated by the intelligentsia, though I do not have exact figures. One example was the worker and farmer inspection groups, which oversaw the functioning of all levels of state and economic administration. See Zimmermann (1984:54–55); and Staatliche Zentralverwaltung für Statistik (1988:411).

5. On these points, see also Neugebauer (1990a:9); Scharf (1984:134); Weber (1988:94); and Keefe (1982:177).

6. Goeckel (1990:37).

7. Interviews in Berlin, spring 1989 and fall 1990. See also Zimmermann (1984:71); and Neugebauer (1990a:12).

8. Scharf (1984:134–35). The fourth Block party, the NDPD (National Democratic Party), targeted craftspeople and some businesspersons (Neugebauer [1990a:23]).

9. Interviews in Berlin, fall 1990, and Bernau, summer 1989. For additional information, see Hancock (1978:141); and Baylis (1974:141).

10. Staatliche Zentralverwaltung für Statistik (1988:401). Urania was another large "society of technical intelligentsia" (Scharf [1984:140]).

11. Staatliche Zentralverwaltung für Statistik (1988:412); Scharf (1984:139 [quote]). See also Zimmermann (1984:69–70).

12. Duncan Smith (1988:178).

13. On the Kulturbund and the *Klubs der Intelligenz,* see Staatliche Zentralverwaltung für Statistik (1988:414); Duncan Smith (1988:179); and Zimmermann (1984:67–69).

14. Baylis (1974:71).

15. See Duncan Smith's (1988:177–78) commentary on the Writers' Union and Rueschemeyer's (1991:38–40) portrayal of the 6,000-member Artists' Union.

16. Eisenstadt (1992:30). Baylis (1974:107) reported that the seven top managers of one enterprise spent an average of seven hours per week on organizational activities outside work, such as those of the Kammer der Technik, the party, and the FDGB. Granick (1975:442–43) noted that 30 percent of managers in the GDR firms he studied held or had held an elected position in a sociopolitical organization, which included the SED and "government bodies." An early study of members of the intelligentsia who had left the GDR revealed that two-thirds held an average of three positions in such organizations (Baylis [1974:107]). Haas (1988:31, 32) showed that unskilled and semiskilled GDR workers had the lowest levels of political and societal participation of all sectors of the working class.

17. Glaeßner (1992:13); Meuschel (1992:155); Neugebauer (1990a:25). Estimates of the number of such groups seem to coalesce around 300–500. Meuschel, who offered

the lowest estimate, said nearly 100,000 people, though not classified as "permanent activists," participated in all sorts of group activities. For additional commentary, see Reißig (1991:16); and Opp, Voss, and Gern (1995:132).

18. Interview in Berlin, fall 1990. See also Zimmermann (1984:73); Offe (1991:26); Meuschel (1989–90:18); Meuschel (1992:155); Musch (1990:96); Wensierski (1982:403); Büscher (1982:429–30, 434); Roland Smith (1985:77); and Sodaro (1983:107).

19. Interview in Berlin, spring 1991. See also Rein (1989:20, 28, 31); Kunze (1990:158); Joppke (1995:118, 120, 127–28); Greenwald (1993:29); and Philipsen (1993:39, 42, 53–55, 77, 161, 167, 238).

20. For examples and discussion, see Philipsen (1993:41, 165, 185); Joppke (1995:143); Kramer (1991:80); and Segert (1993:13, 14).

21. Scharf (1990:6); personal communication, fall 1994.

22. Some members of the intelligentsia also had opportunities to forge relationships with different sets of intellectuals as a result of job changes over the course of their careers. Evidence of this second job-related opportunity for intraclass networking comes from Granick's (1975:447, 449, 464, 485) study of enterprise management; Schröter's (1992:8) research on public administrators; and Baylis's study (1974:78, 106–7), which noted the ease and frequency with which members of the the technical intelligentsia moved back and forth between engineering and managerial jobs and between enterprises, government institutes, party organs, and academic institutions.

23. Rakovski (1978:esp. 44–48, 89–90).

24. Interview in Berlin, winter 1991.

25. Both Connelly (1990:78) and Segert (1993:14) suggested such an argument in passing; however, they focused on middle-class engagement in opposition groups, whereas I argue that those in the intelligentsia acquired their political talents and experience through variety of other pre-*Wende* civil society associations as well.

26. See Opp, Voss, and Gern (1995:133) for data on the frequency with which a sample of opposition group members had participated in various political activities.

27. In the following paragraphs, I focus my attention on oppositional intellectuals, but the logic of my argument, though not the details, also holds for the activist intellectuals who came to the defense of the system.

28. My argument follows that of many studies, which have found that people's intimate personal networks are not the result of free choice. People build their networks of lovers, friends, and confidantes only from among those they encounter in the social contexts in which they participate, but these contexts are not freely chosen. They are shaped by the macrostructural, organizational, and cultural features of the societies in which they exist, such as class structure, race relations, and economic organization. This macrosocial map both limits and provides the pool of people from which individuals build their networks of personal friends. Many have commented on the class-exclusive pattern of the friendship networks of the intelligentsia in other socialist countries. See, for example, Rakovski (1978:65); Staniszkis (1992:101); Konrád and Szelényi (1979:208–9); and Teckenberg (1990:26, 29, 40, 42, 47). My observations during the various social activities I attended in the GDR suggest that the situation there was similar. Moreover, Lamont's (1992:10) comments that interactions between workers and

intellectuals elsewhere were sometimes characterized by a "distance openly marked" by reserve, overly formal courtesy, and a perceptible degree of uneasiness seemed to hold true in the GDR. In addition, members of the intelligentsia I interviewed claimed they had virtually no "direct" connection with workers before the *Wende,* and it appears this included marriage, which, according to G. E. Edwards (1985:10, 11), was heavily class endogenous. Scharf (1984:151, 156) also remarked that there was "little socializing between the [intelligentsia and the working class] apart from the work place." Like their counterparts in East and Central Europe, GDR intellectuals appeared routinely to construct networks of friends that included few, if any, workers.

29. Interview in Berlin, spring 1991. See also Philipsen (1993:84, 230); and Opp, Voss, and Gern (1995:103). Joppke (1995:109–10) cited the Ministry of State Security as the country's largest employer. Trust among revolutionary activists was also made easier by the fact that the networks from which they were drawn were composed of not just friends but friends who had the same class background. In the dangerous and uncertain world of political activism during the *Wende,* it was important for activists to surround themselves with those most like themselves socially, because shared social standing allowed them to be more certain of where fellow activists were "coming from." This socially based trust permitted easier and more rapid communication among activists. It meant activists could collectively respond faster and more flexibly in the heat of the contest. It meant they felt more comfortable leaving decisions up to the discretion of co-activists, whom they might not have known well, at the many junctures when this was required. Kanter (1977:esp. chap. 3) made similar points in her classic analysis of managerial work.

30. Opp, Voss, and Gern (1995:134).

31. Interview in Berlin, spring 1991. See also Philipsen (1993:230).

32. Philipsen (1993:241). That many who were politically active on the side of the challengers during the *Wende* were the same people who had been active in the peace, human rights, women's, ecology, and other oppositional groups beforehand is undoubtedly what many commentators meant when they said the citizens' opposition groups of the revolutionary period were the "outgrowth" of these earlier associations. See, for example, Krisch (1992:93); Sandford (1992:125, 139, 140); Joppke (1995:142); and Musch (1990:96). Many noting this connection, however, did not stress the points most salient to my argument: the largely middle-class character of the pre-*Wende* groups came to be reflected in the social makeup of revolutionary groups, and this connection often was accomplished through tight friendship networks. Opp, Voss, and Gern (1995:106, 109, 112–18, 134) found that opposition group membership (in Neues Forum and church groups) did not affect the frequency of demonstration but that people likely to participate in demonstrations and in general protests had critical *friends.* Their findings pertained to the period before October 9, 1989.

33. Philipsen (1993:297–98).

34. Interview in Berlin, spring 1991. See also Greenwald (1993:130).

35. Philipsen (1993:44); Rein (1989:28 [quote]).

36. Of related interest, McFalls (1995:127) found that demonstrators in his sample were characterized by higher-social-class origins.

37. Interview in Berlin, spring 1991.

38. Ibid.

39. Joppke (1995:143).

40. For examples, see Wierling (1996:52); and Meuschel (1992:144–45).

41. Numerous commentators on other East and Central European socialist societies have also observed workers' proclivity to view society in "us" versus "them" terms. See, for example, Pravda (1979:215); Rakovski (1978:47); Konrád and Szelényi (1979:223); and Connor (1991:103). Class identification through opposition, however, is not the same as class consciousness.

42. Burowoy (1985, 1992).

43. I do not claim that the class divide was equally obvious to every GDR worker in all the ways I will discuss. For different reasons, class distinctions were less perceptible in some areas of life than in others and to some workers than to others. Nonetheless, all the manifestations of class difference discussed below played a part in diverting GDR workers away from political activism during the revolution.

44. Kornai (1992:316–18, 324); interviews in Bernau, spring 1989, and Berlin, spring 1988. Minnerup (1982:22) gave the 1970 earnings ratio between manual or clerical workers and general directors of *Kombinate* as 4.6:1. Other sources reported that the same year the earnings gap between the lowest and the highest paid people in large industrial enterprises was on the order of 9:1 or 10:1 (Dennis [1988:54]; Grätz [1971:37]; see also Granick [1975:135–36]). Krisch (1985:99) reported 1981 ratios for "general workers" and *Kombinat* directors at between 2.4:1 and 6:1. Granick (1975:199–200) wrote that top managerial personnel also received yearly bonuses ranging, in the cases with which he was familiar, up to five-and-a-half times their monthly salaries. Some top managers, however, received no bonuses. 1976 estimates suggested that no more than 10,000 people in the GDR earned over 2,500 marks a month. One direct and effective way some socialist countries, including the GDR, promoted income equality was to increase the minimum wage regularly. For example, in 1976 the GDR raised the monthly minimum wage from 350 to 400 marks and instituted sliding scale increases for those earning between 400 and 500 marks per month. Together these moves benefited one in seven GDR workers (Zimmermann [1977:111]).

45. For example, Dennis (1992:68) reported that people with higher education degrees working in research and technology earned salaries 27 percent above the GDR average.

46. Interview in Berlin, summer 1988; Meier (1987a:6). See also Marcuse (1991:58); Wierling (1996:52); and Baylis (1974:68, 78).

47. Interview in Bernau, spring 1989.

48. For example, see Pravda (1979:218–19); and Ruble (1986:44–46). For early indications of the same sentiments in the GDR, see Baylis (1974:100). On the Soviet intelligentsia's perspective on income differences, see Connor (1991:105); and Teckenberg (1990:30). Commentators have often noted a difference between workers and the intelligentsia, especially its scientific-technical segment, in attitudes toward the periodic economic reforms attempted in socialist countries. In general, those in the scientific-technical intelligentsia were solid supporters of such changes, whereas

workers did not necessarily see them in their interests. See discussions by Connor (1981:170); Rakovski (1978:21, 26–28); Konrád and Szelényi (1979:201–2); Connor (1991:198–99); Pravda (1979:217–18); Cox (1991:188); and Pravda (1981:46–47).

49. In this context, Lamont's (1992:esp. chs. 5 and 6) argument that the relative unimportance of such socioeconomic class markers as money correlates with the relative dominance of the public, nonprofit sector an the economy is interesting.

50. Interview in Berlin, spring 1991. See Konrád and Szelényi (1979:172–73) for a more extended discussion. See also Baylis (1974:70–71).

51. See Leonhard's (1958:376–77) interesting early description of the four-class dining system at the office of the Central Committee.

52. Interview in Bernau, summer 1989.

53. Opp, Voss, and Gern (1995:54). For a discussion of the unsatisfactory working conditions of many unskilled and semiskilled GDR workers, see Haas (1988). Andorka, István, and Gyenei's (1984:36) survey data from Hungary showed between 6 percent and 14 percent of the managerial, professional, and clerical staff worked in unhealthy conditions, while between 26 percent and 48 percent of industrial workers did so.

54. Interview in Berlin, winter 1991.

55. It is not clear that, in aggregate, one group spent substantially more hours at work than the other. Baylis (1974:107) cited GDR studies that put the average work week of factory directors at about 60–70 hours. See also "What It Takes to Be a Boss" (1986:50). Scharf (1984:149) maintained production workers, for whom overtime was common, worked 2–4 hours a week longer than office employees. A survey of one GDR town revealed that the intelligentsia had more leisure time than other groups of employees (Ludz [1981:278, 281]).

56. Jugel, Spangenberg, and Stollberg (1978:140). See ibid., 139, on the relationship between education and shift work in their sample.

57. Ibid., 10; Staatliche Zentralverwaltung für Statistik (1988:152); G. E. Edwards (1985:85); Zimmermann (1978:5–6).

58. See, for example, Dennis (1991:18); Meier (1987a:15); and Rueschemeyer (1988:365). Jugel, Spangenberg, and Stollberg's (1978) study portrayed a less negative picture of shift work than I uncovered in my discussions with workers. See also G. E. Edwards (1985:86).

59. For discussions of various control and organization strategies, see R. Edwards (1979); Fuller and Smith (1991); and Burawoy (1979).

60. Borneman (1988:7–21).

61. Such positions were sometimes referred to as Leerstelle. In German, this was a play on words. Lehrstelle means a traineeship or apprenticeship held prior to assuming a permanent job, while leer means empty.

62. See, for example, Dennis (1991:16, 19); Deppe and Hoß (1989:175); Belwe and Klinger (1986:72); Erbe (1979b:413–14); and Erbe (1979a:108–9). Erbe (1989a:109), who provided detailed information on this topic, cited one GDR study claiming that "no linear dependence exists between [the] development of steps in the introduction of technology in production and the qualification demands and the mental-creative content of work." See also Haas (1988).

63. Steele (1977:138); see, for example, Dennis (1991:11); and G. E. Edwards (1985:83).

64. Baylis (1978:101, 93). For information on working-class involvement in such bodies elsewhere in East and Central Europe, see Pravda (1981:57); Bielasiak (1981:103); and Konrád and Szelényi (1979:173–74).

65. Interview in Bernau, summer 1989; Markovits (1982:550, 582). See also Borneman (1988:25). Borneman (1988:6), however, reported that in the mid-1980s, more than half the members of the *Konfliktkommissionen* were working class. *Konfliktkommissionen* are discussed further in chapter 7.

66. Interview in Berlin, summer 1989. Self-employed intellectuals were rarely even union members.

67. I was told that nonstate workplaces, such as the social service agencies discussed earlier, were also virtually union-free, though for a different reason.

68. Interviews in Berlin, spring 1988 and spring 1991, and Leipzig, summer 1988.

69. See Scharf (1984:149), who argued that production workers "experience more pressure [than office employees] to take part in union and production meetings held after work hours." Shift work, which was performed largely by the working class, created a major obstacle to workers' involvement in union meetings. Working-class women had difficulty staying active in the unions because of their unpaid work obligations, and many brought this up in interviews. Rueschemeyer (1983:31) noted that "nearly all professionals have functions in the union at some time," a claim that could hardly be made about workers. It was not uncommon for middle-class members to dominate workplace unions not only through the union leadership positions they held (see chapter 4) but also because of their higher occupational status. See, for example, Rueschemeyer (1983:35); and Kirschner (1989:10).

70. Wierling (1996:52).

71. Szelényi (1978:77). See also Gleye (1991:197); Marcuse (1991:58, 59, 241); Scharf (1984:157); and Kornai (1992:331–32).

72. Quoted in Philipsen (1993:124–25). This badge of intellectual privilege never corresponded perfectly to official income. See Kornai (1992:42–43, 322, 323); Konrád and Szelényi (1979:173); and Szelényi (1978:70).

73. Laufer (1991:18); Anderson (1990:176). Weber (1988:98) reported that in 1985, GDR households with incomes below 800 marks per month owned 6 passenger cars per 100 living units, while those with incomes above 2,200 marks per month owned 77 passenger cars per 100 living units. The average for the country was 46 passenger cars per 100 households. Fifty-nine percent of McFalls's (1995:175) sample had a technical college or university degree, and 62 percent of that sample owned a car in 1989. Weber (1988:98) also provided figures on washing machine and TV ownership. For some roughly comparable figures from Hungary and the Soviet Union, see Brezinski (1987:94); Andorka, István, and Gyenei (1984:40); and Teckenberg (1990:29).

74. Greenwald (1993:111). See also ibid., 91.

75. Although the intelligentsia was materially more privileged than workers, all members of the intelligentsia were not equally privileged. Gradations of material privilege within the intelligentsia were apparent to those familiar with the GDR and other state socialist societies. On the GDR, see Marcuse (1991:272); and Leonhard (1958:379). On state socialist societies in general, see Kornai (1992:43, 322).

76. For information on the GDR intelligentsia and foreign travel, see Goeckel (1990:209).

77. Interview in Berlin, fall 1990. Many have correctly pointed out that access to hard currency did not follow strict class lines. Anyone with relatives or friends in the West could accept limited gifts of Western currency, and apparently about 30 percent of the population from disparate walks of life had such connections in the 1980s (interview in Berlin, fall 1990). Certain high-level and mid-level (but not top-level) party people, however, were not allowed to have Western contacts and therefore amassed few West German marks in this way. Similarly, permission to travel to the West, which by the mid-1980s had become a good deal easier for those with relatives there, did not totally correspond to class position. Nonetheless, it is incorrect to suggest that access to hard currency was only randomly associated with class.

78. Marcuse (1991:188).

79. On this point, see Konrád and Szelényi (1979:172). Marcuse (1991:187) described a special class of goods, called *Bück-waren* (stoop goods). These were particular items for "special" customers, which GDR shopkeepers had to "stoop" under the counter to retrieve.

80. Darnton (1991:173, 188). On this point, see also Gleye (1991:197); Scharf (1984:119); Zimmermann (1978:5); and Marcuse (1991:48, 111).

81. Leonhard (1958:377–78); Philipsen (1993:125).

82. Szelényi (1978:67). See also Kornai (1992:320, 321).

83. Staatliche Zentralverwaltung für Statistik (1988:262–63). Unfortunately, I have no precise information on the social class of occupants in state subsidized versus private housing in the GDR.

84. Rueschemeyer (1991:43). Nearly 2 billion marks were spent on culture in 1987 (Staatliche Zentralverwaltung für Statistik [1988:262–63]). See also Staatliche Zentralverwaltung für Statistik (1988:272–73); and Hanke (1984:222–23). In a largely working-class sample, Jugel, Spangenberg, and Stollberg (1978:79) found that about 90–100 percent never went to concerts.

85. Staatliche Zentralverwaltung für Statistik (1988:274–75); Greenwald (1993:36). Kornai (1992:43, 322) and Konrád and Szelényi (1979:172) suggested such inequities were not abnormal in other East and Central European socialist countries.

86. Staatliche Zentralverwaltung für Statistik (1988:270–71); Smith (1988:57).

87. Staatliche Zentralverwaltung für Statistik (1988:268–69).

88. Joppke (1995:224); Staatliche Zentralverwaltung für Statistik (1988:272, 273); Michalsky (1984:252, 253). See also Scharf (1984:103); and Keefe (1982:84). In the early days of the republic, when material conditions were far worse, Leonhard (1958:378–79) made the following pertinent comments about the Central Committee rest home: "[The] Rest Home was very luxuriously fitted up for that date. It was surrounded by a huge park and entirely cut off from the outside world. The feeding there was so sumptuous that it made even the rations at the Central Committee building appear poor by comparison. Careful attention was paid to rank in the exercise of all these privileges. At first the Rest Home was used by all officials in the Central Committee *apparat.* Not long afterwards, however, a new distinction was introduced: an even more exclusive Rest Home was established for the most senior members of the Central Secretariat."

89. Staatliche Zentralverwaltung für Statistik (1988:262–63).

90. Scharf (1989:17–18); Zimmermann (1978:28); Szelényi (1978:68, 85).

91. Scharf (1984:117–118). According to Scharf (1989:14–15), income taxes had only a small impact on this equation. He maintained that, in aggregate, personal income taxes appeared "very nearly proportional except for the very lowest income categories." Scharf (1984:99) also noted that bonuses and overtime income were not taxed and that certain intelligentsia occupations enjoyed special tax exclusions. Brezinski (1987:94) reported that up to 3,000 marks a year from "unofficial and unregistered" work were tax-free after 1972.

92. In chapter 1, we also saw that workers held uncomplimentary opinions about intellectuals. No doubt the unfavorable views each class had of the other were reinforcing. However, in my reading of why workers did not join the middle-class challengers during the *Wende*, the latter's attitudes surfaced as the more significant.

93. Interview in Berlin, spring 1991; Philipsen (1993:347); interviews in Berlin, spring 1991 and fall 1990; Philipsen (1993:355). See also Philipsen (1993:173, 210, 247, 275); Joppke (1995:199); Wallace (1992:116–17); and Parmalee (1994:309).

94. There were, of course, exceptions. Some individuals, even some factions of opposition groups, thought the development of a mass base was extremely important. Some of these activists hoped their groups would evolve into a collection of loosely linked, democratic, relatively small, grass-roots groups, to whom an overall leadership would somehow be accountable. Some moves in this direction were made in the local issue-oriented round tables. Some alternative institutions were also formed. Pamphlets were produced and distributed suggesting how people could organize themselves when it was still illegal to do so. Vereinigte Linke, Neues Forum, and Demokratie Jetzt all made some attempts to work within some enterprises (interviews in Berlin, fall 1990 and spring 1991; Pirker et al. [1990:59, 60, 77]). As the *Wende* progressed, tensions mounted between activists who argued for the mass-movement approach to politics, which depended on recruiting and mobilizing more workers, and those who wanted to form traditional political parties and focus on attracting votes, participating in government, and grooming appealing leaders. Within Neues Forum, this split was serious and never resolved to the satisfaction of many members, prompting some to leave for the SPD-DDR and others to joint such groups as the IUG (Initiative for Independent Unions) (interview in Berlin, spring 1991).

95. Philipsen (1993:290). See also Segert (1992:9).

96. Interview in Berlin, spring 1991.

97. *Kran*, March 15, 1990, 2.

98. Interview in Berlin, spring 1991.

99. Joppke (1995:163).

100. See, for example, Philipsen (1993:267).

101. See chapter 6 for elucidation.

102. Interview in Berlin, fall 1990.

103. Interview in Frankfurt Oder, fall 1990.

104. Some middle-class activists were aware of some of these issues. See, for example, Rein (1989:28–29); Musch (1990:98); and Reißig (1991:28). See Lötsch (1992:52)

for mention of why freedom of speech was a less meaningful goal for workers than for the intelligentsia.

105. For mention of such efforts, see *IUG,* December 1989, 2, and March 26, 1990, 1–2; and Pirker et al. (1990:80). Many were undertaken on behalf of the *Angestellten* (white-collar workers). *Angestellten* included white-collar workers as a whole, some of whom were not of the intelligentsia. However, the sectors of *Angestellten* I knew of that pushed for separate unions were overwhelmingly intellectual—doctors, engineers, and administrators, for example. Erbe (1979b:419–20) raised questions about the argument that *Angestellten* and production workers were becoming less distinguishable, and my interviews support this position.

106. Interview in Bernau, fall 1990. The IUG, discussed in the following chapter, waffled on the issue of separate *Angestellten* unions. They received support from an *Angestellten* union in the FRG, held at least one forum on the pros and cons of this union split, and printed letters and articles supporting the formation of a country-wide *Angestellten* confederation in their newsletter (*IUG,* March 26, 1990, 1–2, and February 1, 1990, 11). One IUG activist told me the organization ultimately opposed this idea, however.

107. *IUG,* March 26, 1990, 1.

108. *Kran,* March 15, 1990, 5.

109. While middle-class oppositionists often spoke and behaved in ways that discouraged workers from joining their challenge, party members were not so dissuaded. Lots of SED members were active in Vereinigte Linke; in Neues Forum, which according to one informant was quite open about accepting them (interview in Berlin, spring 1991); and, of course, in the PDS. Party figures often attended street demonstrations; they shared the podium with middle-class activists at some of the biggest of these; and they were cosignatories of some widely distributed political proclamations of the period. Oppositionists' sympathetic estimation of party members was once suggested in an interview with a Neues Forum principal. Some party members, he said, "put as much effort as we do into changing conditions. The only difference is our tactics and maybe our strategy" (Rein [1989:23]). See also Philipsen (1993:44, 240–41, 262).

110. Note that I have not even considered symbolic resources or other material resources, such as money, which would also have accrued disproportionately to intellectuals and would have further solidified their ascendance among *Wende* activists of both types.

111. Greenwald (1993:197).

112. Greenwald's (1993:226) mention of a well-known SED figure who was more widely accepted by workers than were other party people because he "look[ed] and sound[ed] like a Berlin proletarian, not a fluent-in-four-languages intellectual" is relevant here.

113. Surely individual members of both classes enjoyed more positive relations with one another than what I describe here. However, because my interest is working-*class* political behavior, I cannot base my analysis on the relationships between *individuals* of both classes.

114. The workplace was the exception. The overriding feature of interclass contact there, however, was inequality.

115. Parmalee (1994:310).

Chapter 6: Workers on Stage

1. Burawoy and Lukács (1992:159) would not be surprised: "Attempts at [worker] self-organization [most naturally emerge] in production—for that is where the destiny of workers is being determined, where the legacy of past class consciousness is most developed, where mobilizing power is most easily aggregated. . . ." For pertinent worker comments, see Philipsen (1993:289).

2. For information on the *Betriebsräte* of this period, see Moore (1978:esp. chap. 9).

3. For more information on the *Betriebsräte* in the early years of the GDR, see Scharf (1974:chap. 3); Pirker et al. (1990:52–58); and Suckut (1982).

4. Pirker et al. (1990:60–62). See also Grabsch and Kschischan (1990:4).

5. See, for example, Grabsch and Kschischan (1990:4, 5).

6. Grabsch and Kschischan (1990:7–8), however, found a good relationship between the *Betriebsrat* and management in most of the six firms they studied.

7. Interview in Berlin, winter 1990. According to 1972 FRG law, *Betriebsrat* members cannot be dismissed while holding office or for one year thereafter. See also Pirker et al. (1990:61–62). I also encountered examples of workers electing older coworkers to the *Betriebsrat* to protect them from dismissal.

8. Grabsch and Kschischan (1990:10).

9. Interview in Berlin, winter 1990.

10. Ibid., spring 1991.

11. Ibid., winter 1990; Pirker et al. (1990:63, 79); Grabsch and Kschischan (1990:10). According to the German Information Center (1977:11), in the FRG, "Both employer and *Betriebsrat* must avoid any action that could disturb industrial accord on the shop floor. Strikes can only be called by the union and only on a regional or national level, not by the *Betriebsrat*.

12. Interview in Bernau, fall 1990. See also Pirker et al. (1990:75, 77).

13. Interview in Berlin, spring 1991; Kirschner (1990:40–41); Pirker et al. (1990:73). Pirker et al. (1990:60) noted that union opposition to work councils was much stronger in Berlin than in Leipzig.

14. Pirker et al. (1990:61, 69).

15. Interview near Bernau, fall 1990. In some workplaces, the union and the *Betriebsrat* merged structures and personnel. See, for example, Grabsch and Kschischan (1990); and Segert (1992).

16. Pirker et al. (1990:69).

17. Interview in Berlin, fall 1990. For additional discussion of the prominence of production-based intellectuals in the work councils, see Kirschner (1990:40); and Pirker et al. (1990:60, 62, 69).

18. Interview in Berlin, spring 1991; Pirker et al. (1990:59, 60, 62, 73–74).

19. Pirker et al. (1990:62). Grabsch and Kschischan (1990:4–5) reported participa-

tion rates between 72 percent and 50 percent in the *Betriebsrat* elections in the firms they studied. Segert (1992:24) reported on a *Betriebsrat* election with only 44 percent turnout. See also Segert (1992:43).

20. Interview in Berlin, winter 1991. See also Grabsch and Kschischan (1990:7); and Kirschner (1990:31).

21. Pirker et al. (1990:69–70).

22. These illustrations of radical union structural and procedural reform come from *IUG*, December 1989, 4; an interview in Berlin, winter 1990; Kirschner (1990:8, 11–12, 16); and *Kran*, January 18, 1990, 5, February 1, 1990, 1, 2, 5, February 15, 1990, 1, and March 1, 1990, 1, 2. See also Segert (1992:10, 17, 18, 20, 22, 43). On the spokespersons' councils and the social councils, see the following section.

23. Interview in Berlin, fall 1990. Other examples in this paragraph come from interviews near Bernau, fall 1990, and in Berlin, fall 1990; and from Kirschner (1990). See also Segert (1992:19).

24. Emulations and competitions among groups of workers occurred frequently in the GDR. The focus of such campaigns differed, but many centered on increased productivity.

25. *IUG*, December 1989, 3–4.

26. Segert (1992:17, 18).

27. Kirschner (1990:45). See also Grabsch and Kschischan (1990:10).

28. My classification of these union college students as workers is arguable. They were virtually all party members. Prior to enrolling in the union college, many had been *Vertrauensleute*, AGL, or BGL members. Some had even held mid-level union positions, and nearly all were headed for such posts upon graduation. Most, therefore, were only a diploma away from inclusion in the GDR intelligentsia. Nonetheless, as I became acquainted with some of these students before the revolution, I found a number had close connections to workplaces and intimate knowledge of workers' situations, and they appeared genuinely committed to serving workers' interests. Both the concerns and the manner of many were unlike those of numerous BGL chairs and higher union functionaries I talked to before the crisis. So, too, it turned out, was their involvement in revolutionary politics. For a contrasting assessment, see Böhm (1990:10).

29. According to Schießl (1990:50), some union researchers brought the need for union reform to the attention of the organization's leadership in 1988. Their critiques and suggestions, however, were swept under the rug, only to reemerge during the *Wende*. Informal and unofficial discussions on the need for union renewal were also occurring at base levels of the union before the *Wende*. Segert (1992:11) provided an example of a radical reform action immediately prior to the period I consider: in August 1989, the BGL of a Brandenburg steel works refused to go through the ritual of approving the 1990 plan.

30. "Für eine Wende in der Gewerkschaftsarbeit" (1989:3, 5). The unions' relationship with their legislative deputies in the Volkskammer and in lower-level legislative bodies also came under scrutiny. Early on, demands were made for more union control over these representatives. Later, it was suggested that the union dismantle its

legislative faction, since it was more beholden to the party and state than to workers' organizations.

31. Some viewed the law as the FDGB's cynical, last-ditch bid to retain power. See,
for example, Gill (1991:74–77). Others, however, praised it as thoroughgoing and
progressive.

32. Interviews in Bernau and Berlin, fall 1990. In their activism, the students also
differentiated themselves from the BGL at the union college.

33. Two representatives from Fritz Heckert were also regular participants in IUG
(Initiative for Independent Unions) activities in Berlin. IUG representatives were
invited to planning meetings for the Extraordinary FDGB Congress and to this congress itself (interview in Berlin, spring 1991).

34. Pirker et al. (1990:33); interview in Bernau, fall 1990 (quote).

35. See, for example, Schießl (1990:51).

36. See, for example, "Für eine Wende in der Gewerkschaftsarbeit" (1989:1); and
IUG, February 1, 1990, 10. For mention of how representatives to the Extraordinary
FDGB Congress were chosen at one worksite, see *Kran*, January 18, 1990, 5. For discussion of the representative to this congress in one plant, see Segert (1992:24). Gill
(1991:75), who was quite critical of the congress, commented positively on how representatives to the meeting were selected. For interesting commentary on the Extraordinary FDGB Congress itself, see *Tribüne*, February 1, 1990, 1, 2; *Kran*, February 15,
1990, 5; Segert (1992:18); and Schießl (1990:51, 52). According to this last source, FRG
unionists were not invited to the event.

37. Lydike (1990:8).

38. "Für eine Wende in der Gewerkschaftsarbeit" (1989:4); Komitee zur Vorbereitung des außerordentlichen FDGB-Kongresses (1990:side 1)

39. See Schießl's (1990:52, 53) interesting assessment of why the radical union reform movement ultimately failed.

40. Since worker activists adopted these labels somewhat arbitrarily, two spokespersons' councils, for example, might bear little resemblance to each other, or organizations in different workplaces might be known by different names, even though
they operated in a similar fashion.

41. Lohr (1990:4).

42. Spokespersons' councils were relatively rare. Consequently, I never interviewed
a worker or visited a workplace where one had been set up. The following account draws
from the work of Kirschner (1990:6–33). Other *Sprecherräte* were discussed briefly in
IUG, May 13, 1990, 4, and January 1990, 6; and in Grabsch and Kschischan (1990:10).

43. Kirschner (1990:9).

44. Ibid., 10.

45. Ibid., 11. Groups representing workers were also elected in several production
areas of this firm. These groups then came together to form a larger committee representing these particular areas. The demands of this committee were more far-reaching than those of the *Sprecherrat*. It argued for the dismissal of a department manager and won the right of its chair to approve salary agreements and expenditures.
The committee worked as a partner of department-level management, and the in-

troduction of a new salary model became the focus of its activities, which continued past the March union elections. Overall, this committee's existence allowed workers in the areas it represented greater participation in economic reform than workers in other departments of the enterprise enjoyed.

46. Social councils were also relatively uncommon, so it is fortunate that Kirschner (1990:34–46) detailed the formation and functioning of the one discussed below. For mention of another, see Schnibben (1990:29).

47. Kirschner (1990:39).

48. At one point, some production-based intellectuals in the factory suggested transforming the *Gesellschaftliche Rat* into a *Betriebsrat*. The *Vertrauensleute*, however, soundly defeated this idea. They argued that a *Betriebsrat* would be less independent from management (Kirschner [1990:40]).

49. On these events, see Pirker et al. (1990:79); and *Kran,* February 15, 1990, 1, 2. For discussion of a "business committee" that took over the tasks of the old BGL as well as additional ones, see *Kran,* March 1, 1990, 1.

50. Elections for new *Vertrauensleute* in this plant, however, were carried out successfully. This is described in Pirker el al. (1990:78–79).

51. Interview in Berlin, spring 1991. Analogous reasoning made the IUG wary of the *Betriebsrat* movement. "Our people thought that the *Betriebsräte* would create another establishment that would exist totally separated from the majority of workers. There wouldn't be a mobilized base. There wouldn't be any workers who cared about it or who regularly asked the *Betriebsrat* what it was doing or figured out on their own what they wanted from the *Betriebsrat*. The *Betriebsräte* wouldn't have to answer to any specific group of people. They'd just do their own thing" (ibid.).

52. Ibid.

53. Ibid.

54. *IUG,* February 1, 1990, 6–7.

55. For information on the planning meeting prior to this national congress, see *Tribüne,* February 5, 1990, 2.

56. Ibid., February 15, 1990, 2.

57. See, for example, *IUG,* June 9, 1990, 3, 4.

58. Interview in Berlin, spring 1991. In one regional IUG gathering, workers made up only 30 percent of participants (*IUG,* February 1, 1990, 6). The *Tribüne* (February 5, 1990, 2) reported that the IUG was supported by the white-collar union from the FRG but that there were no contacts with the DGB (Confederation of German Trade Unions, FRG). Schießl (1990:50) said the IUG received support from such middle-class-dominated citizens' opposition groups as Neues Forum and Vereinigte Linke.

59. Interviews in Berlin, spring 1991.

60. Ibid.

61. Interview in Berlin, spring 1991.

62. Ibid.

63. A handful of the original IUG members, along with new people from both the eastern and western parts of Germany, eventually reorganized as the Initiative for Critical Union Work. The new group's focus was improving the DGB.

Chapter 7: A Second Look at the Labor Process and Workplace Politics

1. See, for example, Ticktin (1992).

2. Interviews in Bernau, summer 1989 and fall 1990. As a *Kombinat* director put it, "We are world champions in improvisation" (*Leipziger Volkszeitung,* October 20, 1989, 3). After the revolution, Jürgens, Klinzing, and Turner (1992:26) reported a work force in the former GDR that was "used to improvising and problem solving." See also Wierling (1996:54).

3. Limiting workers' control was not the only, or even the manifest, goal of these efforts. The Innovators' Movement was also intended to encourage economically profitable innovation. The rationalization workshops were also an attempt by the *Kombinate* and large enterprises to inject some predictability into their otherwise chaotic supply situations by producing as many of their own inputs as possible. For additional analyses of the goals of the rationalization workshops, their funding, and their contribution to the GDR economy, see Wenzel (1984).

4. Staatliche Zentralverwaltung für Statistik (1988:132). Recall from chapter 5, however, that participation rates in the Innovators' Movement were comparatively low among unskilled workers.

5. Staatliche Zentralverwaltung für Statistik (1988:109); Wenzel (1984:1170, 1172); Voskamp and Wittke (1991:348–349). Edeling (1990:8) observed that while critical to production in the socialist economy after the *Wende,* workers in rationalization workshops were among those most vulnerable to layoffs. Kornai (1992:249) noted that set-ups similar to the GDR rationalization workshops existed in other socialist countries.

6. Markovits (1982:569–70).

7. Interview in Berlin, fall 1990. Recall that, due to the autonomous logic of the economy, labor, like all other production inputs, could be in overall short supply even while it sometimes appeared to be in oversupply in some establishments. The labor shortage in the GDR also had clear implications for how hard people worked. See chapter 3 on these points.

8. Deppe and Hoß (1989:esp. 178–84).

9. Marcuse (1991:283).

10. Voskamp and Wittke (1991:358).

11. Burawoy and Lukács (1992:78).

12. Braverman (1974).

13. Interview in Berlin, summer 1991.

14. Granick's (1975:216) observations provided evidence of workers' management of production in the GDR in the 1970s. Stark (1986) described Hungary's move to institutionalize the economic potential of workers' control of production through enterprise-business-work partnerships (VGMs).

15. Students of the GDR workplace have noted prerevolutionary instances in which workers used their control over production successfully to challenge management, for instance, over norms, the use of such new technologies as robots and computer-controlled machine tools, and the organization of labor time. For examples, see Meier (1987a:5–6, 15); and Voskamp and Wittke (1991:358).

16. Burawoy and Lukács (1992:173).

17. Contrast the following to Haraszti's (1978:92) account of choosing the local union head in Hungary in the early 1970s.

18. See, for example, Allen (1989:87–88).

19. Interviews in Bernau, summer 1989.

20. See also Kirschner (1989:52). In these cases, *Vertrauensleute* were technically chosen by consensus, not by ballot.

21. The *Kollektive* I knew firsthand averaged 22 members.

22. Interview in Bernau, summer 1989.

23. Pirker et al. (1990:78–79); *Kran*, March 1, 1990, 2. Before the *Wende*, Kirschner (1989:49, 50) also found evidence of greater rank-and-file confidence in and respect for *Vertrauensleute* than for higher-level union officials at the worksite. He also found that voter turnout was the highest in *Vertrauensleute* elections and that these posts were always filled, something not always the case with higher-level positions. See also *Kran*, November 9, 1989, 2, 4, and February 1, 1990, 5; and Segert (1992:10).

24. Throughout the discussion of workplace politics in this chapter, recall the analogous argument of chapter 5 regarding members of the the GDR intelligentsia, who, however, had far more extensive opportunities to do politics before the *Wende* than did workers.

25. Interview in Bernau, summer 1989. Or, as a tool finisher told Kirschner (1990:28) approvingly, "Our *Vertrauensmann*, because he always fought for our demands, was a thorn in the department manager's side. They prefer someone who always says 'yes' and 'amen.'"

26. Interviews in Bernau and Berlin, summer 1989. As another *Vertrauensperson* told Kirschner (1990:30, 31), "I was always there for my co-workers. My behavior and appearance left a bad impression on factory leadership, so because of that I was elected *Vertrauensmann* after a couple of years and have kept on getting elected for about 15 years." For another example of *Vertrauensleute* independence, see Philipsen (1993:115). Some workers holding other unpaid union offices, some secured in pre-chewed selection processes, also saw themselves as assertive and worker-identified. The cultural officer of one BGL, for example, who twice interrupted my meeting with his boss, striding confidently into the room without knocking and walking right up to his superior, once to ask a question and once to shove some paper under his nose to be signed, told me, "I like my union work because I'm not afraid of confronting anyone" (interview near Leipzig, summer 1988). I even came across some paid union officials who appeared to be cut from a more activist mold, thereby distinguishing themselves from many of their union counterparts in other workplaces. The BGL chair in an electric motor factory, for example, told me, "I'm very much for strong *Vertrauensleute*. It makes my job better. Myself, I'm a fighter. If there are conflicts, I fight for the interest of the workers I represent. I'm proud of the acceptance the workers give me, and I try to carry through with their proposals and criticisms" (interview in Berlin, summer 1988). Kirschner's (1989:78, 79) survey of union officers in a large plant uncovered interesting suggestions of differences between *Vertrauensleute* and AGL and BGL officers on this issue: 62 percent of *Vertrauensleute*, but only 51 percent of AGL and BGL officers, felt union functionaries must represent work-

ers' interests in order to change enterprise goals and conditions; 16 percent of AGL and BGL officers, but only 9 percent of *Vertrauensleute,* felt that certain enterprise conditions and goals provided the framework for the representation of workers' interests; 29 percent of AGL and BGL officers, but only 17 percent of *Vertrauensleute,* felt unions and state management had basically the same interests; and 51 percent of *Vertrauensleute,* but only 43 percent of AGL and BGL officers, felt that if the union did not assert itself vis-à-vis management, the social needs of workers would be subordinated to economic goals. Later Kirschner (1989:95, 96) noted that the most dissatisfied group of union functionaries in the plant were largely *Vertrauensleute* who were not party members and who strongly emphasized conflict and workers' interests. Kirschner (1989:72–73) also reported that 37 percent of *Vertrauensleute* felt their ability to argue was sufficient to carry out their union tasks.

27. Lötsch's (1992:52) comments are of interest here: "Ordinary workers were already quite used to expressing their opinions in daily life (even at their work-places)." See also Philipsen (1993:123). The *Kollektiv* was the place in the worksite where workers enjoyed the fullest freedom of expression. Stollberg (1988:156) cited research indicating that the best functioning *Kollektive* were those in which everyone was an active union member.

28. For relevant information on the central role of *Kollektiv* leadership, see Stollberg (1988:157–59).

29. See, for example, Kirschner (1990:16); Segert (1992:43); and Pirker et al. (1990: 78–79).

30. See, for example, Rueschemeyer (1983:30, 45); Scharf (1984:131); and Rueschemeyer and Scharf (1986:62, 79, 81, 82). For information on union autonomy at the base level in the 1950s, see Baring (1972:16, 35, 43); and Scharf (1974:57, 84, 87, 91, 92).

31. It may not have been so common for workers to take their problems to *Vertrauensleute* in the 1960s. At that time, Scharf (1974:194) reported a "clear disposition to by-pass immediate functionaries in favor of contacting officials of the BGL." See also ibid., 195, 200.

32. For additional mention of the autonomy of GDR work collectives, see Rueschemeyer and Scharf (1986:78, 79); Rueschemeyer (1983:30); Rueschemeyer (1982:163); and Kirschner (1989:126).

33. See chapter 8 for discussion of why so much of this leadership talent went underutilized during the *Wende.*

34. Lohr (1990:2–3) emphasized noninstitutionalized forms of direct bargaining as vehicles for workers' participation in the GDR.

35. Interviews in Leipzig, summer 1988, and near Bernau, summer 1989. The collective agreement, redrafted annually, contained agreements between management and the enterprise-level union on matters ranging from wages to support for women workers to workers' recreational activities to working conditions.

36. Kirschner (1990:28).

37. Interview in Frankfurt Oder, summer 1989; Kirschner (1990:28). My interviews, as well as the research of others, also revealed union successes in dealing with prob-

lems concerning work hours, work organization, transfers, job evaluations, and promotions, as well as norms and pay. Discipline and bonus distribution also belong on this list, though from chapter 3 we know that the meaning of successful union involvement in these areas was not straightforward. Kirschner's (1989:72–73) intensive prerevolutionary study of one factory contains some survey results consistent with the argument here: 48 percent of the *Vertrauensleute* said their ability to implement their ideas was sufficient to do successful union work, 41 percent said their organizational talents were adequate to do so, and 50 percent felt their insights into the technical and technological connections of the production process were up to this task. Over half of the *Vertrauensleute* said such issues as hygiene, dirt, noise, heat, and the resolution of disputes between workers and managers should be "a" main or "the" main task of the union, and over one third put wages in this category (Kirschner [1989:74]). Over 72 percent of the *Vertrauensleute* agreed or largely agreed that state leaders guaranteed the necessary prerequisites (time, money, space, materials) to allow them to do their jobs, and 32 percent responded similarly to the statement that poor managerial decisions could be quickly corrected through the influence of *Vertrauensleute* (Kirschner [1989:82]). The following are the percentages of *Vertrauensleute* who were either satisfied or more satisfied than dissatisfied with particular areas of union work in this *Betrieb:* conflicts with leaders, 80 percent; discipline, 89 percent; disaggregation of the plan down to the *Kollektiv* and workplace level, 75 percent; actual norm and achievement guidelines in workplaces, 77 percent; executing social and economic policies together and outside the firm, 76 percent (Kirschner [1989:92–93]). Finally, 38 percent of all functionaries who answered all Kirschner's questions about satisfaction with the effectiveness of union work in particular areas (there were many more than those just mentioned) were not dissatisfied in any sphere. This group was made up evenly of *Vertrauensleute* and AGL/BGL functionaries and of party and nonparty members. Leading AGL and BGL functionaries, however, were the most likely to fall into this satisfied group (Kirschner [1989:96]).

38. The *Konfliktkommissionen* are excellent examples of the Janus-faced character of workplace politics in the GDR. Compare the following discussion with that in chapter 5 to understand how these bodies played a role in both encouraging and discouraging working-class activism.

39. Otte, Sahr, and Herzog (1988:10, 15); Lehrstuhl Gewerkschaftsaufbau (1989:2). On the composition of the grievance commissions, see also Borneman (1988:4–5, 9, 22). Sometimes, however, *Konfliktkommissionen* served larger groups of workers, such as one I knew of in a service establishment that resolved disputes for over six hundred employees.

40. Borneman (1988:26). Apparently the chair of the grievance commission sometimes made nominations. Dennis (1988:107) contended that nominations were proposed by enterprise union executives, but I never heard of this happening. Wolfe (1989:69) maintained grievance commission members were "nominated in the union groups and by leaders of the union in a gathering of the workers." See also Keefe (1982:88).

41. Staatliche Zentralverwaltung für Statistik (1988:411); Borneman (1988:6). I was

told that inventory discrepancies and indiscipline accounted for the fact that grievance commissions in the commerce and service sectors were the busiest (interview
in Bernau, summer 1989). Borneman (1988:15–16, 32) reported on a commission in a
hotel that heard twenty cases in one year. Heavy industry reportedly had more cases
than light industry, and health, government administration, and education supposedly had the least. In the workplaces I knew best, the number of *Konfliktkommission*
cases ranged from none in two years to nine cases in one year.

42. Borneman (1988:2).

43. Ibid., 5; Rueschemeyer and Scharf (1986:70). *Konfliktkommissionen* also made
annual reports on their activities to the BGL. Supraworksite union bodies oversaw
the legal quality of grievance commission work.

44. The district union office also dispensed legal advice to workers.

45. See Markovits (1982:594) on this point.

46. One woman felt it so important that the views of the entire *Kollektiv* be presented at grievance commission sessions that she argued every *Kollektiv* should have
its own member on the body (interview in Bernau, summer 1989).

47. Ibid.

48. Borneman told me that some workers complained about party interference
with the grievance commissions (discussion in Berlin, summer 1988). I was told that
the normal amount of time necessary for a grievance commission to handle a case
was two weeks and that the mandated maximum was one month (interview in
Bernau, summer 1989). Borneman (1988:22), however, discussed a case that lasted over
three months.

49. Borneman (1988:9). Borneman told me that union approval was necessary for
someone from outside a worksite to observe grievance commission proceedings
(discussion in Berlin, summer 1988).

50. Interviews in Berlin and Bernau, summer 1989. Borneman (1988:32) was told
between 70 and 80 percent. Of the seven cases he detailed, workers prevailed in five.
(In one of these five, the worker's boss was eventually brought before the grievance
commission and demoted, partly for bringing the case against the worker to the
Konfliktkommission in the first place.) However, both Borneman's and my research
suggested that grievance commissions sometimes blocked cases from proceeding to
a hearing when they did not think the worker could win, and this could help explain
the high percentage of worker wins. The estimates of employee wins both Borneman
and I heard were dramatically higher than Markovits's (1982:558–59) earlier ones of
20–25 percent. Unless there was a sharp rise in worker wins between the 1970s, to
which Markovits's data pertain, and the late 1980s, when Borneman and I conducted
our research, Markovits's low estimate was probably the result of her sample. It consisted of all cases decided by the Supreme Court between the beginning of 1970 and
mid-March 1977 and all labor law cases reported in the GDR labor law journal between 1975 and 1978. There are numerous reasons to suspect that such a sample would
not have been representative of all the cases coming before the *Konfliktkommissionen*.

51. Interview in Berlin, summer 1988. A handful of other people I interviewed commented that management was more afraid of the grievance commissions than of the

union and that workers respected the grievance commissions more than they did the union.

52. For relevant comments on the *Konfliktkommissionen,* see Borneman (1988:35, 36).

53. Each AGL usually grouped between 90 and 300 workers.

54. Interviews in Bernau and Berlin, summer 1989.

55. Interview in Bernau, summer 1989.

56. Ibid.; Kirschner (1990:31). See also Kirschner (1990:16).

57. Interview near Bernau, summer 1989.

58. Interview in Bernau, summer 1989. Some union functionaries Rueschemeyer (1983:30) interviewed faulted themselves for "not talking to workers enough" and "not listening."

59. For further, more theoretical, examination of some of the advantages mentioned here, see Barber (1984); Mansbridge (1983); and Cochrane (1986). See also Calhoun's (1991) discussion of direct interpersonal relationships.

60. Students of face-to-face politics mentioned additional advantages of this form of political practice: strengthening individual and collective accountability and responsibility as well as the opportunity to factor the intensity of a person's interest, feelings, and preferences into the decision-making equation. See, for example, Stollberg (1988:146). Although GDR workers did not speak of these explicitly, I suspect they were also part of their political experiences in the *Kollektive.*

61. Stollberg (1988:154). On the importance of social ties and friendship within the collective, see Rueschemeyer (1982:156, 160, 163); and Rueschemeyer (1988:367). Stollberg (1988:145–48) made interesting comments on this and related matters. Rueschemeyer and Scharf (1986:76–77) cited empirical findings linking work satisfaction and the quality of work to cooperative and collegial relations at work, pointing out that it was quite common for GDR workers to have personal friends among coworkers and revealing that personal friends were more often coworkers in socialist than in capitalist countries. They also cited a study in which respondents ranked "improved personal relations" as the principal achievement of the GDR *Kollektiv.* See Meier's (1987a:15–16) comments as well.

62. Interview in Berlin, fall 1991. Rueschemeyer (1983:29, 35, 36) and Rueschemeyer (1983:40–42) discussed mutual help with work tasks in collectives composed mainly of professionals. On the general importance of mutual help in the *Kollektiv,* see Stollberg (1988:esp. 148–49).

63. Rowbotham (1986:esp. 87–92).

64. Interview in Berlin, fall 1991.

65. Rueschemeyer (1988:367).

66. For interesting comments on this, see ibid, 364; and Stollberg (1988:148).

67. Interviews in Bernau and Berlin, summer 1989. See also Kirschner (1989:110); Kirschner (1990:31); and Scharf (1974:129). Rueschemeyer (1982:160) discussed involvement of the *Vertrauensperson* and collective members in handling "messy sexual relationships" in a professional collective.

68. According to three Humboldt University sociologists, over 50 percent of all

union functionaries were women, and the lower in the leadership ranks one went, the more women one encountered. I visited several enterprises in which a majority of union officers were women, even though the majority of workers appeared to be men.

69. Habermas (1990:7).

70. Marcuse (1990:42); Marcuse (1991:163). See also Voskamp and Wittke (1991:359–60).

71. For information on postrevolutionary opinions of the defunct regime, the unions, and postrevolutionary union membership figures that fit my line of argument, see Fichter (1991:30); Bowers (1990:42, 43); Kreißig and Schreiber (1992:251); Jürgens, Klinzing, and Turner (1992:13); and Philipsen (1993:291). See also Opp, Voss, and Gern (1995:73–75), who found that perceived political influence and belief in the efficacy of collective protest were relatively high in the GDR before October 9, 1989.

72. Reißig (1992:30) was one GDR commentator who argued for greater recognition of the complexities of socialism: "[They] should be borne in mind when undertaking a concrete analysis of real socialist systems, the similarities and differences."

Chapter 8: Workers in the Wings

1. Passive participants probably overlapped most closely with workers Kirschner (1990:25–29) identified as the "exasperated-expectant" group. See also Havel's (1985:64–67) discussion of levels of political activity under socialism.

2. See Philipsen's (1993:13) comments in this regard.

3. For evidence suggesting workers' passive support of the status quo in the Soviet Union, see Burawoy and Krotov (1993:90).

4. On factory newspapers in the GDR, see the appendix.

5. *Kran*, November 2, 1989, 5.

6. See, for example, ibid., October 12, 1989, 4, October 19, 1989, 3, 4, October 26, 1989, 4, and November 2, 1989, 5.

7. Ibid., November 16, 1989 5; *Neues Deutschland,* October 15, 1989, 2. Egon Krenz succeeded Honecker as the head of the GDR in mid-October 1989 and was himself deposed in early December. See also *Kran*, November 2, 1989, 5, and October 12, 1989, 2.

8. *Kran*, November 16, 1989, 3; *Neues Deutschland,* October 15, 1989, 2. See also *Kran,* November 2, 1989, 5, October 12, 1989, 2, October 26, 1989, 2, 4, and December 7, 1989, 3; and *Neues Deutschland,* October 15, 1989, 2. Survey results from November and December 1989 suggested steadily declining support for unification. Among those who were in favor of unification, many supported a confederationist version, which would have allowed the GDR to retain its political autonomy. For corroboration of this general point, see McFalls (1995:90); Philipsen (1993:284); and Greenwald (1993:274–75).

9. Interviews near Bernau, fall 1990, and in Berlin, spring 1991.

10. Interview in Berlin, fall 1990; Philipsen (1993:268). As one worker characterized the situation, "In the majority of companies, the old management, who were good communists at one point and who are the worst capitalists now, are still hold-

ing their positions. Some of these [old managers], though, were good, and they continue to stick up for employees" (interview in Berlin, fall 1990). See also Schnibben (1990:30).

11. *Kran,* December 7, 1989, 3; interviews near and in Bernau, fall 1990.

12. See, for example, Grabsch and Kschischan (1990:6–6). Alternately, Pirker et al. (1990:78) suggested an instrumental motivation for passive support of the unions. Workers may merely have worried that the allocation of vacation spots and cures and the approval of sick leaves would not be binding without official union approval.

13. My interviews, as well as the research of Kirschner (1990) and Grabsch and Kschischan (1990), uncovered many such examples. See also *IUG,* April 9, 1990, 4; and Philipsen (1993:268). The survival of workplace unions was in marked contrast to the fate of party structures at analogous levels, most of which were rapidly disbanded with workers' vocal approval.

14. Interview in Bernau, fall 1990. See also Philipsen (1993:289, 290). Pirker et al. (1990:78) argued that, in general, the BGLs that endured the revolution did so in name only. While the situation in some workplaces would surely corroborate their assessment, it was far from uniformly the case.

15. Grabsch and Kschischan (1990:4); Kirschner (1990:15).

16. See, for example, *Kran,* January 18, 1990, 5; and Segert (1992:14, 20). Burawoy and Lukács (1992:159) reported the same situation in the Soviet Union. "Official trade unions," they wrote, "continue to retain the allegiance of the overwhelming proportion of workers in industry." See also Clarke and Fairbrother (1993:94). *Kran,* February 1, 1990, 5, reported that 93 percent of a Leipzig company's employees retained their union memberships.

17. Kirschner (1990:15).

18. Segert (1992:15).

19. Interview in Berlin, fall 1990. For other examples, see Segert (1992:20, 21, 44).

20. Kirschner (1990:16, 30, 42); Grabsch and Kschischan (1990:4, 5). Also of interest are the ex-union officers and party members who were elected to *Betriebsräte* and some of the newly created organs of worker representation. I encountered many of these, including one in a refrigeration enterprise, where a woman told me, "Our *Betriebsrat* head, Uwe, is still in the party. He won't leave. But we don't hold that against him. We voted for him for *Betriebsrat,* and we couldn't get a better man. He does a lot of work. He always tries to find a way" (interview in Berlin, fall 1990). See also Segert (1992:24); and Philipsen (1993:289). I also learned of a case in which a prerevolutionary union leader, who had served at the district level of the FDGB, was elected to head a branch union in his district (interview in Apolda, fall 1990). See also Schnibben (1990:28) for the story of one of "many SED members who remained workers, even as they were party comrades, [and who] were the objects of sympathy, not hatred, from other workers."

21. *Neues Deutschland,* October 18, 1989, 1. For other examples, see Pirker et al. (1990:73); and Philipsen (1993:120, 281).

22. See, for example, *Kran,* November 9, 1989, 5, November 30, 1989, 3, and December 14, 1989, 1; and Kirschner (1990:36).

23. *Kran,* October 19, 1989, 4–5; interviews in Berlin, fall 1990 and spring 1991.

24. Kennedy (1991:215–21).

25. See Bachrach and Baratz's (1970:esp. chap. 3) classic discussion of nondecisions.

26. As one BGL member explained this move, "We would not let ourselves be sorted into good and bad, big and little potatoes" (Kirschner 1990:38). See also Segert (1992:16).

27. See, for example, Schnibben (1990:30). Higher-level party, state, and union officers were known to do the same. Kennedy (1991:219), referring to Soviet-type societies before their demise, wrote, "One commonly employed . . . strategy when a decision of consequence has to be made is to pick up one's briefcase and leave."

28. Segert (1992:8–9); Philipsen (1993:63, 127).

29. Interviews in Berlin, spring 1991.

30. The wall newspapers consisted of a miscellany of notices, critiques, demands, announcements, denunciations, and calls to action, together with responses to all of these. They were often signed by individuals or groups. A common critique in the wall newspapers at many worksites concerned the privileges of union and party leaders and their cozy relationship with one another. See Marcuse (1991:95–96).

31. Prominent among these were criticisms of worker housing; the quantity, quality, and distribution of consumer goods and services ("What can one get in the shops and stores after 4 P.M. at the end of the shift? Which services can one still obtain? [*Kran,* October 26, 1989, 4]); the scarcity of materials and spare parts at workplaces; the incongruity between work performance and remuneration; and swollen administrative ranks. In view of earlier chapters on the class divide, the labor process, and workplace politics, these criticisms, as well as others mentioned in the text, come as no surprise.

32. Pirker et al. (1990:16); *Kran,* November 2, 1989, 3, and December 21, 1989, 3.

33. Schnibben (1990:29). See also Philipsen (1993:116–20).

34. *Kran,* December 7, 1989, 1. Workers also strongly objected to the planned hirings and retentions of party and state officials and state security functionaries. See, for example, Segert (1992:14, 15).

35. *IUG,* January 1990, 5–6. As this passage hints, workers commonly called for reductions in administrative and management personnel. See, for example, *Kran,* November 23, 1989, 3; and Kirschner (1990:44, 45).

36. Pirker et al. (1990:21). See also Philipsen (1993:116–20).

37. Kirschner (1990:37). See also *Kran,* November 30, 1989, 4.

38. See, for example, the demands and proposals of union groups in *Kran,* November 16, 1989, 5, and November 30, 1989, 5.

39. Interview in Apolda, fall 1990; *Kran,* February 1, 1990, 5; *IUG,* January 1990, 6; Kirschner (1990:15).

40. Kirschner (1990:15, 42). See also Segert (1992:16); and *Kran,* November 9, 1989, 2.

41. See, for example, *IUG,* March 19, 1990, 7.

42. Kirschner (1990:15, 42); Grabsch and Kschischan (1990:4); Pirker et al. (1990:78). Thirty-seven percent did not vote in the steelworks Segert (1992:20) studied. On the first page of its factory newspaper, one BGL virtually begged workers to participate

in the union elections they had demanded in October and November (*Kran,* March 1, 1990, 1). Kirschner (1990:15–16) attributed low turnout to workers' definitive rejection of the old unions, whereas I see it as only passive participation on behalf of the opposition.

43. *Neues Deutschland,* October 31, 1989, 3; Schnibben (1990:28). See also *IUG,* December 1989, 3–4; *Kran,* Novmeber 9, 1989, 2; and Philipsen (1993:116–20).

44. For good examples, see Kirschner (1990:36); and *Kran,* March 1, 1990, 2. Some worker leaders began to demonstrate passive support of the opposition as early as August (Philipsen [1993:119]).

45. Interview in Berlin, spring 1991.

46. *Leipziger Volkszeitung,* October 20, 1989, 3.

47. On revelations of union corruption, see Gill (1991:72, 74).

48. *Leipziger Volkszeitung,* October 20, 1989, 3; interview in Berlin, fall 1990. See also Segert (1992:12).

49. Neugebauer (1990b:20, 21) and (1990a:7). Not all of these were workers, though Philipsen (1993:397) wrote that 70 percent of the over 200,000 party members who had resigned in October and November were.

50. Segert (1992:14). Exactly what kind of work this person did is not clear, but he apparently held no leadership position in the party.

51. *Neues Deutschland,* October 23, 1989, 1. See also *IUG,* December 1989, 3; and Philipsen (1993:116–20).

52. Segert (1992:10, 13).

53. Workers Philipsen (1993:127–29) interviewed corroborate some of these points.

54. The situation was even more complicated, for many activist workers also strove to protect certain features of GDR socialism and to dismantle others, further contributing to workers' hesitant involvement in revolutionary politics.

Chapter 9: Class, the Labor Process, and Workplace Politics in Comparative Perspective

1. Laba (1991) and Goodwyn (1991) are two such convincing accounts. As Laba (1991:3–7) noted, there has been a good deal of debate on this issue. My focus is limited to workers' role in *initiating* the demise of socialism in Poland. The entire process took nearly a decade, in the course of which the role of workers and Solidarity changed dramatically. On the later years of the transformation, see Ost (1990:chaps. 6, 7, 8, epilogue).

2. See Pravda (1981:60); Pravda (1986:139); Kolankiewicz (1981:102, 145); and Goodwyn (1991:54).

3. Goodwyn (1991:71).

4. Laba (1991:33). The quote refers to Gdańsk in 1970. See also Laba (1991:36, 62).

5. Pravda (1986:130–31).

6. See chapter 7.

7. Pravda (1986:131, 136–37); Woodall (1982:181, 182); Bielasiak (1983:236–37).

8. See, for example, Weinstein (1996:96–99); and Pravda (1986:139).

9. Weinstein (1996:90).

10. Pravda (1986:131). See also ibid., 137–38; and De Weydenthal (1981:197–98).

11. Goodwyn (1991:71).

12. Ibid., 76; Pravda (1986:133).

13. Laba (1991:40, 45). The government allowed workers free union elections after the unrest of 1970–71, but this was soon rescinded (Ost [1990:52, 56, 83]).

14. Laba (1991:157).

15. Pravda (1986:135). Emphasis added.

16. Ibid., 134, 139. See also Kennedy (1991:52); Pravda (1981:57); and Kolankiewicz (1973a:141).

17. Weinstein (1996:89); Laba (1991:22 [quote], 37). At the same time, some party members reportedly won workers' confidence by joining workers' protests in 1970, 1971, and 1980, in places becoming among the most militant worker leaders (Laba [1991:30, 67, 81]; Pravda [1981:61]; Ost [1990:93]; Kolankiewicz [1973a:150]; Kolankiewicz [1981:151]).

18. Pravda (1986:138, 144) offered a somewhat more positive assessment of low-level Polish union organizations.

19. Weinstein (1996:47–48); Goodwyn (1991:51, 52).

20. Kolankiewicz (1973a:149).

21. De Weydenthal (1981:195).

22. Laba (1991:78).

23. Ibid, 92; Weinstein (1996:102–3); Goodwyn (1991:154, 155, 157, 206).

24. Pravda (1981:55, 58); Kolankiewicz (1981:139); Ost (1990:93); Kennedy (1991:51).

25. On the importance and development of workers' communication by 1980, see Goodwyn (1991:15, 160, 173, 180, 212).

26. See Laba's (1991:81–82) description of a 1971 meeting of Łódź workers, the premier, and a Politburo member.

27. Sadly, the most brutally honest among the working class also discovered that state-perpetrated violence and repression, which occurred periodically after the late 1940s, actually rallied fervent support to their cause, albeit often with tragic consequences that they needed to do everything in their power to avoid (De Weydenthal [1981:194]; Goodwyn [1991:147–48, 154–55]; Weinstein [1996:49]; Pravda [1981:61]; Kolankiewicz [1981:138]; Laba [1991:27, 30, 36, 55]). The personal report of a future national vice chair of Solidarity illustrates this: "Up until [the violence in Gdańsk on December 17, 1970] I wasn't interested in politics. I returned home that night tremendously upset. My mates, my friends had already come over. All spoke up, one after another. We knew we had to do something" (quoted in Laba [1991:64]).

28. Goodwyn (1991:32, 208) made these points well.

29. Kolankiewicz (1973a:149–51).

30. Goodwyn (1991:7, 53, 156–57) is clear on this matter.

31. Kennedy (1991:53, 252–53); Kolankiewicz (1981:145); Gömöri (1973:161); Weinstein (1996:33); Goodwyn (1991:98).

32. Pravda (1981:51); Ost (1990:45); Gömöri (1973:160, 162–68); Kolankiewicz (1973b:195–98); Taras (1973:269–72); Weinstein (1996:43); and Woodall (1982:135) all offer relevant comments.

33. Starski (1982:195).

34. Kennedy (1991:89); Goodwyn (1991:38).

35. Kennedy (1991:53); Goodwyn (1991:111). Goodwyn emphasized the kitchen table as an early and important working-class space.

36. Goodwyn (1991:31).

37. On intellectuals' perceptions of workers in Poland, see Laba (1991:174–76).

38. Kennedy (1991:256–57).

39. Starski (1982:48).

40. Ninety-five percent of enterprise directors were party members in 1955 (Weinstein [1996:104–5]), and though I do not have figures from the 1960s and 1970s, Woodall (1982:146, 148) suggested the percentages remained high during these decades.

41. Kennedy (1991:275); Woodall (1982:144, 150); Laba (1991:46).

42. Laba (1991); Goodwyn (1991).

43. Kennedy (1991:41); De Weydenthal (1981:201); Goodwyn (1991:143, 149, 151, 441).

44. Goodwyn (1991:153).

45. Weinstein (1996:45). See also Goodwyn (1991:197–200), who cited *Robotnik*'s editorial preference for reforming existing trade unions rather than forming independent ones.

46. On these points, see Ost (1990:12–13); Goodwyn (1991:143, 203); and Starski (1982:58–59).

47. If Polish workers learned something during this period, intellectuals probably learned even more. They began to assemble some real knowledge about workers' lives, their grievances, and their decades-long struggle to better the former by resolving the latter. They began to understand more of the connections between their own private troubles and the public sphere. Finally, they came to recognize the necessity of collective political action for change. The numerous, largely intellectual groups that became active throughout the late 1970s are testimony to this. For brief commentary on these groups, see Kennedy (1991:41–42); Laba (1991:94); Kolankiewicz (1981:139); and Goodwyn (1991:142).

48. Goodwyn (1991:141).

49. Starski (1982:87); Laba (1991:107).

50. Goodwyn (1991:56, 60); Laba (1991:123); De Weydenthal (1981:186).

51. Quoted in Laba (1991:122). See also Goodwyn (1991:135–36).

52. On this point, see Biezenski (1994); and Woodall (1982:esp. chap. 6).

53. Weinstein (1996:97).

54. Laba (1991:164); Ward (1981:415); Weinstein (1996:92, 97); Ost (1996:34). Pravda (1986:137–38), however, offered a different analysis.

55. On these points, see Weinstein (1996:97–99); and Kolankiewicz (1973a:133). Kolankiewicz (1981:41) is also excellent here.

56. Burawoy and his collaborators (Burawoy [1985]; Burawoy and Lukács [1992]; Burawoy and Krotov [1993]) are a major exception.

57. Laba (1991:120).

58. See for example, Bielasiak (1983:231–32); Kolankiewicz (1973a:123); Montias (1981:186); Laba (1991:68, 162, 165, 233); and Starski (1982:50, 65, 186).

59. Bielasiak (1983:228–29). On this topic, see also Laba (1991:40, 123–24); Kolankie-wicz (1973b:200, 201); Kennedy (1991:275); Bielasiak (1983:227); and Kolankiewicz (1973a:132).

60. On this topic, see Laba (1991:121); Kolankiewicz (1973a:125–26, 130, 137–49); and Montias (1981:181–82). On workers' councils, see Biezenski (1994). On conferences on workers' self-management, see Woodall (1982:chaps. 5 and 6).

61. Kolankiewicz (1981:145).

62. Starski (1982:22, 185); Bielasiak (1983:233, 226).

63. Bielasiak (1983:234); Laba (1991:162–63).

64. Laba (1981:82); Goodwyn (1991:160, 161).

Appendix

1. Krisch (1992:89–90) has lamented the lack of this kind of data from before the *Wende*.

2. The most obvious change accompanying this shift was the sudden appearance of photos of nude women in nearly every issue.

3. I had one minor brush with the security apparatus while researching this book. During the first days of my first research trip, I lived in West Berlin and had to se-cure a visa to cross the border daily. After about a week this aroused suspicion, and one morning I was asked to step out of the line of people seeking entry into East Berlin, escorted into the proverbial concrete-walled room with glaring fluorescent lights, one metal desk, and two chars, and instructed to wait. The heavy lock clicked behind me as the border official left with my passport, my address book, and my research materials. I sat alone in the small room, imagining the worst as I studied the bleak walls for hidden cameras and the furniture for microphones. About two hours later, an armed, high-ranking security official entered the room with a smile on his face, ready to chat. This we did for some time, occasionally skirting the topic of why I had been visiting the GDR every day for a week. At one point in the conver-sation I mentioned I would probably be late for an appointment I had that day at the university. "My goodness! I studied at that university," was his spirited response. Then, after a monologue recalling details of his curriculum and his favorite profes-sors, he rose, wished me great success with my work (though he offered no apology or explanation for my detention), ushered me graciously out the door, and person-ally escorted me through the remaining border checkpoints.

4. Opp and Gern (1993:666) recognized the potential for this type of distortion in their work also.

5. Greenwald (1993:278–79), a U.S. diplomat, recognized this, but the most com-pelling discussion of this matter was in Duncan Smith (1988:20–21, 30, 124, 150, 206–7).

6. Philipsen (1993:330–31, 337–38) offered good descriptions.

7. In the social research meaning of the term, validity refers to researchers' ability to gather data on what they want to gather data on and what they think they are gathering data on.

Works Cited

Allen, Bruce. 1989. *Germany East.* Montreal: Black Rose Books.

Altvater, Elmar. 1981. "The Primacy of Politics in Post-Revolutionary Societies." *Review of Radical Political Economics* 13 (Spring): 1–10.

Anderson, Edith. "Town Mice and Country Mice." In *Without Force or Lies,* edited by William Brinton and Alan Rinzler, 170–92. San Francisco: Mercury House, 1990.

Andorka, Rudolf, Harcsa István, and Marta Gyenei. 1984. "First Results of a Survey of Social Stratification." In *Stratification and Inequalities,* edited by Rudolf Andorka and Tamás Kolosi, 1–15. Budapest: Institute for Social Sciences.

Ash, Timothy Garton. 1990. *The Magic Lantern.* New York: Random House.

Åslund, Anders. 1983. "Private Enterprise in Soviet-Type Economies: A Comparison between Poland and the GDR." *Osteuropa Wirtschaft* 28 (September): 175–93.

Bachrach, Peter, and Morton Baratz. 1970. *Power and Poverty.* Oxford: Oxford University Press.

Bahro, Rudolf. 1978. *The Alternative in Eastern Europe.* London: Verso.

Baier, Lothar. 1990. "Enemies of the People." *New Statesman,* June 22, 16–19.

Barber, Benjamin. 1984. *Strong Democracy.* Berkeley: University of California Press.

Baring, Arnulf. 1972. *Uprising in East Germany: June 17, 1953.* Ithaca, N.Y.: Cornell University Press.

Baylis, Thomas. 1974. *The Technical Intelligentsia and the East German Elite.* Berkeley: University of California Press.

———. 1978. "Participation and Ideology." In *The German Democratic Republic,* edited by Lyman Legters, 85–102. Boulder, Colo.: Westview.

———. 1994. "Scapegoating GDR Research? A Commentary." *Eastern German News,* April (supplement), 1–2.

———. 1995. "Leadership Change in Eastern Germany: From Colonisation to Integration?" In *The Federal Republic of Germany at Forty-five,* edited by Peter Merkl, 243–62. New York: New York University Press.

Belwe, Katharina. 1982. *Die Fluktuation Werktätiger als Ausdruck sozialer Konflikte in der DDR.* Bonn: Gesamtdeutsches Institut.

Belwe, Katharina, and Fred Klinger. 1986. "Der Wert der Arbeit." In *Tradition und Fortschritt in der DDR,* 61–86, XIX Tagung zum Stand der DDR-Forschung in der Bundesrepublik Deutschland, May 20–23. Cologne: Edition Deutschland Archiv im Verlag Wissenschaft und Politik Berend von Nottbeck.

Bielasiak, Jack. 1981. "Workers and Mass Participation in 'Socialist Democracy.'" In *Blue-Collar Workers in Eastern Europe,* edited by Jan Triska and Charles Gati, 88–107. London: Allen and Unwin.

———. 1983. "Inequalities and the Politicization of the Polish Working Class." In *Communism and the Politics of Inequalities,* edited by David Nelson, 221–47. Lexington, Mass.: Lexington Books.

Biermann, Wolf. 1990. "Nur wer sich ändert, bleibt sich treu." *Die Zeit,* August 24, 43–45.

Biezenski, Robert. 1994. "Workers' Self-Management and the Technical Intelligentsia in People's Poland." *Politics and Society* 22 (March): 59–88.

Böhm, Renate. 1990. "Radnotizen." *IUG,* February 1, 10.

Borneman, John. 1988. "The Practice of Democratic Socialism: An Ethnography of People's Courts in the GDR." Unpublished paper.

Bourdieu, Pierre. 1991. *Die Intellektuellen und die Macht.* Hamburg: VSA-Verlag.

Bowers, Stephen. 1990. "Honecker's Legacy." *GDR Monitor* 23 (October): 39–51.

Braverman, Harry. 1974. *Labor and Monopoly Capital.* New York: Monthly Review Press.

Brezinski, Horst. 1987. "The Second Economy in the GDR—Pragmatism Is Gaining Ground." *Studies in Comparative Communism* 20 (Spring): 85–101.

Burawoy, Michael. 1979. *Manufacturing Consent.* Chicago: University of Chicago Press.

———. 1985. *The Politics of Production.* London: Verso.

Burawoy, Michael, and Pavel Krotov. 1993. "The Soviet Transition from Socialism to Capitalism: Worker Control and Economic Bargaining in the Wood Industry." In *What about the Workers?* edited by Simon Clarke, Peter Fairbrother, Michael Burawoy, and Pavel Krotov, 56–90. London: Verso.

Burawoy, Michael, and János Lukács. 1992. *The Radiant Past.* Chicago: University of Chicago Press.

Büscher, Wolfgang. 1982. "Unterwegs zur Minderheit: Eine Auswertung konfessionsstatistischer Daten." In *Die Evangelischen Kirchen in der DDR,* edited by Reinhard Henkys, 422–36. Munich: Chr. Kaiser.

Calhoun, Craig. 1991. "Indirect Relationships and Imagined Communities: Large-Scale Social Integration and the Transformation of Everyday Life." In *Social Theory for a Changing Society,* edited by Pierre Bourdieu and James Coleman, 95–121. Boulder, Colo.: Westview.

Clarke, Simon. 1993. "The Contradictions of 'State Socialism.'" In *What about the Workers?* edited by Simon Clarke, Peter Fairbrother, Michael Burawoy, and Pavel Krotov, 5–29. London: Verso.

Clarke, Simon, and Peter Fairbrother. 1993. "Trade Unions and the Working Class." In *What about the Workers?* edited by Simon Clarke, Peter Fairbrother, Michael Burawoy, and Pavel Krotov, 91–120. London: Verso.

Cochrane, Allan. 1986. "Community Politics and Democracy." In *New Forms of Democracy,* edited by David Held and Christopher Pollit, 51–77. Beverly Hills, Calif.: Sage.

Collins, Patricia Hill. 1990. *Black Feminist Thought.* Boston: Unwin Hyman.

Connelly, John. 1990. "Moment of Revolution: Plauen (Vogtland), October 7, 1989." *German Politics and Society* 20 (Summer): 71–89.

Connor, Walter. 1981. "Workers and Power." In *Blue-Collar Workers in Eastern Europe,* edited by Jan Triska and Charles Gati, 157–72. London: Allen and Unwin.

———. 1991. *The Accidental Proletariat.* Princeton, N.J.: Princeton University Press.

Cox, Robert. 1991. "'Real Socialism' in Historical Perspective." In *Socialist Register,* edited by Ralph Miliband and Leo Panitch, 169–93. London: Merlin.

Darnton, Robert. 1991. *Berlin Journal, 1989–1990.* New York: W. W. Norton.

Dennis, Mike. 1988. *German Democratic Republic.* London: Pinter.

———. 1991. "Scientific-Technical Progress, Ideological Legitimation, and Political Change in the German Democratic Republic." In *Studies in GDR Culture and Society,* vol. 10, edited by Margy Gerber, 1–29. Lanham, N.Y.: University Press of America.

———. 1992. "'Perfecting' the Imperfect: The GDR Economy in the Honecker Era." In *The German Revolution of 1989,* edited by Gert-Joachim Glaeßner and Ian Wallace, 57–83. Oxford: Berg.

Deppe, Rainer, and Dietrich Hoß. 1989. *Arbeitspolitik im Staatssozialismus.* Frankfurt: Campus.

De Weydenthal, Jan. 1981. "Poland: Workers and Politics." In *Blue-Collar Workers in Eastern Europe,* edited by Jan Triska and Charles Gati, 187–208. London: Allen and Unwin.

Edeling, Thomas. 1990. "Organisationswandel ostdeutscher Betriebe im Übergang zu Marktwirtschaft." Institut für Soziologie. Humboldt University, Berlin. Mimeo.

Edwards, G. E. 1985. *GDR Society and Social Institutions.* London: Macmillan.

Edwards, Richard. 1979. *Contested Terrain: The Transformation of Work in the Twentieth Century.* New York: Basic Books.

Eisenstadt, S. N. 1992. "The Breakdown of Communist Regimes and the Vicissitudes of Modernity." *Daedalus* 121 (Spring): 21–42.

Erbe, Günter. 1979a. "Annäherung von Arbeiterklasse und Intelligenz?" *Deutschland Archiv,* June, 103–13.

———. 1979b. "Klassen und Schichten." In *Politik, Wirtschaft und Gesellschaft in der DDR,* edited by Günter Erbe, 403–24. Opladen: Westdeutscher.

Feffer, John. 1992. *Shock Waves.* Boston: South End.

Fichter, Michael. 1991. "From Transmission Belt to Social Partnership? The Case of Organized Labor in Eastern Germany." *German Politics and Society* 23 (Summer): 21–39.

Frowen, Stephen. 1985. "The Economy of the German Democratic Republic." In *Honecker's Germany,* edited by David Childs, 32–49. London: Allen and Unwin.

Fulbrook, Mary. 1991. *The Divided Nation*. London: Fontana.

Fuller, Linda. 1990. "Union Autonomy at the Socialist Workplace: A Comparison of Cuba and the German Democratic Republic." *Socialism and Democracy* 11 (September): 75–108.

Fuller, Linda, and Vicki Smith. 1991. "Consumers' Reports: Management by Customers in a Changing Economy." *Work, Employment, and Society* 5 (March): 1–16.

"Für eine Wende in der Gewerkschaftsarbeit." 1989. Discussion paper from the Gewerkschaftshochschule Fritz Heckert, Bernau, October 29.

Galtung, Johan. 1992. "Eastern Europe Fall 1989—What Happened, and Why?" *Research in Social Movements, Conflicts and Change* 14: 75–97.

Gann, Lewis. 1992. "German Unification and the Left-Wing Intelligentsia: A Response." *German Studies Review* 15 (February): 98–110.

German Information Center. 1977. *Co-determination: Worker Participation in German Industry*. New York: German Information Center.

Gill, Ulrich. 1991. *FDGB: Die DDR-Gewerkschaft von 1945 bis zu ihrer Auflösung 1990*. Cologne: Bund.

Glaeßner, Gert-Joachim. 1984. "The Education System and Society." In *Policymaking in the German Democratic Republic*, edited by Klaus von Beyme and Hartmut Zimmermann, 190–211. Aldershot, England: Gower.

———. 1986. "Wissenschaftliche-technische Revolution—Intelligenz Politik in der DDR." In *Tradition und Fortschritt in der DDR*, 11–28, XIX Tagung zum Stand der DDR-Forschung in der Bundesrepublik Deutschland, May 20–23. Cologne: Edition Deutschland Archiv im Verlag Wissenschaft und Politik Berend von Nottbeck.

———. 1988. "Am Ende der Klassengesellschaft? Sozialstruktur und Sozialstrukturforschung in der DDR." *Aus Politik und Zeitgeschichte* 32 (August): 3–12.

———. 1992. "Political Structures in Transition." In *The German Revolution of 1989*, edited by Gert-Joachim Glaeßner and Ian Wallace, 3–22. Oxford: Berg.

Gleye, Paul. 1991. *Behind the Wall*. Carbondale: Southern Illinois University Press.

Goeckel, Robert. 1990. *The Lutheran Church and the East German State*. Ithaca, N.Y.: Cornell University Press.

Gömöri, George. 1973. "The Cultural Intelligentsia: The Writers." In *Social Groups in Polish Society*, edited by David Lane and George Kolankiewicz, 152–79. New York: Columbia University Press.

Goodwyn, Lawrence. 1991. *Breaking the Barrier: The Rise of Solidarity in Poland*. New York: Oxford University Press.

Grabsch, Brigit, and Karel Kschischan. 1990. "Betriebliche Mitbestimmung in der DDR." Institut für Soziologie, Humboldt University, Berlin, July. Mimeo.

Granick, David. 1975. *Enterprise Guidance in Eastern Europe*. Princeton, N.J.: Princeton University Press.

Grätz, Frank. 1971. "Extras für die Bosse in der DDR." *Die Zeit*, September 3, 37.

Greenwald, G. Jonathan. 1993. *Berlin Witness*. University Park: Pennsylvania State University Press.

Grote, Manfred. 1979. "The Socialist Unity Party of Germany." In *The Communist*

Parties of Eastern Europe, edited by Stephen Fischer-Galati, 167–200. New York: Columbia University Press.

Haas, Winfried. 1988. "Die soziale Gruppe der Un- und Angelernten in der Sozialstruktur der Arbeiterklasse in der DDR." *Informationen zur soziologischen Forschung in der Deutschen Demokratischen Republik* 24, no. 4: 25–34.

Habermas, Jürgen. 1990. "What Does Socialism Mean Today?" *New Left Review* 183 (September–October): 3–21.

Hancock, M. Donald. 1978. "Intellectuals and System Change." In *The German Democratic Republic,* edited by Lyman Legters, 133–54. Boulder, Colo.: Westview.

Hanhardt, Arthur, Jr. 1990. "Demonstrations, Groups, Parties and the *Volkskammer* Election: Aspects of Political Change in East Germany." Paper delivered at the meeting of the American Political Science Association, San Francisco, August 30–September 2.

Hanke, Irma. 1984. "Continuity and Change: Cultural Policy in the German Democratic Republic since the Eighth SED Party Congress in 1971." In *Policymaking in the German Democratic Republic,* edited by Klaus von Beyme and Hartmut Zimmermann, 212–41. Aldershot, England: Gower.

Haraszti, Miklós. 1978. *A Worker in a Workers' State.* New York: Universe Books.

Harding, Sandra. 1986. *The Science Question in Feminism.* Ithaca, N.Y.: Cornell University Press.

———. 1991. *Whose Science? Whose Knowledge?* Ithaca, N.Y.: Cornell University Press.

Harman, Chris. 1983. *Class Struggles in Eastern Europe, 1945–1983.* London: Pluto.

Havel, Václav. 1985. "The Power of the Powerless." In *The Power of the Powerless,* edited by John Keane, 23–96. Armonk, N.Y.: M. E. Sharpe.

Heller, Agnes. 1990. "The Nature of Post-Communist Civil Society in Eastern Europe." *PAWSS Perspectives* 1 (December): 4–8.

Herminghouse, Patricia. 1991. "Confronting the 'Blank Spots of History': GDR Culture and the Legacy of Stalinism." *German Studies Review* 14 (May): 345–36.

Huspek, Michael. 1994. "Oppositional Codes and Social Class Relations." *British Journal of Sociology* 45 (March): 79–102.

IUG (Berlin).

Joppke, Christian. 1995. *East German Dissidents and the Revolution of 1989.* New York: New York University Press.

Jugel, Martina, Barbara Spangenberg, and Rudhard Stollberg. 1978. *Schichtarbeit und Lebensweise.* Berlin: Dietz.

Jürgens, Ulrich, Larissa Klinzing, and Lowell Turner. 1992. "Scrapping the East German Industrial Relations System." Unpublished paper.

Kanter, Rosabeth. 1977. *Men and Women of the Corporation.* New York: Basic Books.

Keefe, Eugene, ed. 1982. *East Germany: A Country Study.* Washington, D.C.: Department of the Army.

Kennedy, Michael. 1991. *Professionals, Power, and Solidarity in Poland.* Cambridge: Cambridge University Press.

Kirschner, Lutz. 1989. "Gewerkschaftsarbeit im sozialistischen Industriebetrieb." Ph.D. diss., Humboldt University, Berlin.

———. 1990. "Zum Wandel von Belegschaftsvertretungen im Industriebetrieb der DDR." Institut für Rechtsgeschichte und Rechtstheorie, Humboldt University, Berlin.

Klier, Freya. 1990. *Lüg Vaterland.* Munich: Kindler.

Knabe, Hubertus. 1990. "Politische Opposition in der DDR," *Aus Politik und Zeitgeschichte* 1–2 (January): 21–32.

Kolankiewicz, George. 1973a. "The Polish Industrial Working Class." In *Social Groups in Polish Society,* edited by David Lane and George Kolankiewicz, 88–151. New York: Columbia University Press.

———. 1973b. "The Technical Intelligentsia." In *Social Groups in Polish Society,* edited by David Lane and George Kolankiewicz, 180–232. New York: Columbia University Press.

———. 1981. "Poland, 1980: The Working Class under 'Anomic Socialism.'" In *Blue-Collar Workers in Eastern Europe,* edited by Jan Triska and Charles Gati, 136–56. London: Allen and Unwin.

Komitee zur Vorbereitung des außerordentlichen FDGB-Kongresses. 1990. "Aufruf an Alle!" two sides.

Konrád, George, and Ivan Szelényi. 1979. *The Intellectuals on the Road to Class Power.* New York: Harcourt Brace Jovanovich.

Kornai, János. 1986. *Contradictions and Dilemmas.* Cambridge: MIT Press.

———. 1992. *The Socialist System.* Princeton, N.J.: Princeton University Press.

Kramer, Jane. 1991. "Letter from Berlin." *New Yorker,* November 25, 55–108.

Kran. Takraf. Betriebszeitung. Leipzig.

Kran. Takraf. Organ der Leitung der Grundorganisation der SED. Leipzig.

Kreißig, Volkmar, and Erhard Schreiber. 1992. "Participation and Technological Alternatives in the German Democratic Republic: The Dilemma of Scientific Prediction and Co-management by Trade Unions in the Past and Present." In *Labour Relations in Transition in Eastern Europe,* edited by György Széll, 249–60. Berlin: Walter de Gruyter.

Krejci, Jaroslav. 1976. *Social Structure in Divided Germany.* New York: St. Martin's.

Krisch, Henry. 1985. *The German Democratic Republic.* Boulder, Colo.: Westview.

———. 1992. "Changes in Political Culture and the Transformation of the GDR, 1989–1990." In *The German Revolution of 1989,* edited by Gert-Joachim Glaeßner and Ian Wallace, 87–99. Oxford: Berg.

Kunze, Reiner. 1990. "Life and Consequences: Being a Writer in Divided Germany." In *Without Force or Lies,* edited by William Brinton and Alan Rinzler, 152–69. San Francisco: Mercury House.

Kuran, Timur. 1991. "Now Out of Never: The Element of Surprise in the East European Revolution of 1989." *World Politics* 44 (October): 7–48.

Laba, Roman. 1991. *The Roots of Solidarity.* Princeton, N.J.: Princeton University Press.

Lamont, Michèle. 1992. *Money, Morals, and Manners.* Chicago: University of Chicago Press.

Lasky, Melvin. 1991. *Voices in a Revolution.* Southwick, Sussex: Grange.

Laufer, Peter. 1991. *Iron Curtain Rising.* San Francisco: Mercury House.

Lehrstuhl Gewerkschaftsaufbau. 1989. "Fakten." Unpublished document, Bernau.

Leipziger Volkszeitung (Leipzig).

Leonhard, Wolfgang. 1958. *Child of the Revolution.* Chicago: Henry Regnery.

Lewin, Moshe. 1988. *The Gorbachev Phenomenon.* Berkeley: University of California Press.

Lohr, Karin. 1990. "Zur Entwicklung des Systems der industriellen Beziehungen in Betrieben der ehemaligen DDR." Institut für Soziologie, Humboldt University, Berlin.

Lötsch, Manfred. 1992. "From Stagnation to Transformation: The Sociology of the 'GDR Revolution.'" In *The German Revolution of 1989,* edited by Gert-Joachim Glaeßner and Ian Wallace, 43–56. Oxford: Berg.

Ludz, Peter. 1981. "German Democratic Republic." In *Survey Research and Public Attitudes in Eastern Europe and the Soviet Union,* edited by William Welsh, 242–318. New York: Pergamon.

Lydike, Mathias. 1990. "Gewerkschaftstreffen in Bernau." *IUG,* February 1, 7–10.

Maier, Harry. 1987. *Innovation oder Stagnation.* Cologne: Deutsches Institut.

Mansbridge, Jane. 1983. *Beyond Adversary Democracy.* Chicago: University of Chicago Press.

Marcuse, Peter. 1990. "Letter from the German Democratic Republic." *Monthly Review* 42 (July–August): 30–62.

———. 1991. *Missing Marx.* New York: Monthly Review Press.

Markovits, Inga. 1982. "Law or Order—Constitutionalism and Legality in Eastern Europe." *Stanford Law Review* 34 (February): 514–613.

McCauley, Martin. 1981. "Power and Authority in East Germany: The Socialist Unity Party (SED)." *Conflict Studies* 132 (July): 1–28.

McFalls, Laurence. 1992a. "Different Strokes for Different *Volks:* German Cultural (Dis-)Unity and Reunification." Paper presented at the GDR Studies Association, Washington, D.C., November 12–15.

———. 1992b. "The Modest Germans: Towards an Understanding of the East Germans' Revolution." *German Politics and Society* 26 (Summer): 1–20.

———. 1995. *Communism's Collapse, Democracy's Demise?* New York: New York University Press.

Meier, Artur. 1987a. "In Search of Workers' Participation—Implementation of New Technologies in GDR-Firms." Institut für Soziologie, Humboldt University, Berlin.

———. 1987b. "Transition from School to Work in GDR and USSR: Universals and Peculiarities of Socialist Educational Systems." Paper presented at the American Sociological Association, Chicago, August 17–21.

Meuschel, Sigrid. 1989–90. "The End of "East German Socialism." *Telos* 82 (Winter): 3–26.

———. 1992. "Revolution in a Classless Society." In *The German Revolution of 1989,* edited by Gert-Joachim Glaeßner and Ian Wallace, 144–59. Oxford: Berg.

Michalsky, Helga. 1984. "Social Policy and the Transformation of Society." In *Policymaking in the German Democratic Republic,* edited by Klaus von Beyme and Hartmut Zimmermann, 242–71. Aldershot, England: Gower.

Minnerup, Günter. 1982. "East Germany's Frozen Revolution." *New Left Review* 132 (March–April): 5–32.

———. 1989. "The Revolution in East Germany." *Labour Focus on Eastern Europe,* no. 3: 5–9.

———. 1990. "Kohl Hijacks East German Revolution." *Labour Focus on Eastern Europe,* no. 1: 4–7.

Montias, J. M. 1981. "Observations on Strikes, Riots and Other Disturbances." In *Blue-Collar Workers in Eastern Europe,* edited by Jan Triska and Charles Gati, 171–86. London: Allen and Unwin.

Moore, Barrington, Jr. 1978. *Injustice: The Social Bases of Obedience and Revolt.* White Plains, N.Y.: M. E. Sharpe.

Musch, Reinfried. 1990. "Die Linke und die Revolution in der DDR." In *Linke Politik in Deutschland,* edited by Axel Lochner, 96–106. Hamburg: Galgenberg.

Mushaben, Joyce. 1984. "Swords to Plowshares: The Church, the State, and the East German Peace Movement." *Studies in Comparative Communism* 17 (Summer): 123–35.

Neues Deutschland (Berlin).

Neugebauer, Gero. 1990a. "Von der Führung an das Ende—Die SED und das Parteiensystem der DDR bis zur Bundestagswahl 1990." Unpublished paper, Free University of Berlin.

———. 1990b. "Von der Wende zur Wahl—Der Zusammenbruch des politischen Systems der DDR." Unpublished paper, Free University of Berlin.

———. 1991. "Privatisierung in der ehemaligen DDR." Berliner Arbeitshefte und Berichte zur Sozialwissenschaftlichen Forschung, no. 58, Zentralenstitut für sozialwissenschaftliche Forschung, Free University of Berlin.

Offe, Claus. 1991. "Prosperity, Nation, Republic: Aspects of the Unique German Journey from Socialism to Capitalism." *German Politics and Society* 22 (Spring): 18–32.

Opp, Karl-Dieter, and Christiane Gern. 1993. "Dissident Groups, Personal Networks, and the East German Revolution of 1989." *American Sociological Review* 58 (October): 659–80.

Opp, Karl-Dieter, Peter Voss, and Christiane Gern. 1995. *Origins of a Spontaneous Revolution: East Germany, 1989.* Ann Arbor: University of Michigan Press.

Ost, David. 1990. *Solidarity and the Politics of Anti-Politics.* Philadelphia: Temple University Press.

———. 1996. "Polish Labor before and after Solidarity." *International Labor and Working-Class History* 50 (Fall): 29–43.

Otte, Stefan, Siegfried Sahr, and Bettina Herzog. 1988. *Die Konfliktkommission.* Berlin: Verlag Tribüne.

Page, John. 1985. "Education under the Honeckers." In *Honecker's Germany,* edited by David Childs, 50–65. London: Allen and Unwin.

Parmalee, Patty Lee. 1994. "Workers and Intellectuals in the German Democratic Republic." In *Socialist Register,* edited by Ralph Miliband and Leo Panitch, 290–311. London: Merlin.

Philipsen, Dirk. 1993. *We Were the People.* Durham, N.C.: Duke University Press.

Pirker, Theo, Hans-Hermann Hertle, Jürgen Kädtler, and Rainer Weinert. 1990. *FDGB—Wende zum Ende.* Cologne: Bund.

Pravda, Alex. 1979. "Industrial Workers: Patterns of Dissent, Opposition and Accommodation." In *Opposition in Eastern Europe,* edited by Rudolf Tökés, 209–62. Baltimore: Johns Hopkins University Press.

———. 1981. "Political Attitudes and Activity." In *Blue-Collar Workers in Eastern Europe,* edited by Jan Triska and Charles Gati, 43–69. London: Allen and Unwin.

———. 1986. "Poland in the 1970s: Dual Functioning Trade Unionism under Pressure." In *Trade Unions in Communist States,* edited by Alex Pravda and Blair Ruble, 125–47. Boston: Allen and Unwin.

Radcliffe, Stanley. 1972. *25 Years on/of the Two Germanies.* London: Harrap.

Rakovski, Marc. 1978. *Towards an East European Marxism.* London: Allison and Busby.

Ratsch, Traude. 1984. "Unilateralism in the East." *Labour Focus on Eastern Europe 7,* no.1: 20–22.

Rein, Gerhard, ed. 1989. *Die Opposition in der DDR.* Berlin: Wichern.

Reißig, Rolf. 1991. "Der Umbruch in der DDR und das Scheitern des 'realen Sozialismus.'" In *Das Ende eines Experiments,* edited by Rolf Reißig and Gert-Joachim Glaeßner, 12–59. Berlin: Dietz.

———. 1992. "The Failure of 'Real Socialism.'" In *The German Revolution of 1989,* edited by Gert-Joachim Glaeßner and Ian Wallace, 23–42. Oxford: Berg.

Rowbotham, Sheila. 1986. "Feminism and Democracy." In *New Forms of Democracy,* edited by David Held and Christopher Pollit, 78–109. Beverly Hills, Calif.: Sage.

Ruble, Blair. 1986. "Industrial Trade Unions in the USSR." In *Trade Unions in Communist States,* edited by Alex Pravda and Blair Ruble, 23–52. London: Allen and Unwin.

Rueschemeyer, Marilyn. 1982. "The Work Collective: Response and Adaptation in the Structure of Work in the German Democratic Republic." *Dialectical Anthropology 7,* no. 2: 155–63.

———. 1983. "Integrating Work and Personal Life: An Analysis of Three Professional Work Collectives in the German Democratic Republic." *GDR Monitor,* no. 8 (Winter): 27–47.

———. 1988. "New Family Forms in a State Socialist Society." *Journal of Family Issues 9* (September): 354–71.

———. 1991. "State Patronage in the German Democratic Republic: Artistic and Political Change in a State Socialist Society." *Journal of Arts, Management, and Law 20* (Winter): 31–55.

Rueschemeyer, Marilyn, and C. Bradley Scharf. 1986. "Labor Unions in the German Democratic Republic." In *Trade Unions in Communist States,* edited by Alex Pravda and Blair Ruble, 53–84. Boston: Allen and Unwin.

Sandford, John. 1992. "The Peace Movement and the Church in the Honecker Years." In *The German Revolution of 1989,* edited by Gert-Joachim Glaeßner and Ian Wallace, 124–43. Oxford: Berg.

Scharf, Carl Bradley. 1974. "Labor Organizations in East German Society." Ph.D. dissertation, Department of Political Science, Stanford University.

———. 1984. *Politics and Change in East Germany*. Boulder, Colo.: Westview.

———. 1989. "Social Policy and Social Conditions in the GDR." In *The Quality of Life in the German Democratic Republic*, edited by Marilyn Rueschemeyer and Christiane Lemke, 3–24. Armonk, N.Y.: M. E. Sharpe.

———. 1990. "Social Welfare and Citizen Participation in the GDR: Intermediate Linkages before the 1989 Revolution." Paper presented at the American Political Science Association, San Francisco, August 30–September 2.

Schießl, Karin. 1990. "Vom Aufbruch in die Übername—Gerwerkschaften in der DDR 1990." In *Linke Politik in Deutschland*, edited by Axel Lochner, 47–56. Hamburg: Galgenberg.

Schnibben, Cordt. 1990. "Was nun, Harry Dolch?" *Der Spiegel*, January 1, 28–31.

Schröter, Eckhard. 1992. "Administrative Cultures in Eastern and Western Germany: As Different as Fire and Water?" Paper presented at GDR Studies Association Conference, Washington, D.C., November 12–15.

Segert, Astrid. 1992. "Wie ein streifähiger Betriebsrat entsteht." Berliner Arbeitshefte und Berichte zur Sozialwissenschaftlichen Forschung, no. 71, Zentralenstitut für sozialwissenschaftliche Forschung, Free University of Berlin.

———. 1993. "Ulf Schmitt—Ein "Schillernder Typ." Unpublished paper, Berlin.

Singer, Daniel. 1991. "Privilegentsia, Property and Power." In *Socialist Register*, edited by Ralph Miliband and Leo Panitch, 211–23. London: Merlin.

Smith, Dorothy. 1987. *The Everyday World as Problematic*. Boston: Northeastern University Press.

Smith, Duncan. 1988. *Walls and Mirrors*. New York: Lanham.

Smith, Roland. 1985. "The Church in the German Democratic Republic." In *Honecker's Germany*, edited by David Childs, 66–82. London: Allen and Unwin.

Sodaro, Michael. 1983. "Limits to Dissent in the GDR: Fragmentation, Cooptation, and Repression." In *Dissent in Eastern Europe*, edited by Jane Curry, 82–116. New York: Praeger.

Staatliche Zentralverwaltung für Statistik. 1988. *Statistisches Jahrbuch der Deutschen Demokratischen Republik*. Berlin: Staatsverlag der Deutschen Demokratischen Republik.

Staniszkis, Jadwiga. 1991. "Patterns of Change in Eastern Europe." In *Upheaval against the Plan*, edited by Peter Weilemann, Georg Brunner, and Rudolf Tökés, 5–26. Oxford: Berg.

———. 1992. *The Ontology of Socialism*. Oxford: Clarendon.

Stark, David. 1986. "Rethinking Internal Labor Markets: New Insights from a Comparative Perspective." *American Sociological Review* 51 (August): 492–504.

Starski, Stanislaw. 1982. *Class Struggles in Classless Poland*. Boston: South End.

Steele, Jonathan. 1977. *Socialism with a German Face*. London: Jonathan Cape.

Stollberg, Rudhard. 1988. *Soziologie der Arbeit*. Berlin: Die Wirtschaft.

Suckut, Siegfried. 1982. *Die Betriebsrätebewegung in der sowjetischen Besatzungszone Deutschlands, 1945–1948*. Frankfurt/Main: Haag und Herchen.

Süß, Walter. 1989. "East Germany's Defensive Politics." *Telos* 79 (Spring): 163–80.

Szelényi, Ivan. 1978. "Social Inequalities in State Socialist Redistributive Economies." *International Journal of Comparative Society* 19 (March–June): 63–87.

―――. 1979. "Socialist Opposition in Eastern Europe: Dilemmas and Prospects." In *Opposition in Eastern Europe*, edited by Rudolf Tökés, 187–208. Baltimore: Johns Hopkins University Press.

―――. 1986–87. "The Prospects and Limits of the East European New Class Project: An Auto-critical Reflection on *The Intellectuals on the Road to Class Power.*" *Politics and Society* 15, no. 2: 103–44.

Taras, Ray. 1973. "The Local Political Elites." In *Social Groups in Polish Society*, edited by David Lane and George Kolankiewicz, 233–301. New York: Columbia University Press.

Teckenberg, Wolfgang. 1990. "The Stability of Occupational Structures, Social Mobility, and Interest Formation." In *Class Structure in Europe*, edited by Max Haller, 24–58. Armonk, N.Y.: M. E. Sharpe.

Ticktin, Hillel. 1992. *Origins of the Crisis in the USSR*. Armonk, N.Y.: M. E. Sharp *Tribüne* (Berlin).

"Umgeschult." 1963. *Der Spiegel*, April 10, 30–33.

Urnov, M. Iu. 1990. "How Ready Are We for Democracy?" *Soviet Sociology* 29 (July–August): 6–31.

Volkmer, Werner. 1979. "East Germany: Dissenting Views during the Last Decade." In *Opposition in Eastern Europe*, edited by Rudolf Tökés, 113–41. Baltimore: Johns Hopkins University Press.

Voskamp, Ulrich, and Volker Wittke. 1991. "Industrial Restructuring in the Former German Democratic Republic (GDR): Barriers to Adaptive Reform Become Downward Development Spirals." *Politics and Society* 19 (September): 341–71.

Wallace, Ian. 1992. "The Failure of GDR Cultural Policy under Honecker." In *The German Revolution of 1989*, edited by Gert-Joachim Glaeßner and Ian Wallace, 100–123. Oxford: Berg.

Ward, Barclay. 1981. "Poland." In *Survey Research and Public Attitudes in Eastern Europe and the Soviet Union*, edited by William Welsh, 389–435. New York: Pergamon.

Weber, Hermann. 1985. "The Socialist Unity Party." In *Honecker's Germany*, edited by David Childs, 1–14. London: Allen and Unwin.

―――. 1988. *Die DDR, 1945–1986*. Munich: R. Oldenbourg.

Weinstein, Marc. 1996. "The Remaking of the Polish Industrial Relations System: The Institutional and Ideational Antecedents of Firm-Level Employment Practices." Ph.D. diss., Alfred P. Sloan School of Management, MIT.

Wensierski, Peter. 1982. "Kirche Unterwegs: Von der Volkskirche zu . . . ?" In *Die Evangelischen Kirchen in der DDR*, edited by Reinhard Henkys, 400–421. Munich: Chr. Kaiser.

Wenzel, Manfred. 1984. "Leistungsstarker Rationalisierungsmittelbau bringt dem Kombinat hohen Zuwachs an Effektivität." *Wirtschaftswissenschaft* 32, no. 8: 1170–82.

"What It Takes to Be Boss." 1986. *Economist*, February 22, 50.

Wierling, Dorothee. 1996. "Work, Workers, and Politics in the German Democratic Republic." *International Labor and Working-Class History* 50 (Fall): 44–63.

Wolfe, Nancy. 1989. "Social Courts in the GDR and Comrades' Courts in the Soviet

Union: A Comparison." In *East Germany in Comparative Perspective,* edited by David Childs, Thomas Baylis, and Marilyn Rueschemeyer, 60–79. London: Routledge.

Woodall, Jean. 1982. *The Socialist Corporation and Technocratic Power.* Cambridge: Cambridge University Press.

Woods, Roger. 1986. *Opposition in the GDR under Honecker, 1971–1985.* London: Macmillan.

Zeman, Z. A. B. 1991. *The Making and Breaking of Communist Europe.* Oxford: Basil Blackwell.

Zierke, Irene. 1993. "Das politisch-alternative Milieu in Brandenburg: Recherchen über die Konstituierung eines neuen Milieus in einer ostdeutschen Mittelstadt." Unpublished paper, Berlin.

Zimmermann, Hartmut. 1977. "In der DDR wird das Lohnsystem reformiert." *Die Quelle* 3: 114–17.

———. 1978. "The GDR in the 1970s." *Problems of Communism* 27 (March–April): 1–39.

———. 1984. "Power Distribution and Opportunities for Participation: Aspects of the Socio-political System of the GDR." In *Policymaking in the German Democratic Republic,* edited by Klaus von Beyme and Hartmut Zimmermann, 1–108. Aldershot, England: Gower.

Index

AGL (department-level union committee), 49, 64, 67, 68, 69, 72, 109, 111–12, 114, 115, 116, 128, 129, 131–32, 135, 143, 146, 149, 150, 192n. 46, 194n. 1, 195n. 9, 209n. 28, 213–14n. 26, 214–15n. 37, 217n. 53

Ash, Timothy, 39

Bahro, Rudolf, 15, 16, 17, 22, 55

Baring, Arnulf, 31–32

base wage, 52, 53, 54, 193n. 50

Baylis, Thomas, 20, 81, 92

Betriebsräte (enterprise-level work councils): in FRG, 107–8, 109, 208nn. 7, 11; and working-class activism, 107–10, 120, 150, 135, 145, 208nn. 2, 3, 6–7, 13, 15, 208–9n. 19, 211nn. 48, 51, 219n. 20

BGL (enterprise-level union committee), 49, 51, 55, 57, 58, 60, 62–76, 109, 110, 111, 114, 115, 116, 117, 128, 129, 132, 139, 143, 146, 147, 149, 150, 151, 175, 193n. 55, 194nn. 1, 7, 195n. 9, 196nn. 23, 25, 27, 197nn. 30, 34, 198n. 44, 209nn. 28, 29, 210n. 32, 211n. 49, 213n. 26, 214nn. 31, 37, 216n. 43, 219n. 14, 220nn. 26, 38, 42

Biermann, Wolf, 28

bonuses, 52–54, 59, 91, 135, 191n. 33, 193nn. 48, 54, 55, 202n. 44, 206n. 91, 214–15n. 37. *See also* labor process

Borneman, John, 91, 132, 134

Braverman, Harry, 125

Burawoy, Michael, 29, 87, 125, 126

CDU (Christian Democratic Union), 38, 68, 79, 180nn. 8, 10, 189n. 22

citizens' commissions, 79, 199n. 4

citizens' opposition groups, 5, 35, 36–38, 84, 85–86, 100–101, 103, 106, 109, 147, 150, 189n. 11, 201n. 32, 206n. 94. *See also* Demokratie Jetzt; Demokratischer Aufbruch; Neues Forum; Vereinigte Linke

civil society, 77–86, 103, 162, 199nn. 3, 10, 15, 16, 200n. 22. *See also* citizens' commissions; discussion circles; elected government positions; intelligentsia, pre-*Wende* organizations and networks of; political parties; social service groups

class: and education, 18–23, 183n. 26; and families, 18, 19–20, 183nn. 29, 30, 31, 184nn. 41, 44; and occupational structure, 18, 21–24, 184nn. 39, 40–41, 43–44; and political system, 18, 20–21, 22, 23, 24, 183nn. 34, 36, 184nn. 38, 44; reproduction of, 2, 10, 18, 22–23, 184n. 44; structure, 9–10, 13, 19, 200–201n. 28. *See also* intelligentsia; working class

collective agreements, 60, 69, 73, 76, 132, 214n. 35

conglomerates. *See Kombinate*
CSU (Christian Social Union), 180n. 8
Cuba, 1, 6, 192n. 37
Culture League. *See* Kulturbund

DA (Democratic Awakening), 180nn. 8, 10
DBD (Democratic Farmers' Party), 80
Demokratie Jetzt, 5, 36, 37, 86, 114, 180n. 10, 206n. 94. *See also* citizens' opposition groups
Demokratischer Aufbruch, 5, 36, 85, 86, 180nn. 8, 10. *See also* citizens' opposition groups; political parties
Deppe, Rainer, 125
De Weydenthal, Jan, 159
discussion circles (pre-*Wende*), 81, 82, 84, 85, 86
DSU (German Social Union), 180nn. 8, 10

elected government positions, 79, 84, 199nn. 3, 16
elections (March 1990), 5, 38–39, 112, 114

FDGB (Confederation of Free German Trade Unions), 66, 71–72, 96, 101, 102, 107, 109, 111, 112, 113–14, 119, 146, 149, 150, 195n. 7, 198nn. 46, 49, 199n. 16, 210nn. 31, 33, 36, 219n. 20
FDJ (Communist Youth Organization), 73
feminist scholarship, 2, 11–13, 24, 138
FRG (Federal Republic of Germany), 1, 148, 176; *Betriebsräte* in, 107–8, 109, 208nn. 7, 11; involvement in *Wende*, 5, 38–39, 120, 146, 152; unions in, 118, 119–20, 207n. 106, 210n. 36, 211n. 58; work in, 42, 190n. 8
Fritz-Heckert. *See* union college (Fritz-Heckert)
Fulbrook, Mary, 26

gender. *See* women
Gern, Christiane, 37
Gesellschaftliche Räte (social councils), 111, 114, 115–16, 120, 211nn. 46, 48
Glaeßner, Gert-Joachim, 18
Gleye, Paul, 31, 67

Goeckel, Robert, 79
Gömöri, George, 162
Goodwyn, Lawrence, 156, 162, 163, 166, 167
Grabsch, Brigit, 108, 145, 146, 149
Granick, David, 22
grievance commissions (*Konflikt-kommissionen*), 58, 63, 91, 92, 132–35, 204nn. 64, 65, 215nn. 38–40, 215–16n. 41, 216nn. 46, 50, 216–17n. 51, 217n. 52
Grote, Manfred, 26

Habermas, Jürgen, 140
Hancock, M. Donald, 25
Hertle, Hans-Hermann, 110, 150
Heym, Stefan, 115
Honecker, Erich, 27, 76, 218n. 7
Hoß, Dietrich, 125
Hungary, 20, 97, 125, 184n. 46, 190n. 17, 192n. 35, 203n. 53, 204n. 73, 212n. 14, 213n. 17

Innovators' Movement, 91–92, 123–24, 212nn. 3, 4
intelligentsia: activism of, during *Wende*, 32, 33, 36–39, 73, 78–86, 103, 106, 107, 120–21, 189n. 17, 200nn. 22, 25–27, 201nn. 29, 32, 207n. 110, 213n. 24; definitions of, 2, 14–18, 175, 181n. 8, 181–82n. 14, 182nn. 15, 21–22; divisions within, 23–28, 33, 34, 35, 39, 185n. 49, 188n. 7; friendships among, 84–86, 103, 200–201nn. 28–29, 32; involvement with SED, 25–28, 29, 69, 79, 144, 185n. 56, 186n. 68–69; pre-*Wende* organizations and networks of, 37, 78–86, 96, 103, 199nn. 3, 10, 15–16, 200n. 22; relationship with working class, 29–30, 88, 98–102, 104, 187nn. 76–77, 79, 206nn. 92, 94, 206–7n. 104, 207nn. 105, 109, 112, 113; and social change, 16, 17, 30; and unions, 80, 92–93, 101–2, 119, 204nn. 66, 69. *See also* citizens' opposition groups; civil society; discussion circles; KdT; *Klubs der Intelligenz*; Kulturbund; political parties; social service groups; working class, activism during *Wende*

IUG (Initiative for Independent Unions), 102, 114, 117–20, 206n. 94, 207n. 106, 210n. 33, 211nn. 51, 55, 58, 63

Joppke, Christian, 100
Jugel, Martina, 89

Kädtler, Jürgen, 110, 150
KdT (Chamber of Technology), 80, 81, 102, 199n. 16
Kennedy, Michael, 17–18, 21, 22–23, 146, 162, 165
Kirschner, Lutz, 43, 67, 72, 145, 146, 149
Klier, Freya, 20
Klubs der Intelligenz (intelligentsia clubs), 81, 199n. 13
Kolankiewicz, George, 162, 172
Kollektive (work collectives), 6, 43, 54, 57, 63, 69, 83, 116, 125, 127–41, 145, 153, 192nn. 41, 44, 194nn. 1, 7, 213n. 21, 214nn. 27, 28, 32, 214–15n. 37, 216nn. 46, 48–49, 217nn. 60–62, 67. *See also Vertrauensleute*
Kombinate (conglomerates), 21, 51, 87, 123–24, 131, 202n. 44, 212nn. 2, 3
Konfliktkommissionen. See grievance commissions
Konrád, George, 17, 22, 26, 28
Kornai, János, 19
Krenz, Egon, 143, 148, 218n. 7
Kschischan, Karel, 108, 145, 146, 149
Kulturbund (Culture League), 80, 81, 199n. 13

Laba, Roman, 165, 166
labor code (*Arbeitsgesetzbuch*), 50, 70, 76, 114
labor process, 30, 32, 40–56, 78, 152; dishonesty of, 5, 40, 44, 47–50, 53, 55, 68, 152, 191nn. 29–30, 32–33, 193n. 49, 197n. 33; disorganization of, 5, 40, 44–47, 50, 55, 150, 152, 191n. 27; hard work in, 42–44, 50, 55, 190nn. 8, 9, 13, 16–18, 191n. 20, 212n. 7; management control of, 88, 90–91, 135, 203nn. 59, 61–62; remuneration and disciplinary systems of, 5, 40, 44, 50–55, 56, 59, 61, 63, 152, 192nn. 44,

46–47, 193nn. 49–50, 193–94n. 62, 214–15n. 37, 220n. 31; workers' control of, 6, 123–26, 135, 152. *See also* base wage; bonuses; overtime; remuneration system; shiftwork; shortages
LDPD (Liberal Democratic Party of Germany), 38, 79–80, 180nn. 8, 10, 189n. 22
Lukács, János, 29, 125, 126

managers, 22, 26–27, 29, 43, 46–47, 49, 50–51, 54, 55, 57, 59, 60, 61, 62–64, 66, 67, 68, 69, 70, 72, 73, 75, 76, 78, 80, 82, 84, 87–92, 96, 102, 108, 110, 111, 112, 115, 116, 117, 118, 124, 125, 126, 131–132, 133, 134, 144, 148, 149, 153, 175, 176, 186n. 64, 190n. 15, 191n. 25, 193nn. 55, 61, 193–94n. 62, 196nn. 12, 17–18, 199n. 16, 200n. 22, 202n. 44, 203n. 55, 207n. 105, 208n. 6, 210–11n. 45, 212nn. 2, 15, 213n. 25, 213–14n. 26, 214n. 35, 214–215n. 37, 216n. 50, 216–17n. 51, 218–19n. 10, 220nn. 31, 35. *See also* labor process; unions (workplace level)
Marcuse, Peter, 95, 125, 140
Markovits, Inga, 124
Marx, Karl, 10, 181n. 8
Meier, Artur, 87
methodology, 175–77, 218n. 4, 224nn. 4–7
Michalsky, Helga, 30
Mielke, Erich, 76

NDPD (National Democratic Party of Germany), 189n. 22, 199n. 8
Neues Forum, 5, 36, 37–38, 85–86, 100, 101, 109, 113, 180n. 10, 201n. 32, 206n. 94, 207n. 109, 211n. 58. *See also* citizens' opposition groups
Neugebauer, Gero, 81
nomenclature, 21, 30, 184nn. 39–40. *See also* class, and occupational structure; class, reproduction of

Opp, Karl-Dieter, 37
opposition groups (pre-*Wende*), 81–82, 84–85, 199–200n. 17, 200nn. 25, 26
overtime, 43, 53, 59, 132, 135, 190n. 15, 193n. 49, 203n. 55, 206n. 91

Parmalee, Patty Lee, 105
PDS (Party of Democratic Socialism), 38, 85, 109, 180nn. 8, 10, 207n. 109
performance principle (*Leistungsprinzip*), 52, 55, 192n. 46
Philipsen, Dirk, 30, 42
Pirker, Theo, 110, 150
planning, 40–41, 43, 47, 48, 49, 50, 53, 54, 58, 60–61, 69, 75, 132, 136, 189nn. 2–3, 189–90n. 4, 190n. 15, 191n. 25, 192n. 37, 193nn. 54–55, 194n. 5, 195n. 9, 209n. 29, 214–15n. 37
Poland, 6, 7, 49, 154–74; Communist party in, 20, 156, 157, 158, 159, 160, 163, 164, 165, 168, 172, 222nn. 17, 26, 223n. 40; intelligentsia in, 155, 162, 164, 166–69, 221n. 1, 223nn. 37, 45, 47; labor process in, 169–71; managers in, 156, 157, 160, 162, 163, 164, 165, 170, 171–72, 223n. 40; unions in, 155, 156–57, 222nn. 13, 18
—working class: activism, explanations for, 158–61, 163–64, 165–69, 170–71, 173, 222nn. 25–27, 223nn. 35, 45, 47, 56; activism before 1980, 157, 158–61, 163, 165, 166–67, 172, 222nn. 13, 17, 26–27, 223n. 47; activism in 1980, 6, 83, 154–55, 157, 158, 167–69, 172, 221n. 1, 222n. 17; political noninvolvement of, 169–70, 171–73, 223n. 54; relationship with intelligentsia, 161–69, 171, 172; and Solidarity, 6, 82, 155, 168, 221n. 1
political parties, 5, 20, 38–39, 77, 79–80, 84, 85, 103, 106, 189n. 27, 199n. 8, 206n. 94. *See also* DA; CDU; CSU; DBD; DSU; LDPD; NDPD; PDS; SPD-DDR
Pravda, Alex, 157
Protestant church, 27–28, 37, 80, 82, 85, 186nn. 69–70, 201n. 32

race and ethnicity, 3, 24, 164, 179n. 5, 200–201n. 28
Rakovski, Marc, 83
rationalization workshops, 123–24, 212nn. 3, 5
Reich, Jens, 36
remuneration system, 87–88, 102, 132, 135,

202nn. 44–45, 214n. 35, 214–15n. 37. *See also* labor process, remuneration and disciplinary systems of
round tables, 5, 38, 39, 106, 113, 206n. 94
Rowbotham, Sheila, 138
Rueschemeyer, Marilyn, 96, 138

Scharf, Carl Bradley, 30, 38, 52, 54, 82, 97
Schröter, Eckhard, 22
SED (Socialist Unity Party of Germany), 14, 20–21, 21–22, 25–29, 30, 31, 36, 37, 38, 46, 49, 57, 58, 61, 62–66, 67, 68, 70, 72, 73, 76, 78, 79, 80, 82, 84, 91, 92–93, 94, 95, 97, 101, 111, 113, 114, 143, 144, 145, 146, 148, 149, 150, 151, 153, 176, 180n. 8, 181n. 6, 183nn. 34, 36, 184nn. 39, 44, 185nn. 56, 58, 191n. 32, 196nn. 12, 18–20, 22–23, 25, 197nn. 39–40, 199n. 16, 200n. 22, 205nn. 77, 88, 207nn. 109, 112, 209n. 28, 210n. 30, 214n. 26, 214–15n. 37, 216n. 48, 218–19n. 10, 219nn. 13, 20, 220nn. 30, 34, 221nn. 49–50. *See also* intelligentsia, involvement with SED; unions (workplace level)
Segert, Astrid, 145–46
shiftwork, 89–90, 203n. 58, 204n. 69
shortages, 40–48, 55, 76, 90, 123–25, 138, 152, 189nn. 2, 3, 189–90n. 4, 192n. 41, 212n. 7, 220n. 31. *See also* labor process, hard work in
Smith, Dorothy, 11–13, 24, 180n. 3
Smith, Duncan, 81, 96
social councils. *See Gesellschaftliche Räte*
social service groups (pre-*Wende*), 81, 82, 84, 204n. 67
Sodaro, Michael, 26
Soviet Union, 80, 187n. 77, 190nn. 9, 10, 18, 202–3n. 48, 204n. 73, 218n. 3, 219n. 16
Spangenberg, Barbara, 89
SPD-DDR (Social Democratic Party of Germany in the GDR), 38–39, 86, 180nn. 8, 10, 189n. 27, 206n. 94
Sprecherräte (spokespersons' councils), 111, 114, 115, 120, 210n. 42
Stasi (Ministry of State Security), 27, 30, 76, 96, 176, 200n. 29, 220n. 34, 224n. 3

Steele, Jonathan, 91
Stollberg, Rudhard, 89
Szelényi, Ivan, 17, 22, 24, 26, 28, 93, 95–96

taxes, 53, 97, 102, 206n. 91
Ticktin, Hillel, 16–17
Tisch, Harry, 149, 151

Ulbricht, Walter, 15, 31
union college (Fritz Heckert), 43, 67, 112–
  13, 191n. 20, 209n. 28, 210nn. 31, 33
unions (above workplace level), 38, 48, 57,
  67, 68, 69, 70, 71, 72, 111, 112, 114, 129, 130,
  145, 150, 194n. 1, 195n. 7, 197nn. 34, 38,
  198nn. 46, 49, 209nn. 28–29, 216nn. 43–
  44, 219n. 20, 221n. 47
unions (workplace level), 57–76, 78; dependence on party and management,
  5, 6, 35–36, 57, 59, 62–66, 73–76, 97, 149,
  153, 157, 195n. 10, 196nn. 12, 16–18, 204n.
  69, 220n. 30; functioning of, 5–6, 57,
  58–66, 62, 73–74, 76, 153, 156, 194n. 5,
  194–95n. 7, 195n. 9; leaders of, 31, 35, 36,
  37, 38, 41, 42, 43, 48, 49, 51, 57, 58, 59, 60,
  63, 64–70, 71, 72–73, 74–76, 108, 109, 110,
  111, 113, 128–31, 134, 135, 136, 137, 139, 140,
  141, 143, 145–46, 147, 149, 150–52, 153,
  175, 181n. 6, 191n. 32. 192n. 46, 194n. 7,
  196nn. 17–18, 19, 22, 196–97n. 27, 197nn.
  28, 35, 39, 198nn. 46, 54, 213n. 26, 214n.
  33, 215n. 40, 217n. 58, 217–18n. 68, 219n.
  20, 220n. 30, 221nn. 44, 49–50; leadership selection procedures of, 5, 6, 57–
  58, 66–68, 69, 73–75, 153, 156–57, 197nn.
  30, 32–35; political practice of, 6, 58,
  68–73, 74–76, 150, 156, 198nn. 44–45, 48,
  51. *See also* AGL; BGL; *Vertrauensleute*
United States, 72, 87

Vereinigte Linke, 5, 36, 86, 109, 180n. 10,
  206n. 94, 207n. 109, 211n. 58. *See also*
  citizens' opposition groups
Vertrauensleute (*Kollektiv*-level union
  officer), 35–36, 41, 48, 58, 59, 62, 63, 64,
  65, 67, 68, 70, 72, 76, 109, 111, 112, 116,
  127–33, 135–39, 143, 145, 146, 150, 151, 153,

190n. 8, 194nn. 1, 7, 195n. 9, 196n. 20,
  196–97n. 27, 197n. 39, 198n. 44, 209n. 28,
  211nn. 48, 50, 213nn. 20, 23, 25, 213–14n.
  26, 214n. 31, 214–15n. 37, 217n. 67
Volkmer, Werner, 31
Volkskammer (national legislature), 5, 79,
  80, 112, 199n. 3, 209–10n. 30
Voskamp, Ulrich, 125
Voss, Peter, 37

Wałęsa, Lech, 163, 166, 167
Weber, Hermann, 21
Weinert, Rainer, 110, 150
Weinstein, Marc, 162
white-collar workers (*Angestellten*), 42,
  89, 102, 118, 181n. 9, 207nn. 105–6
Wierling, Dorothee, 93
Wittke, Volker, 125
women, 3, 35, 43–44, 58, 69, 81, 85, 139, 159,
  164, 175, 185n. 51, 188n. 7, 190n. 17, 197n.
  40, 201n. 32, 204n. 69, 214n. 35, 217n. 66,
  217–18n. 68, 224n. 2
Woodall, Jean, 165
work councils. *See Betriebsräte*
work collectives. *See Kollektive*
workers' uprising (June 1953), 31–32, 188n.
  88, 196n. 16
working class:
—activism, explanations for: 122–23, 126–
  27, 140–41, 158, 159, 161, 218nn. 71–72;
  class, 97–98; labor process, 122, 123–26,
  131, 152, 212n. 2–5, 14–15; workplace
  politics, 57, 74, 76, 123, 127–40, 153,
  213nn. 20, 25, 213–14n. 26, 214nn. 27, 28,
  30–32, 34, 214–15n. 37, 216n. 50, 216–17n.
  51, 217nn. 59–62, 66–67, 221n. 53
—activism before *Wende*, 31–32, 147, 188n.
  88, 209n. 29.
—activism during *Wende*, 4, 6, 37, 57, 100,
  101, 106–21, 154, 188n. 4, 189n. 17, 208n.
  1; and *Betriebsräte*, 107–10, 120, 135, 145,
  150, 208nn. 2, 3, 6–7, 13, 15, 208–9n. 19,
  211nn. 48, 51, 219n. 20; and intelligentsia, 109–10, 113, 114, 115, 116, 117, 118, 119,
  120, 121, 208n. 17, 209n. 28, 211n. 48;
  and radical reform of unions, 100, 107,

110–14, 120, 135, 150, 209nn. 24, 28–29, 209–10n. 30, 210nn. 32–33, 36, 39; and workers' self-representation, 107, 109, 111, 114–20, 135, 145, 150, 210n. 40, 210–11n. 45, 211n. 49, 219n. 20.

—definitions of, 2, 13–18, 181nn. 6, 8, 181–82n. 14, 182nn. 15, 22

—homogeneity or heterogeneity of, 3, 34, 35, 43–44, 58, 69, 179n. 5, 185n. 51, 188n. 7, 197n. 40, 204n. 69

—passive political involvement of, 4, 142–43, 154, 218nn. 1–2, 221n. 54; on behalf of challengers, 4, 97–98, 143, 147–52, 220nn. 30–31, 34–35, 38, 220–21n. 42, 221nn. 44, 49; on behalf of status quo, 4, 143–47, 218n. 8, 219nn. 12–14, 16, 20–21, 220n. 26; explanations for, 6, 68, 152–53, 221n. 54

—political noninvolvement of, 4, 5, 32–39, 154, 188n. 4

—political noninvolvement of, explanations for: class, 6, 77, 78, 79, 81, 83, 84, 97–105, 200n. 25, 202n. 43, 206n. 92, 215n. 38; labor process, 34–36, 40–56,

102–3, 122, 191nn. 27, 29, 192nn. 41, 46, 193n. 48–50, 193–94n. 62; workplace politics, 57–76, 103, 122–23, 126–27; 135, 136, 153, 198nn. 44, 46, 217n. 58.

—relationship with intelligentsia: lack of contact with, 28, 31–32, 77, 78–86, 100, 104–5, 162, 199n. 2, 200–201n. 28; perception of difference between themselves and intellectuals, 28, 32, 78, 86–98, 104, 105, 202n. 43, 202–3n. 48, 203nn. 49–51, 53, 55, 58, 204n. 65, 72–73, 75, 205nn. 76–77, 79, 83–84, 88, 207n. 112; poor nature of, 29–32, 55, 88, 98, 103, 187nn. 76, 79–80, 88, 193n. 61, 206n. 92, 207n. 14; view of intelligentsia as homogenous, 23–29, 32, 78, 103–4, 169, 186n. 66

—and social change, 3–4, 16, 17, 30, 98–99, 154, 173–74, 179n. 4, 179n. 5. *See also Gesellschaftliche Räte;* IUG; *Sprecherräte;* workers' uprising

Zetkin, Clara, 94
Zimmermann, Hartmut, 52, 97